AF228370

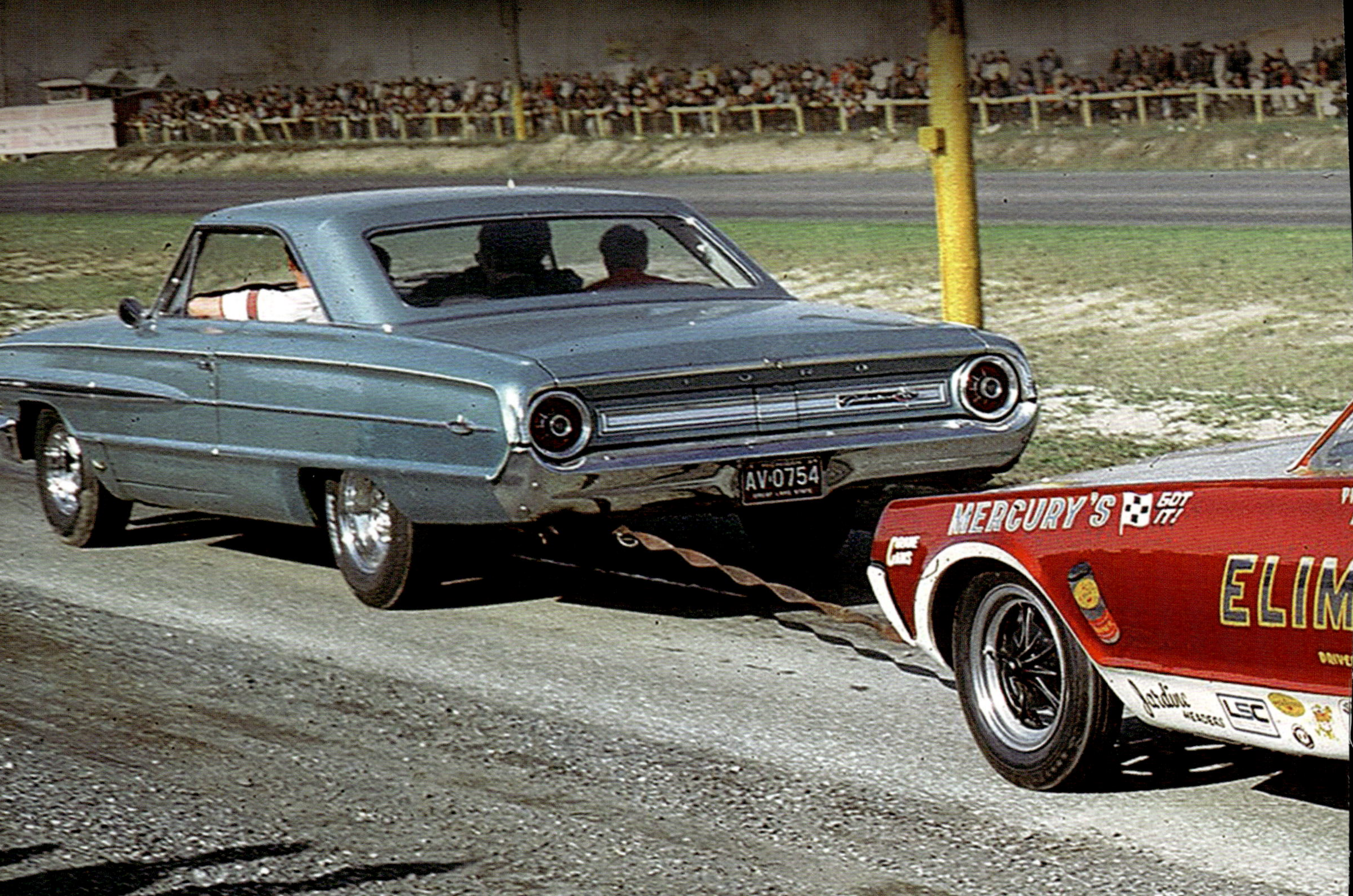

"DYNO"
DON
DOUG BOYCE

THE CARS AND CAREER OF DYNO DON NICHOLSON

CarTech®

CarTech®, Inc.
838 Lake Street South
Forest Lake, MN 55025
Phone: 651-277-1200 or 800-551-4754
Fax: 651-277-1203
www.cartechbooks.com

Edit by Bob Wilson
Layout by Hailey Samples

ISBN 978-1-61325-405-9
Item No. CT631

Library of Congress Cataloging-in-Publication Data

Names: Boyce, Doug, author.
Title: Dyno Don : the cars and career of Dyno Don Nicholson / Doug Boyce.
Description: Forest Lake, MN : CarTech Books, [2018] | Includes index.
Identifiers: LCCN 2017055510 | ISBN 9781613254059
Subjects: LCSH: Nicholson, Don, 1927-2006. | Automobile racing drivers–United States–Biography. | LCGFT: Biographies.
Classification: LCC GV1032.N534 B68 2018 | DDC 796.72092 [B] –dc23
LC record available at https://lccn.loc.gov/2017055510

Edited and designed in the U.S.A.
Printed in China
10 9 8 7 6 5 4 3 2

PUBLISHER'S NOTE:
In reporting history, the images required to tell the tale will vary greatly in quality, especially by modern photographic standards. While some images in this volume are not up to those digital standards, we have included them, as we feel they are an important element in telling the story.

PUBLISHER'S NOTE:
In reporting history, the images required to tell the tale will vary greatly in quality, especially by modern photographic standards. While some images in this volume are not up to those digital standards, we have included them, as we feel they are an important element in telling the story.

DISTRIBUTION BY:

Europe
PGUK
63 Hatton Garden
London EC1N 8LE, England
Phone: 020 7061 1980 • Fax: 020 7242 3725
www.pguk.co.uk

Australia
Renniks Publications Ltd.
3/37-39 Green Street
Banksmeadow, NSW 2109, Australia
Phone: 2 9695 7055 • Fax: 2 9695 7355
www.renniks.com

Canada
Login Canada
300 Saulteaux Crescent
Winnipeg, MB, R3J 3T2 Canada
Phone: 800 665 1148 • Fax: 800 665 0103
www.lb.ca

Contents

ACKNOWLEDGMENTS

Without a doubt, first and foremost on the list of acknowledgements is the Nicholson family. Specifically I'd like to give a big thanks to Don's daughter Cindy, his granddaughter and probably his biggest fan Candace, his nephew Richard, and Richard's son, Don. They each contributed in numerous ways and their input added immensely to the finished work. I was able to spend some quality time with the Nicholsons and I have to say, they truly are special people. They're the type who invite you into their lives and immediately make you feel part of the family. They graciously shared their family history, which allows us all a glimpse of a side of Don that most of us never knew. I am eternally grateful to them for the hospitality shown while welcoming me into their lives.

A special thanks has to go out to Bob Frey. Bob spent 46 years announcing a countless number of NHRA-IHRA races, but facts be known, Bob is also quite the drag race historian. It seemed no matter what question I threw at him, and trust me there were a lot of them, he was there with a well-researched answer. Bob has been a tremendous help through a number of past projects of mine and I can't thank him enough for his ongoing support. Equally, John Jodauga, long with the *National Dragster* has been an ongoing contributor to my work. When he heard I had a Dyno Don book in the works, he immediately stepped up and offered to assist in any way he could. Thanks once again, John.

It's impossible to tell a story such as this without great photographs, so a big thanks to all those who contributed. It feels like I spent hours picking through photos before settling on the 300+ included here. Take some time examining each of these great shots, as they all tell a story of their own.

The list of contributors below prove positive the love and appreciation those within the drag racing community have for Don. Without hesitation each contributed in one form or another, and without them this book would have fallen far short.

C. J. Batten, Bob Bayles, Brian Beattie, Arnie Beswick, Dave Bishop, Jack Bleil, Forrest Bond, Phil Bonner Jr., Bob Boudreau, Darren Boyce, Dick Brannan, Sonny Bryant, Steve Call, Joe Carson, Mike Cochran, Tony Conover, Bill Coon, Ariel Cordero, Ray Cunningham, George Cureton, John Durand, Lloyd Eggstaff, Dick Estevez, Arlen Fadely, Jim Fuerer, John Gacioch, Robert Genat, Terry Gilkes, Bob Glidden, Jim Glover, Sherman Gunn, Ken Gunning, James Handy, Brian Hankins, Don Hardy, Lou Hart, Randy Hernandez, Mike Hoag, Samuel Hoff, Keith Hudak, Daryl Huffman, Jerry Jardine, Jim Kampmann, Tom Kasch, Brian Kennedy, Irwin Kroiz, Larry Knapp, Ray Kobe, Wayne Langford, Butch Leal, Jim Marlett, John Marsh, Bob Martin, Jason McGrane, Robin McQueen, Ed Meyer, Michael Mihalko, Connell Miller, Don Montgomery, Gordon Moore, Charlie Morris, Thomas Nagy, Robert Nielsen, Dan Nowak, Frank Oglesby, Charlie Pepper, Dan Pfeiffer, Larry Pfisher, Britt Pike, Allen Platt, Alex Polewik, Barrie Poole, Rob Potter, Michael Pottie, Peter Quinn, Steve Reyes, Jack Roush, Ed Schartman, Jim Schild, Tom Schiltz, Tim Schmackpfeffer, Paul Shedlik, Rod Short, Frank Sicinski, Mick Smallridge, Gary Smith, Mike Sopko Sr., Jim Sottile, Roy Steffey, Mike Strickler, Geoff Stunkard, Jan Suhr, Doug Thorley, "Big Gene" Townley, Allen Tracy, Al Turner, Curt Vogt, Fred Von Sholly, Carl Weisinger, Tom West, Bob Wenzelburger, Dan Williams, Todd Wingerter, Ralph Woodall, and Jeff Wright.

Additionally, information compiled for this book came from publications released by: Lopez, Argus, Magnum, Petersen and Dobbs. A big help as well were the *National Dragster, Drag News,* and *Drag World* newsprints. A special thanks to Thomas Voehringer, Archivist at TEN: The Enthusiast Network, for digging through the Petersen Publishing vault and coming up with a number of the more favorable shots included here. Of course, I have to give a shout out to those who I have connected with on the World Wide Web. The Internet sure has made chasing leads and hunting contacts so much easier for us writers. Dot com websites that proved to be resourceful included competitionplus, draglist, nhra, jalopyjournal, boss302, fordmuscle, catsccc, 348-409, hemmings, hotrod, nitromater, mercurycougar.net, and 351.net.

INTRODUCTION

Look up the word *legendary* in the Oxford English Dictionary and you will read, "Remarkable enough to be famous; very well known." When it comes to Don Nicholson, the man and the impact he had on the sport of drag racing, he definitely fits the bill. What made him remarkable? To begin with, his number of drag racing firsts is unmatched. As a small sample, he had the first Funny Car in the 7s, the first Pro Stock in the 7s, and reportedly the first unblown door car faster than 150 mph. A diverse racer, Don is just one of two people to have made a final-round appearance in six different drag race categories. He's been there in Funny Car, Pro Stock, Super Eliminator, Street Eliminator, Comp Eliminator, and Stock. And unlike most racers who have a difficult enough time winning with one brand of automobile, Don did it in Chevrolets, Fords, and Mercurys. The man was always a threat regardless of the category he chose to run or the car he chose to race.

If those stats aren't remarkable enough for you, during drag racing's golden era, his track record and overall popularity saw sanctioning bodies and numerous publications vote him Funny Car Driver of the Year in 1965, 1966, 1967, and 1968. Don was the first racer to have a nationwide fan club, a club created during the early days of Funny Car. He was so popular that drag racing promoters voted him their number one draw.

With the birth of Pro Stock in 1970, Don led the charge for Ford, winning AHRA, IHRA, and NHRA World Championships in 1972, 1975, and 1977. These feats made Don just one of three Pro Stock competitors to have ever won world championships in all three sanctioning bodies; the other two are Ronnie Sox and Lee Shepherd. Even though Don's number of national event wins is quite impressive, he always seemed to gravitate toward match racing, where, throughout his career, he maintained a slightly greater than 90-percent win record. Not an easy feat considering that in the early days he faced guys including Arnie Beswick, "Jungle" Jim, and Gary Dyer. I grew up with the Dyno Don of the 1970s; he's the one who gave fits to guys such as Bill "Grumpy" Jenkins, Sox & Martin, and Dick Landy.

Don's track record, from the dry lakes of the 1940s through the quarter-mile in the 2000s, was as remarkable as the man himself. A real champion to the underdog, he was genuine and generous to a fault. As you read this book, it will be easy to see that the sport of drag racing just wouldn't have been the same without the prowess and personality of the legendary man they called "Dyno" Don.

BIRTH OF A LEGEND (1927–1961)

Donald Ray Nicholson was born, along with his twin sister Dorothy May, to Logan and Hallie Nicholson in Springfield, Missouri, on May 28, 1927. The pair was numbers five and six in a family that eventually numbered seven children. Don spent his early years helping on the family's Missouri farm. As he grew older, his chores included handling the reins of the horses and plow mules. When Don was around 10 years old, his father built a tractor using a cut down 1930 Oakland as a base. It was on this "heap" that Don first gained driving experience. Even though it was no comparison to what was waiting around the corner for him, Don once said, "You might say that was when I got my first taste of speed."

Don's mechanical aptitude came genetically. This picture of Don's father, Logan, was taken in his saw shop located behind the family home in Pasadena. Logan perfected and patented a special water method of sharpening blades and tools. (Photo Courtesy Nicholson Family Collection)

This is the building where, after the war, Don and his brother Harold set up their first speed shop. The building was a hangout and doubled as a gym for the Nicholson boys and their friends. Its location was off the alley behind the Nicholson home on Los Robles Avenue in Pasadena. (Photo Courtesy Nicholson Family Collection)

A four-year-old Don is shown here standing beside the Nicholsons's 1930 Chevy in front of their Missouri home. Seeking greener pastures, Don's father and grandfather had initially gone to California around 1925 and purchased a lot in Pasadena. (Photo Courtesy Nicholson Family Collection)

Don and his brother Harold ran Nick's Speed Shop. The brothers performed bodywork, paint, and performance upgrades. Note the dual rear wheels to harness the power of the 1941 Chevy 6. Performance upgrades included a fabricated intake, Stromberg carbs, and a Ken Harman camshaft. An aluminum nose helped aerodynamics. That's believed to be Harold Nicholson standing on the left of the truck. (Photo Courtesy Don Montgomery)

Here's a rare shot of Don in his Navy gear with his brothers Harold (right) and Warren (left). This photo was snapped near the end of World War II. The two elder Nicholsons were home on furlough while it looks like Don was preparing for his stint. (Photo Courtesy Nicholson Family Collection)

In 1939, the Nicholsons had been hit hard by the Great Depression, so they loaded up their 1934 Chevy and headed for the promised land of southern California. After a turbulent 1,500 miles that included driving through the brunt of a Texas tornado, the family finally touched down in their new home of Pasadena. The Nicholsons purchased a Victorian house on Los Robles Avenue, where Logan, a carpenter by trade, opened a saw-sharpening shop in one of the two out-buildings off the back alley.

By 1941, Don had a paper route, and he had taken over the other out-building to repair bikes and scooters. Within a few years, Don and his older brother Harold used the garage to open their first "speed shop." The Nicholsons, led by eldest son Warren the beekeeper, also jarred and sold honey out of the front of the home.

While attending Pasadena Junior College, Don studied mechanical engineering. After class, he worked in a local body shop, honing a trade that he returned to on and off through his life. It seemed that every spare moment was spent toying with his 1934 Chevy. The car was originally Harold's, but he passed it to Don when he joined the service in 1942. Don was close to Harold, who was a little more than three years older; the pair spent plenty of time street racing. It's said that back then the serious action was taking place down in the Los Angeles River bed. And serious it was. There were times when Nichol-

The Nicholsons's 1934 Ford coupe cum roadster at Paradise Mesa in San Diego, circa 1951. Crude as it appears, the Car was one of the most feared cars of the period. To the right is Don Blair's lakes roadster. (Photo ©TEN: The Enthusiast Network. All Rights Reserved.)

Chevy came home with bullet holes in the back. Running a 235-ci Chevy mill hopped up with a Harman & Collins cam, Stromberg carbs, a Spaulding ignition, and a reworked head, the Chevy had no problem putting away the flathead Fords that were supposed to be faster.

By 18, Don had racked up more than his share of speeding tickets, which eventually led to a date in front of a judge. Said judge gave Don the option of either joining the U.S. Navy or going to jail. Don immediately joined the navy. In doing so, his less-than-stellar driving record was wiped clean and his stack of tickets dismissed. In 1945, Don was sent to boot camp in San Diego and he wrapped up training at the end of June. Reportedly, he was on his way to the Philippines when the war ended in September. Once he was free of the navy, Don joined Harold and the pair returned to their racing activities. Their interests included the dry lakes and a trip to El Mirage in April 1948 for an event sanctioned by the Southern California Timing Association (SCTA). At this event, Don drove away with a record of 128.38 mph. Considering

Don had a great personality and always seemed to have a smile on his face. In the late 1940s, he ran with the California Roadster Association, rubbing fenders with future Indy champ Troy Ruttman, among others. Safety was low on the totem pole and Don valued his life more than the racing, so he gave up the dirt tracks after a couple seasons. (Photo Courtesy Nicholson Family Collection)

That's Don standing on the left and his brother Harold behind the wheel of the pair's A/Modified Roadster. Though Don was a good driver, he found working on the car to make it go faster a lot more fun. Here at Santa Maria in 1954, the Bantam is powered by a 296-inch Merc, which propelled it to 118.11 mph times this day. The Jimmy 6 in the Bantam featured a Wayne F. Horning 12-port head and a side-mount GMC blower on a fabricated intake. (Photo ©TEN: The Enthusiast Network. All Rights Reserved.)

the competition, which included Ak Miller, Stu Hilborn, Dick Kraft, and others, the relatively unknown Nicholson brothers were quickly making a name for themselves.

Showing their diversity, the brothers were members of the California Roadster Association and ran a 1926 Chevy-powered T Roadster for a couple years around southern California tracks. The Roadster appeared in the November 1950 issue of *Hot Rod* magazine, which covered a 75-lap race at Porterville. At that 33-car race, Don came in second. In a *Rodder's Journal* magazine article, Don was quoted to say, "I quit running track roadsters because the cars weren't safe at all. A guy ran up over the back of me and hit my helmet with his wheel."

In 1950, Don went to work for Ollie Prather at his Arcadia Body Shop on 1st Avenue. According to Prather, at the time Don was running a 1950 Chevy. In a previous interview, Prather stated, "Don worked for me a couple years but his heart wasn't really in it. He wanted to race and ran his Chevy as far away as the San Fernando Valley."

The Chevy appeared in the first issue of *Rod & Custom*, which was called *Rods and Customs* for that first issue in May 1953. By then, the Chevy was powered by a 302-inch GMC that produced an estimated 240 hp and had no problem dusting off hot Caddys, Fords, and the top-end charge of foreign jobs such as the Jaguar XK-E. Showing a little ingenuity, Don tricked out the 302 with fabricated headers, intake, and high energy ignition. The

highly modified mill was backed by an overdrive transmission Don built using 1949 Ford and Lincoln-Zephyr parts. The Chevy held the Gas Coupe record for its weight class at Pomona, running 95.94 mph. In 1952, Don left Prather's but didn't go far. He and Harold opened the Nicholson Bros. Speed Shop right next door.

Prior to C. J. "Pappy" Hart opening the nation's first dragstrip at Santa Ana in 1950, Don and other like-minded souls were out racing on the airstrip, to the disdain of local constables. When Hart opened the gates, Don and Harold were among the first to enter. At the time, the brothers were running a GMC-powered 1934 Ford. The car was typical of the stripped-down racers of the day: no fenders, no roof, and no interior. To aid traction, the Chevy ran a set of dual rear wheels. It was said to be the quickest car at Santa Ana in 1950, clocking 120 mph. Don followed with a number of primitive cars, including an Altered, again powered by a Jimmy 6. In 1952, he showed no fear in propelling the A/Dragster of Bubby Walton to 150 mph.

However, for Don, life wasn't all about cars. On May 22, 1950, he married his sweetheart, Patricia McNamara. Patty was a local Pasadena girl who met Don through mutual friends in 1948. Neither wanted a large wedding, so they eloped and were married by a Catholic priest in Las Vegas. Don, raised in a Protestant home, took the necessary classes to convert. This flew in the face of Don's strict father and drove a wedge between the

Proud parents, Don and Patty, pose with their little bundle of joy, Cindy, who is approximately five months old in this photo. Cindy was the only child for the couple and, when old enough, she often traveled to the races with Mom and Dad. Don enjoyed hunting, and the mounted deer seen hanging to the rear in the photo was one he bagged in the San Bernardino Mountains. (Photo Courtesy Nicholson Family Collection)

Don purchased this house in Duarte, his first, in 1950. By the middle of the decade, he had added this three-bay garage. Working without the luxury of a lift, the far-left bay (partially hidden) featured a pit so that Don could access the underside of cars. Cindy Nicholson recalls with a sense of pride that "we were the only family in Duarte with a paved backyard." The Nicholsons lived here through mid-1962. This was also where Jerry Jardine built his first set of headers in 1959. (Author's Collection)

family. This didn't affect Patty and Don's relationship; the two proved to be the consummate lovebirds and were inseparable through the years.

In 1956, the pair celebrated the birth of their only child, a bright-eyed girl they named Cindy. At the time of Cindy's birth, Don and Harold were running their operations, calling it Horsepower Specialties, out of an old service station on Lime Avenue in Monrovia. In 1957, Don was toying with a hopped-up 1952 Lincoln, taking it out to Riverside where he clocked 100 mph times. Patty also got in on the action, making a pass or two of her own. Family friend Lloyd Eggstaff recalled, "Don was always so calm and cool. We were all in the Lincoln driving to the track one day down Route 66, doing about 100 when a car coming in the opposite direction took a slow turn into our path. Don remained calm and said that the driver may want to open both doors because we were driving right through."

Don assisted in building three identical small-block Chevys for the Bonneville streamliner of Chet Herbert. He crewed on the car and warmed it up, but, because he had a wife and daughter, it was felt he shouldn't make the timed runs, which were handed to Dave Ryder. At Bonneville, Mickey Thompson's twin-Chrysler *Challenger*, which clocked 294 mph, overshadowed it. Ryder was the second fastest, hitting 267.359 on his first pass. Any hopes of surpassing Thompson that weekend were

dashed when, according to Don, on the return run "Ryder got it all 'loaded up' with fuel and blew the engines."

Further dry lake ventures for the brothers included running a roadster in conjunction with Don Blair out of his speed shop in Pasadena. With his own shop just down the road, Don regularly relied upon Blair's to perform machine work. A number of trips to El Mirage followed for the Nicholsons, as Harold ran a Coupe on the dry lake bed. It was at El Mirage where Don first met 14-year-old Earl Wade. Wade tagged along with friends, the Price Brothers, who themselves ran a Fuel Coupe.

Tragedy struck the Nicholson family in November 1959 when Harold, driving the Akins and Hawkins dragster at San Fernando, was killed when a front wheel broke loose at speed. Don, racing elsewhere at the time, had told Harold he thought the car was unsafe and recommended not driving it. Needless to say, the loss hit the Nicholsons hard, Don especially. He lost a brother who was also a dear friend. Don rarely spoke of the accident and, more than likely, it's why his parents never took a keen interest in his career.

In 1959, Don went to work for C. S. Mead Chevrolet, handling high-performance tune-ups and operating the Clayton dynamometer that was brought over from his Monrovia shop. He buried himself in his work, and his reputation as a master tuner exploded. It was while at

The Nicholson brothers, Don and Harold, flipped a couple bucks for this advertisement in the 1954 Arcadia High School yearbook. Customers' cars ranged from hot rods to salt-flats to circle-track cars. If you Google the Arcadia address, you'll find that the building still stands.

Don ordered his 1960 Chevy with a tri-power 348 and BorgWarner 4-speed. The Fleetmaster was a no-frills model that lacked deadweight such as a rear seat, radio, and heater. The trophies lined up here were won by a proceeding owner; Don garnered his share running B/S with the car. (Photo Courtesy Gary Stith)

hold. You want to talk about a man in demand? Some mornings when Don arrived at work, cars were lined up waiting for a dyno tune. And not just local racers, Don had customers coming from as far away as Ohio.

Don raced a tri-powered 348 Biscayne in 1959 and out of approximately 75 races that year lost just 2. Recalled Don in a 1990s interview with Robert Genat, "Beyond a 'trick' valve job, I never had the engine apart. I pulled the front end off and built a set of over-the-frame wheelwell headers for it. Nobody built headers but Hedman and they were the conventional inside-the-frame type. Everybody wanted me to build headers for them but it took me two weeks to build those. I didn't have the ambition to build headers. It was a pretty good art to cutting and fitting. I did it all with a hacksaw. I built those headers on the floor of my home garage in Duarte. Jerry Jardine came down and started building headers there. That was the start of Jardine Headers."

With the new free-flowing exhaust in place, Don's Chevy had pretty much everyone covered. He entertained the thought of attending his first NHRA Nationals at Indy, but after putting his Chevy on the dyno, he felt the car just wasn't making enough power. On September 12, Don raced eventual NHRA World Champion Bruce Morgan at San Gabriel and defeated him with a 14.10 at 99.55 mph. I guess he should have put a little more consideration into that trip to Indy.

In February 1960, the NHRA was holding the predecessor to the Winternationals at Pomona and Don was making an appearance in his 348-powered B/S 1960 Chevy. Don's lightweight Fleetmaster grabbed Top Stock with a 13.69 at 101.01 mph by defeating 15 competitors, including the Plymouth of Allen Villa Dyno tuner and future Stock and Super Stock legend Dave Kempton. Dyno's record with the car equaled that of his 1959.

Butch "the California Flash" Leal remembers Don well. "I was quite a bit younger, and he took me under his wing after I raced him with my 348-powered El Camino one day at Lions. He beat me by half a car length and said it was the quickest 348 he ever ran against. When it came to the 348 and 409s, Don was the man everyone turned to for guidance."

C. S. Meads became Service Chevrolet in 1961 and it's where Don first teamed up with Earl Wade. The pair complemented each other well, with Don working his magic on ignition, injection, and carbs while Wade specialized in work on heads and fuel injection. Don had stated that, "We had guys who wouldn't run on weekends unless we tuned their cars. I had a system where I'd loosen the distributor a little bit. I'd power time it while Earl was running the dyno." Wade became Don's right-hand man, doing most of the Corvette stuff while Don focused mainly on the 348 and 409s. Eventually, the dynamic duo moved on from Service Chevrolet. Wade had been splitting his time working alongside another finer tuner, Dick Bourgeois, and the pair operated a successful tune-up and speed shop business. As for Don, well, the 1960s were underway and his storied career was just taking off.

A BEVY OF CHEVYS (1961–1963)

One of Don's fondest memories was winning his first national event, the Winternationals in 1961. He recalled the thrill of coming down the return road that passes by the Pomona grandstands and seeing everyone standing and cheering him. Rather than towing the car to the track (as his competition did), Don drove his Impala as a way to heat the oil in the driveline to create less friction. (Photo ©TEN: The Enthusiast Network. All Rights Reserved.)

Although Dyno Don has been claimed by Ford and Mercury fans as one of their own, his roots were firmly planted in Chevrolets. Yes, his greatest success came while running Fords and Mercurys, but he ran Chevys for a longer period. There's a good chance that if General Motors hadn't ceased all racing activity in 1963, Don would have stuck with Chevrolet. In the period between 1961 and 1963, few enjoyed the same level of success as Don, regardless of the brand they drove or the category they raced. Even Patty got in on the action, racing her Chevy Corvair and winning more than a dozen races.

1961

Don established his reputation nationally by taking Stock Eliminator at the 1961 NHRA Winternationals. He managed the feat in his 409-powered 1961 Impala that was built in a marathon three days. Don received the engine even before he had a car lined up. Bill Thomas, who had worked at Meads as the service manager before contracting with Chevrolet (and opening Bill Thomas Race Cars), arranged a pair of 409s to be shipped from Daytona where NASCAR's Speedweek was being held. The second 409 went into the Roman Red Biscayne that Frank Sanders was preparing. Even though Service Chevrolet in Pasadena employed Don, it was Don Steves Chevrolet in La Habra that provided him with a 348 Impala to build on. Service Chevrolet wasn't prepared to cough up a car. "They weren't interested. Don Steves was kind of into performance at the time."

The Impala had a number of options attached to it, including power windows and a radio. Don was definitely doing it in style. As described in an old *Motor Life* magazine article, Don built his Chevy to the strict rules of the day; he honed the block, as opposed to going the legal .060-over bore route, and retained the factory-forged pistons. He set main bearing clearance at .003 inch and rod bearings at .0025 inch. The single Carter 4-barrel saw metering rods on the primary side reworked to enrich the mixture. The secondary jets were drilled out .003 inch. The advance curve was reworked an amount Don chose to keep to himself. Jerry Jardine built the Tri-Y headers on the 348 prior to the engine being swapped for the 409.

According to Jardine, the headers were welded up on the floor of Don's Duarte home garage and fitted by trial and error. Jardine found that the pri-mary tubes that were 1/8-inch smaller in diameter than the 1¾-inch exhaust port gave the best per-formance. The headers, as crude as they were, were said to be worth an additional 20 hp. Or 5 and 50, as Jardine advertised. That's 5 mph and a .50 improvement in quarter-mile times compared to the stock exhaust manifolds. Backing the factory-rated 360-hp 409 was a 2.54–first gear BorgWarner and a 4:56 gear rear end. The third member was the weak link, and Don went through a number of them. He had mentioned keeping stock early on by "lifting" center sections from cars on the Service Chevrolet lot. Getting the power to the ground was a set of 8.50x14 Firestone soft-compound Butyl tires or a pair of Casler cheaters.

When he prepared the car, Don raised the front suspension by 1.5 inches and lowered the rear 2 inches. In 1961, these mods were commonly accom-plished with the help of heavy-duty springs, spring spacers, and a torch. It was felt that raising the front and lowering the rear helped weight transfer and plant the narrow rear tires. With only a day to go before the Winternationals, final details were but-toned up and the car was tuned. To loosen the new car suspension, Don had Hugh "Putzel" Osterman, who assisted Don on and off well into the decade,

Les Ritchey's 390-powered Ford Starliner had recorded a 13.33 at 106 mph, thanks in part to the newly released tri-carb setup. As good as the times were, they weren't quite good enough for Don's 409 Impala, which recorded a best of 13.29. (Photo ©TEN: The Enthusiast Network. All Rights Reserved.)

At the 1961 Winternationals, Don and his Impala took Mr. Stock Eliminator honors by defeating cars such as the 390-powered Ford of Bud Harris. Only two 409s made Pomona, the other being the Biscayne of Frank Sanders. Don had prepped the heads for Sanders's 409, which won Super Stock class. (Photo ©TEN: The Enthusiast Network. All Rights Reserved.)

take the car out the night before and rack up 400 or 500 highway miles, while he himself caught some much needed z's.

The Winternationals, or the "Big Go West" as it was also called, kicked off at Pomona with time trials on Friday, February 17. Cars to beat included the 389 Pontiac of Mickey Thompson, driven by Pete Petrey; it was the quickest of the Pontiacs in the program. In addition, the Fords of Les Ritchey, Pete McCarroll, and Bud Harris were tough competition. McCarroll was running the recently released 3 x 2-barrel setup, giving the Ford a 375-horse rating. Frank Sanders, in the only other 409 car, proved to be Don's toughest competition. Sanders defeated Don in Saturday's final on a holeshot, 13.63 at 105.26 mph.

The 50 fastest Stockers ran on Sunday for the Mr. Stock Eliminator crown. The cars consisted of S/S stick and automatic as well as A/S and B/S cars. Dyno Don defeated Ritchey in the semifinals before getting around Sanders in the final with a 13.59 at 105.88. Low ET of the meet went to Don, who tripped the clocks with a 13.25 at 107.27 mph.

Don's 1961 was the first Super Stocker to break 110 mph and the first to run consistently in the 12-second zone. Its Carter carb has reworked metering rods and the secondary jets are drilled .003. Tri-Y headers were the work of Jerry Jardine. Don blueprinted the engine. The factory clutch and flywheel were behind the 409. (Photo ©TEN: The Enthusiast Network. All Rights Reserved.)

Don should be recognized as the first of the Stock-class racers to go out on tour. Early in 1961, he was living in Duarte and reading all about the Hot Stockers back East (the Platts, Phil Bonner, Dave Strickler, and others), and he wondered how his Impala would measure up. Well, he'd find out soon enough.

Don jumped at the chance when offered the opportunity to travel to Indiana for a match then head south to North Carolina. Don hit the road, flat towing his Chevy behind the 1957 Chevy of Ida and Jim Barth, who were Earl Wade's "adopted" parents. At Henderson, North Carolina, Don drove through the 16-car field that included 13 Fords, 2 Chevrolets, and 1 Pontiac. Ronnie Sox was there but was unable to compete. The final round came down to Don and a local Ford.

Don later recalled, "There were no guard rails and the asphalt ended before the track did. The crowd had gotten so bad they were all over the track. I almost hit some a couple of times and I told the strip operator that I wasn't going to run again unless he cleared the people off the track. It had gotten so you couldn't even see the track for all the people. So the operator gets on the PA and tells the guy with the Ford, Dallas Parkinson, to go out there and clear the track off. So he comes out of the pits sideways, kicking up sand. I don't know how he didn't kill anyone. On his way back up the track, people were mad and

This photo was shot in early August at Jerry Jardine's aunt's home in Ohio. It was an eventful trip east that saw the tow car lose an axle in Virginia and jackknife in a rainstorm in Arizona. At the time the photo was shot, Don was in Detroit visiting with Chevrolet's Vince Piggins, picking up parts, and hammering out a deal. The gentleman in the photo is Jerry Jardine. (Photo Courtesy Jerod Jardine)

throwing rocks and bottles at his car, breaking the windows out. He gets back to the pits and here come about a thousand people gunning for him. The track operator came out to the middle of the track and started shooting his shotgun in the air to stop them. They finally got them cleared out, and then I almost got 'home town'ed.' The guy jumped the flag and almost beat me. I fumbled second gear but still managed to catch him. To make it a big deal, the $600-dollar winnings was all in one-dollar bills in a wheelbarrow." A wheelbarrow full of cash it was, plus an extra $200 dollars for showing. "Some of the Ford guys said the only reason I beat them was because I had a 4-speed and they didn't. I told them I'd use first and fourth and they block off either second or third and I'd run them. I still got no takers."

It was while towing the Impala (on slicks) back up north for a match at the Detroit Dragway that the tow car lost control on the rain-soaked Virginia turnpike. The cars jackknifed, leading to the tow bar bracket tearing from the Impala's frame. Don, who was attempting to catch some sleep in the back seat, woke in time to see the Impala leaving the road and rolling over in a shallow ditch, coming to a stop back on its wheels. The incident tore up the left front suspension and bent up the roof and many of the body panels. A wrecker was called to haul the Impala into Beckley, where the suspension was repaired at a Chevy dealer.

Don called Gil Kohn at Detroit and tried to beg out of the match, but Kohn wouldn't hear of it. He had Garlits and Ivo lined up but Garlits bailed after getting burned in a fire. Kohn insisted that Don be there, as without him, there was no show. Kohn arranged to have a body shop straighten the Impala, doing what they could before the Sunday match. The car looked like crap but did manage to win the match, defeating the Ace Wilson Royal Pontiac driven by Jim Wangers in convincing fashion.

Back home, the Impala was repaired and repainted in preparation for a planned second trip east early in July to Easy Street Dragstrip near Newton Grove, North Carolina. This time, Jerry Jardine came along to assist Don. The pair borrowed Big John Mazmanian's stubby trailer

> **To make it a big deal, the $600-dollar-winnings was all in one-dollar bills in a wheelbarrow.**

and loaded up Don's 1955 Chev with spare parts. As Jardine recalls, "To balance the load [on the hitch], tools and spare parts, including a spare rear-end section, were tucked under the hood of the '61."

Don has often been credited as the father of the bleach box–style burnout, first using bleach to clean the tires. By trial and error, he found the best water/bleach mix for his Vogue (or Caslers) slicks was 50/50. People use to question the fact that he ran his 7-inch cheater slicks on 4-inch rims, without realizing the advantage it gave him by increasing the footprint.

At the 1961 NHRA Winternationals, Don ran a set of borrowed Atlas Bucrons before switching to Vogue slicks prior to the Nationals. Don was reported to be the first to run the soft-compound tire. The Chevy was repainted and relettered after a wreck in the spring. (Photo ©TEN: The Enthusiast Network. All Rights Reserved.)

By August, Chevrolet was producing upgraded performance parts for the 409. The over-the-counter parts included larger valve heads, a longer duration high-lift camshaft, and a pair of deep-breathing Carter 4-barrel carburetors on an aluminum intake manifold. The parts brought the horsepower rating of the 409 up to an equal 409. Chevrolet slipped Don the parts, which were installed on his 409 prior to the NHRA Nationals on Labor Day weekend. It was after the Winternationals that Don's tie with General Motors strengthened. He'd had indirect contact with Chevrolet but after the winters' win, he had an open line to Vince Piggins. Even though cash and cars were not in the cards from the manufacturer, parts were generally there for the asking. With Don going through transmissions and weak-link third members, it proved to be a beneficial arrangement.

At Indy in September for the NHRA Nationals, the Stockers ran Saturday afternoon and stealing the show were the cars in Optional Super Stock (O/SS). The category was created in 1961 and designed specifically for limited-production cars or cars featuring high-performance parts made available after June 1, 1961, by Detroit's Big Three. Leading the way in O/SS was the 368-horse Pontiac of Mickey Thompson, driven

Don was ready to take on the world when he headed east in July. Prior to doing so, he won a Super Stock meet at Vaca Valley on July 8, setting the track record with a 13.21 at 108.42 mph. Don actually preferred to run a hose to the carbs rather than the Enderle scoop but was not allowed to do so at Indy. (Photo Courtesy Mike Strickler)

by Hayden Proffitt. Proffitt held the low ET and top speed with a 13.07 at 112.21. Close behind was Don with a 13.25 at 110.29 mph. Opening day eliminations saw Proffitt defeat Dave Strickler's Biscayne for honors. Proffitt ran a phenomenal 12.55 during the meet and walked into Sunday's 50-car Mr. Stock Eliminator as the favorite.

In an unorthodox semifinal's move, precipitated by a burning desire to defeat his opponent, Al Eckstrand in the Ramchargers Dodge, Mickey Thompson replaced Proffitt behind the wheel of his Pontiac. Thompson and the Pontiac faithful's hopes were dashed when the Pontiac got hung up in gear. The same thing happened the next round to Eckstrand when the 3-speed in his Dodge failed against Don. The final round came down to the O/SS cars of Dyno Don and the *Passionate Poncho* of Arnie "the Farmer" Beswick. Because of Eckstrand's failed gear in the previous round, Don and Beswick agreed that the overall Stock Eliminator winner should come back to run in a best-of-three grudge race against the 413 Dodge. At the flag, Don and Beswick left bumper to bumper. On the top end, it was Don inching ahead for the win with a 13.37 at 108.69 mph. In the grudge race, Don lost the first round but came back to take the next two. As was usual, after the final race, the cars of both Beswick and Dyno Don were torn down for inspection. Both were disqualified.

As Don recalled, "They started picking on stuff. They pulled the valve springs off my heads. Took the shims from underneath and checked them in their little tester. They checked them at minimum height. I showed them how

In mid-1961, Chevrolet released a twin 4-barrel option for the 409, bringing the horsepower rating up to an even 409. As noted by the cutouts in the hood, Don was running the Chevy in Optional Super Stock at this point. Note the deep-groove generator pulley and additional crankcase breathers, as well the lack of a heater. (Photo ©TEN: The Enthusiast Network. All Rights Reserved.)

Don's reputation preceded him to the East Coast, and from day one the crowds began to gather. Seen here at Indy, fans wanted to know what made the baddest Chevy in the nation tick. As you can see, in 1961, the luxury of paved pits at Indy was still only a dream. (Photo Courtesy Mike Strickler)

to check them at the stock height. Actually the springs were down on pressure because as the runs went on, they went away. The car started missing on me a little bit in the lights and was getting a little worse with each run. I was sure it was the valve springs going away. When we checked them, there was no problem. Then they started mic'ing the heads of the valves. I had never mic'd a head of a valve unless I was making a valve for something. I just pulled the valves out of the Chevrolet boxes and put them in the heads. There were some they found a few thousand over size. I was arguing with Farmer Dismuke, the tech inspector; Chevrolet didn't say $1^{11}\!/_{16}$, +/- 10, or 15 thousand as Chrysler, Pontiac, and most others did. They just had the size, no plus or minus. The valves were sitting right out on the edge, which was the way I did a valve job. We got that squared away and then they said the intake was matched. The factory or whoever made the castings for them had used a die grinder to clean off the burrs as opposed to using a hand scraper. I told them it wasn't matched as it was out a 1/4-inch in spots." It all got very ridiculous with Farmer arguing that Don had received special parts. Chevrolet's Paul Prior, who was there, got involved, arguing the point along with Don. In the end, the disqualification stood with no reason given, and no discussion allowed.

"As far as they were concerned, Beswick and I were just a couple of farm boys who didn't know what we were doing and if we go out there and beat that big Mickey Thompson Pontiac, we must be cheating." Don was prepared to sue but eventually cooled off and let it go. Beswick put it all down to politics. "They had their favorite."

Rounding out Don's trip was a match against the East Coast's finest, Dave Strickler in the *Old Reliable* Chevy, at York US-30 on September 23. Also making an appearance was Arnie Beswick and his potent 389 Pontiac. It was quite a show put on by the three, with each reportedly making in the neighborhood of 20 runs by the end of the day. The hometown biased–news failed to report an overall winner, but you can be sure it wasn't hometown favorite, Dave Strickler. Don was clearly the winner, running consistent 13.0s and low ET of the day with a 13.02. Strickler was close behind with a best of 13.05 and Beswick with a 13.09. Don had more than measured up to the best the east had to offer. To paraphrase Julius Caesar from long ago, Dyno Don came, he saw, and he conquered.

Don campaigned the Impala well into December while the finishing touches were being completed on his new 1962 Bel Air. In one of his last races in the Impala, Don won Stock Eliminator at Pomona on December 8. The Impala clocked a 12.74 at 112.64 mph for low ET and top speed in class. At the same event, Don also drove Dean Lowe's A/SR in Competition but lost in the first

JERRY JARDINE

Jerry Jardine was a young teenager in the early 1950s with little more than cars on the brain. He had the ideal after-school job, working at Pearly's Muffler Shop in Pasadena. It wasn't long before the proprietor taught Jardine how to weld and he was forming exhaust work of his own.

Jardine had owned a few hot rods in his teens and by the time he finished high school he had saved enough for a new 1958 Impala powered by the all-new 315-horse 348. The cost was $400 dollars down and $88 dollars a month. On a trip to the dry lake of El Mirage with the Chevy, Jardine topped 140 mph. The first time out to the drags with the car was a trip to the old San Gabriel track, where Jardine defeated a number of the Les Ritchey Performance Unlimited cars, including the bored and stroked 354-ci Chevys disguised as injected 283s. The next day, Jardine drove out to Don Nicholson's shop (which, in 1958, was located in Monrovia), looking for some help in making the Chevy go even faster.

Jardine recalled that Don said, "I don't know why you bought that thing, it'll never run." Jardine proceeded to tell him how he just beat all of Les Ritchey's cars and the 1957 Chevy that Don had tuned for Dave Fenn. "Don's response was a surprised, 'What?!' Don was all over my car after that; rejetting the carbs, playing with the timing so the advance came in sooner, and upgrading the ignition." This was the beginning of Don's involvement with the 348–409-powered Chevys.

Jerry recalled that the only one who ever beat his 348 was Shirley Shahan. "I went up to Bakersfield one Sunday and had the class covered, running quicker than all the other cars. Shirley had a red 1958 Bel Air. I didn't know they had any women running up there. Over her door was written 'Red and Ready.' The car was red and Shirley had red hair at the time. I was busy looking over at the car when the flagger gave the sign. Needless to say, I came in a late second."

Jardine built his first headers in 1959, a pair of fenderwell Tri-Ys welded together on the floor of Don's garage in Duarte. He adopted the Tri-Y design after looking at a cutaway drawing of a 1956 Maserati. Jardine was doing most of his work out of a sheet metal shop owned by a friend's dad in Pasadena. An exploding aftermarket eventually allowed him to open his own place in Garden Grove around 1960. At its peak, Jardine Headers were producing roughly 100 sets of headers a day. By the late 1960s, fly-by-night header manufacturers had flooded the market and eventually killed the business. Jardine turned to building headers for motorcycles and saw a major boost in business when Tom McMullen at *Chopper* magazine gave him some positive ink. The bike business took off and became larger than the automotive business had ever been. By the end of 1972, Jardine no longer made headers for cars.

"We moved into a new building in 1973, 40,000 square feet and didn't even put a lift in for cars." Jardine Headers survives today in Casper, Wyoming, and is operated by Jerry's son. And yes, once again the company does build headers for cars. Although he's retired, Jardine likes to keep busy and builds the odd set.

Why a wagon? With tire width limited by rules, Don was well aware that the added rear weight aided traction. The B/FX winning School Bus, *as Don pegged the Chevy II, helped with his decision to run the Comet wagon in 1964. (Photo ©TEN: The Enthusiast Network. All Rights Reserved.)*

round. At the end of the year, the Impala found a new owner in David Heath. Heath campaigned the car as the *Kentucky Colonel*, running S/S, B/Factory Experimental, and match racing the car through the next few seasons. The Impala seems to have disappeared after Heath sold it in 1965. It was last known to be in Muncie, Indiana, sporting blue paint.

1962

Don had three cars at the first national event of the year, the NHRA Winternationals; a Super/Super Stock Bel Air, an A/FX Chevy II sedan, and a B/FX Chevy II station wagon. It appears that the sedan never competed, but both the Bel Air and wagon came up winners. The Super/Super Stock class was reserved for Detroit's latest top-of-the-line, showroom-available performance offer-

The winning records of Dyno's cars meant that he never had an issue finding new owners when it was time to move them. David Heath of Owensboro, Kentucky, purchased Don's 1961 and christened it the Kentucky Colonel. *Note the Enderle bug catcher scoop still in use. (Photo Courtesy Jack Bleil)*

ings, such as Don's 409/409 Bel Air. With the issues he had at Indy in 1961, Don ensured his 409 was built to a T; he installed .060-over ForgedTrue pistons with step seal rings, and he mic'd everything before putting it back together.

Don found the opposition a little tougher this year, with stiff competition coming from Les Ritchey's 406 Ford, the Mickey Thompson 421 Pontiac driven by Hayden Proffitt, and East Coast nemesis Dave Strickler and his similarly equipped 409 Bel Air. It was Strickler who eliminated Dyno Don during Saturday's class runoffs in the too-close-to-call semifinal match. Strickler faced Hayden Proffitt in the final, losing to an unbelievable 12.52. In Sunday's 50-car Mr. Stock Eliminator runoffs, Don defeated the Fords of Les Ritchey and Gas Ronda and the S/SA Pontiac of Whittier, California's, Carol Cox. Meanwhile, Strickler, on his way to a final round appearance, did everyone a favor by defeating favorite, Hayden Proffitt, in the first round. With the twin white Chevys lined up for the final go, the flag went up and off they went on a clean start. Dyno Don took a slight holeshot lead and held off Strickler's hard-charging 12.55 with a 12.84 at 109.22 mph. As proof that the sport of drag racing was still in its infancy, part of Don's winnings included a color television donated by Mr. and Mrs.

Sopps, owners of Sopps Car Wash in Los Angeles.

In a 1962 interview, Don discussed his driving technique with automotive journalist Roger Huntington. With the narrow 7-inch tires allotted to Stock, he came off the line at 3,000 rpm. Don stated that the higher (than most racers) revs gave him more flywheel inertia and torque to play with. When the flag went up, Don eased into the throttle and rode out the clutch. For him, this prevented bogging that he felt many cars suffered from. By the time he's halfway through low gear, about 100 feet out, he was full throttle. Shift points came at 6,000 rpm, 6,500 with the new mid-season factory upgrades, which included intake, cam, and heads. These changes did not change the factory 409-hp rating. Don found that there were no performance gains above this. "Wild 7,000 rpm shift points didn't do anything for my times. They just beat up the engine." Chevrolet had released 409 upgrade parts in the spring (.480 lift cam, valve springs, etc.) and again in the fall. The late-season parts included high-port heads that worked in conjunction with a two-piece aluminum intake manifold and a .511-lift camshaft with a little more overlap. These parts were used in 1963 on the Z11 Impala and raised the advertised horsepower to 425.

In the shadow of Don's Mr. Stock Eliminator winning Bel Air were a pair of fuel-injected, 327-powered Chevy II's.

At the 1962 NHRA Winternationals, Don parlayed a nice holeshot in the Mr. Stock Eliminator final to defeat Dave Strickler's Old Reliable. *A 12.84 against Strickler's 12.55 did the trick. Don's Chevy grabbed many track records through 1962, including the half-mile mark at Riverside, where he recorded a 133.90 mph. (Photo ©TEN: The Enthusiast Network. All Rights Reserved.)*

Could Dyno's Winternationals-winning 409 Bel Air be the car that inspired the Beach Boys to pen their April 1962 hit song "409"? There is no doubt that it had to have been a contributing factor. After winning the NHRA winter meet, Don was runner-up to Bill "Maverick" Golden at the AHRA Winter Nationals, turning a best of 12.87 at 112.50 mph. (Photo ©TEN: The Enthusiast Network. All Rights Reserved.)

Both cars were plain 100 series models in Ermine White. There was little difference between the new for 1962 Factory Experimental category and 1961's Optional Super Stock category, it was still meant as a place for the Detroit manufacturers to showcase their limited-production high-performance cars and parts. This category consisted of classes A, B, and C, and each class was based upon a weight to cubic-inch factor. A/FX consisted of cars weighing 8 pounds or less for every cubic inch. B/FX consisted of cars weighing between 9.00 and 12.99 pounds, and C/FX cars that weighed more than 13 pounds per cubic inch. Don won class with the wagon, turning a 12.55 at 108.96 mph. Although it wasn't until late 1964 that Chevrolet released the V-8 Chevy II option to the general public, by early 1962 it did offer over-the-counter kits for the do-it-yourselfer. Don completed the swap on his Chevy II's with the help of Bill Thomas, whose factory ties helped him procure parts before their general release. Don's Chevy IIs were showroom models pulled directly from the dealer's lot. The Corvette mill was factory rated at 360 hp and featured a .060 overbore, Jardine fenderwell headers, and was backed by a Borg-

Even more rare than Don's Chevy II wagon was his A/FX Chevy II sedan, captured here at Motor City Dragway in Michigan. Don hauled all three of his 1962 cars to Atlanta when he relocated there in April 1962. Like the wagon, power came by way of a fuel-injected 327. A 1961 "SS" emblem is on the lower fender. It's unknown what became of this car. (Photo Courtesy John Marsh)

A 360-hp Corvette mill propelled Don's Chevy II wagon to B/FX honors at the Winternationals in 1962. Don Steves supplied the car, which was built with over-the-counter GM parts. Don's Top Stock–winning Bel Air is on the left. (Photo Courtesy Nicholson Family Collection)

Warner transmission. Single-leaf rear springs with track bars harnessed the power. Because the 100 series wagon (with the 327) weighed nearly bang-on to the B/FX minimum, there was no need to remove excess weight. As an example, the wagon retained the rear seat, windshield wiper motor, and heater but the coolant hoses weren't plumbed. All indications are that the sedan was built in the same manner.

Earl Wade was showing success of his own at the winter meet. Previously, Wade had pulled wrenches for John Mazmanian, helping him win AA/MSP at the 1961 Winternationals with his Corvette. Mazmanian had bought the Corvette new at Porter Chevrolet in Pasadena and the first thing he did was drive it over to Service Chevrolet and let Wade and Nicholson have at it. At the 1962 Winternationals, Wade himself won Street Eliminator while driving the A/SP injected Corvette of Mike Lenke. In total, there were eight class winners at the 1962 meet that had visited the dyno at Service Chevrolet. At a huge Super Stock meet at Fontana late in February, Don defeated Hugh "Putzel" Osterman, driving the Grassman-Osterman-Wade-Nicholson (as the records

There was no way that the Chevy II's original 8.2 rear end would hold up to the injected 327, so in went a full-size housing carrying 4:56 gears. Note the class-required exhaust system. Present but difficult to see here are the metallic brake linings, a coil-over shock on the right side only, and a long traction arm. Rear wheels were 15 inches while the fronts were the original 13-inch wheels. (Photo ©TEN: The Enthusiast Network. All Rights Reserved.)

Don's dyno tuning helped at least eight class winners at the 1962 NHRA Winternationals. One was this fuelie Corvette owned by Brendan Grassman. Hugh Osterman drove the B/Sport Production class winner to a best of 12.70 at the Winternationals and took class with a 13.23 at 106 mph. Here, Osterman faces the 421 Tempest owned by Mickey Thompson and driven by Hayden Proffitt. (Photo Courtesy Robert Genat)

Dyno Don's reputation only grew greater when he moved East in the spring of 1962 and took up residence at Nalley Chevrolet, Atlanta's largest Chevrolet dealership. People came from hundreds of miles around to have Don dyno-tune their car. Nalley promised Don the run of the dealer's speed shop/tune up shop as well as a race car, which came in the form of a Z11 Impala in 1963. (Author's Collection)

show) Corvette. Dyno, exhibiting skills that would take him far, read the track and flagman to perfection, and he cleaned Osterman's clock with a 12.87 at 112.35 mph to a trailing 13.24 at 109.22.

Within a couple of months of winning the Winternationals, Don took up a job offer from Nalley Chevrolet in Atlanta, Georgia, to run its dyno and the dealer's speed shop. The move was a bit of a no-brainer for Don, as he looked to make a living drag racing and there was no better place than in the southeast, home of the big-dollar match races. The added bonus was that Nalley was headquarters for the Southern Engineering and Development Company (SEDCO), a front for Chevrolet's clandestine racing program. Don's wife and daughter waited until the end of the school year, when Cindy finished kindergarten, before joining him for the summer.

In July 1962, Chevrolet celebrated its 50th year in production. To commemorate the special occasion, it produced a limited run of 20 409-powered aluminum-nose Impalas via the Central Office Production Order (COPO). Don received one to race at the NHRA Nationals. It's believed that either Don or Dave Strickler received the first car produced. Powering the Impalas was the late-season 409 with the good Z11 parts. Due to its limited production numbers and heavier weight, the car

fell into B/FX. In the class final, Don's yellow Impala defeated Dave Strickler's *Old Reliable III* with a 12.93 to a 12.96. It's questionable as to whether Don drove the car at all after the Nationals, instead focusing his attention on the lighter and quicker Bel Air. Fellow racer Hubert Platt, who worked alongside Don at Nalley, is known to have driven the car after the Nationals, match racing it through the end of the season.

Don also drove the Bel Air at the Nationals but failed to repeat the previous year's showing. Hayden Proffitt took Top Stock, defeating the Ramchargers' Jim Thornton in the final. In a Robert Genat interview, Don states that Proffitt won that race because he was running at shipping weight rather than curb weight; the difference was 3,440 pounds versus 3,620 pounds.

Earl Wade and Dyno Don have reason to be all smiles as they pose proudly with the Bel Air at Vineland, New Jersey, in June 1962. The Chevy was rarely beaten. It was torn down because of official protest 18 different times in 1962; each time it was found to be legal. (Photo Courtesy Nicholson Family Collection)

Even with the aluminum front clip dropping approximately 125 pounds, and without frills such as heater or radio, the 409 Impala still weighed in at close to 3,400 pounds. Reportedly, 18 to 20 of these "lightweights" were built; only two are known to remain. Backing the 409-hp mill was a Hurst-equipped BorgWarner 4-speed. (Photo ©TEN: The Enthusiast Network. All Rights Reserved.)

"It took us a while to catch on. That's why Proffitt's Bel Air car ran so good. Bill Thomas helped build that car. It was a frame-off. They cut up the dashboard, cut

> ## They cut up the dashboard, cut out the bottoms of the ashtrays, and whatever to get the weight out.

out the bottoms of the ashtrays, and whatever to get the weight out. I couldn't believe the NHRA allowed them to get away with that [aluminum] dash. [Stock] those things are heavy with that big pot metal casting."

Hubert Platt left Nalley at the end of 1962, quitting to become a full-time drag racer. Before doing so, he hauled Dyno's 1962 Bel Air down to Tampa on November 22 for an eight-car Super Stock show and proceeded to clean house, defeating Dave Heath in Dyno's old 1961 Chevy and Don Garlits, who made a rare appearance in his new 1963 Dodge, among others. It was Garlits who fell to Platt in the final as the Dodge proved to be no match for

the well-tuned, bored, and stroked Chevy that recorded an 11.77. Jerry Jardine recalled a little trick that Dyno had performed on the match-race engine; he left the two front cylinders of the 409 at stock bore and stroke while all of the other cylinders were enlarged.

"We built headers so that the way they were plumbed, it was nearly impossible to access the plugs for P & G measurement." Topping the big-cubic-inch match-race mill were the late-season Z11 parts. In addition, the Bel Air received lightweight aluminum front-end panels. Ed

The B/FX class final boiled down to the two fastest-running Chevy Impalas in the nation: Dyno Don's and the Old Reliable III of Dave Strickler. Don took a slight holeshot lead and hammered through the 4-speed to take the win with a 12.39. (Photo ©TEN: The Enthusiast Network. All Rights Reserved.)

Under darkening Indiana skies, the B/FX class final gets under way. While Strickler's Impala carried Ermine White paint, Don's Impala appears to wear GM Golden Yellow. Note the OEM steel wheels; aftermarket wheels were just coming into vogue in 1962 and still weren't class legal. (Photo Courtesy Mike Strickler)

After the Nationals, Hubert Platt took over the controls of the Impala. Working alongside Don at Nalley, Platt had stated that "sometimes we'd drive each other's cars." Platt raced the Impala through the remainder of 1962 as the Bounty Hunter before getting a 1963 Z11 Chevy and striking out on his own. The 1962 was sold to a wealthy businessman in Atlanta, and its whereabouts today is unknown. (Photo ©TEN: The Enthusiast Network. All Rights Reserved.)

Those Mopars back East had nothing on Don's Chevy. Dyno's move East in 1962 was based on economics. The West Coast–tracks were paying $25 war bonds (worth $17 according to Don) to the Stockers. In the East and the South, he could make $600 and up for a match race. Great money, considering maintenance on the car was next to nil. (Photo Courtesy Robert Genat)

At the NHRA Nationals in 1963, the aluminum front clip and Z11 engine parts put the Bel Air in B/FX. This photo was shot at the 500 Shopping Center in Indianapolis, where pre-race inspection was carried out. Cut rear coils and stiffer springs up front gave the Chevy its stance. Don used a stiffer coil spring on the left rear to help load the right side upon acceleration. (Photo Courtesy Jack Bleil)

Schartman, who came to work for Don in 1963, raced the Bel Air as late as the spring of 1964. Eventually, the well-worn and stripped car ran 10-second times.

Ken Simpson became the new owner of the Bel Air when Don finally parted with the car sometime in 1965. The historic piece was wrecked by its third owner in Alabama and was scrapped around 1974. The Chevy II wagon was sold and raced out of Florida for a couple season's before disappearing. What became of the Chevy II sedan is still unknown.

1963

Between December 1962 and January 1963, Chevrolet produced in the neighborhood of 57 lightweight Z11 Impalas. Built specifically for drag racing, the heart of the $1,240 Z11 package was the 427-ci engine. Conservatively rated at 430 hp, the 427 was a stroked 409 fitted with large-port heads, 13:5.1 compression, and

Ken Simpson became the second owner of Don's Bel Air, seen here in 1965. All indications are that Don last drove the car at the Nationals in 1963. By its third owner, the Chevy was wrecked; it was finally scrapped in 1974. (Author's Collection)

Ed Schartman is caught coming hard off the line at Cecil County where, in the spring of 1964, the Chevy was competing in A/Modified Production. At this point, the Chevy was running Z11 parts and aluminum front body panels. Note the body was slid back on the chassis, a hood blister was added, and the traction arm was extended. (Photo Courtesy John Durand)

This (yellow) Biscayne was campaigned by Hubert Platt, an employee of Nalley Chevrolet in 1962. Hubert's son Allen believes that Don may have initially campaigned the car. What's known for sure is that Don did drive the car at least on occasion. The 409 helped push the no-frills Biscayne (no radio, heater, or rear seat) to low-12 times. (Photo Courtesy Tom Schiltz)

By 1963, Don was one of the most feared racers in the nation; his Chevys were nearly untouchable. Dyno Don figured that if the Mercury deal hadn't come along for 1964, he could have had another successful year with his Chevys. (Photo Courtesy Nicholson Family Collection)

a camshaft featuring .556 lift. A two-piece aluminum intake manifold mounted twin Carter carburetors that drew fresh air plumbed in from an opening in the cowl. To save weight, the Z11 cars were produced with aluminum parts, 149 in total, including front-end panels and front and rear bumpers. In addition, the cars were delivered without the front sway bar, heater, radio, sound deadener, and sealant. Backing the 427 was a BorgWarner 4-speed transmission, and even though it was delivered with 4:11 rear gears, Don ran 4:56 or 4:88s. With Nalley Chevrolet's close ties to the factory, it's believed Dyno received the first Z11 Impala pro-

duced. Originally running A/FX, by the end of January 1963 Chevrolet had produced the required number of Z11 Impalas, thus allowing the car to run NHRA Super Stock.

Modifications that Don made to the Impala included a thorough blueprinting of the 427. Starting with the Carter carbs, the primary jets were drilled out from .101 to .104 while the secondary jets went from .068 to .073, or larger. On Don's existing 409 Bel Air, jets were drilled to .104 and .067. The distributor was reworked giving 34 degrees total advance between 2,000 and 3,000 rpm. To prevent movement, the breaker plate was welded to

Caught on Detroit's return road during a June 1963 match, Don's 26-gauge aluminum-nose Impala is looking a little worse for wear. Note the high-low stance and 10-inch M&H slicks, standard wear for 1963. Don's Chevy was one of the tops in the nation. (Photo Courtesy Robert Genat)

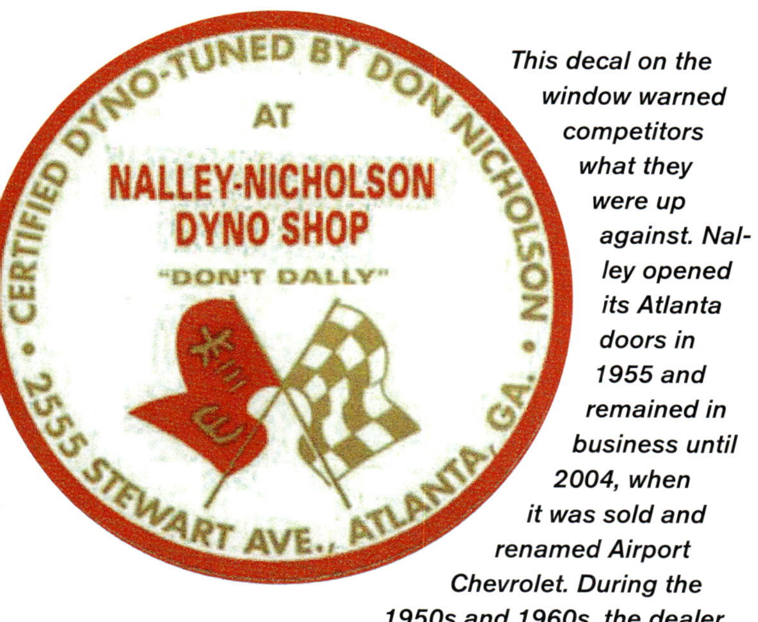

This decal on the window warned competitors what they were up against. Nalley opened its Atlanta doors in 1955 and remained in business until 2004, when it was sold and renamed Airport Chevrolet. During the 1950s and 1960s, the dealer had a direct line to Chevrolet that included all of the rare and one-off performance goodies that the manufacturer had to offer. (Author's Collection)

Don shows off some of the Impala's winnings outside of the Nalley Dyno Shop he operated. The expansive shop was located at the rear of the dealership and featured not only a Clayton dyno but also a loaded machine shop. (Photo Courtesy Nicholson Family Collection)

the housing. The heads were resurfaced and Don reamed out the ports below the seats, per NHRA rules of the day, but no additional grinding was done. All valves were checked and seated to the same depth. As required, shims were placed under the valve springs to restore pressure. Replacing the factory Delco spark plugs were hotter, extended-tip Champion J61 Ys. The plug change was said to be worth 10 more horsepower on the dyno. As far as headers go, Don built his own Tri-Y fenderwells. As for the suspension, a half of a coil was cut from the rear springs and Don fabricated square tube track bars that ran from the rear end to a pivot point on the chassis ahead of the transmission crossmember. With 40 to 50 pounds of air in the front tires and as little as 20 in the rear, the Impala left the line at 3,000 to 3,500 rpm.

On May 12, Don took the Impala to Tampa, Florida, where he claimed the number-9 position on the *Drag News* Top Stock list by defeating Ed Garlits in a best-of-three match. Ed, brother of "Big Daddy" Don Garlits, was a respected driver in his own right and was driving the Dodge sedan of Don's on this day. Nicholson went on to win the Super Stock Eliminator the same day by beating the Z11 Impala of Bob Tucker in the final round, setting the track record in the process with an 11.96 at 119 mph.

The *Drag News* Top 10 Stock list was started in 1962, bringing some organization to the match-race scene and boosting racers' status. The way the list worked was that anyone could challenge those in positions 2 through 10, but to challenge for the number-1 spot, you had to be in the top 10 already. Once he was challenged, the spot holder could shop for a venue, and then take the challenge to any drag strip he chose for the two-out-of-three match. Obviously, money mattered and the racers went to the track that paid the most. Don grabbed the number-1 spot on the list July 7 by defeating the Chevy of Frank Sanders in two at Ohio's Dragway 42 during the *Drag News* Invitational. By this point in the year, Don's Chevy had already been hitting 11.80 times. Prior to the race, Don was protested and, upon inspection, found to be legal. In the match against Sanders, Don ran quick enough to win: 12.33 at 115.53 mph and 12.23 at 116.42 to Sander's best of 12.52 at 114.64. Dyno retained the top spot on the list for the next five months before losing it in December to the Pontiac of Arnie Beswick. Driving his 1962 Chevy, Dyno dropped the match to Beswick in three with a best of 11.83.

In what seems amusing today but was not so much in 1963, Don was tossed at the NHRA Nationals after red lighting on a bye run. It was the first national event where the Christmas tree replaced the flagman start and the two B/FX favorites, Don in his 1962 Bel Air and Arnie Beswick in his Pontiac, were about to face off. Beswick had two cars at the race, a Tempest and a Swiss-cheese Catalina, and had just completed a run in the Tempest. While making the

The Impala's high-in-front, low-in-back stance came courtesy of spring spacers and cut coils. Back in the day, the going theory was that this helped weight transfer. Dyno's relationship with Chevy was informal. Unlike the Ford and Chrysler racers, he had no paperwork or reporting to do. He was under no obligation to the manufacturer, which supplied necessary parts but never money. (Photo Courtesy Robert Genat)

Detroit Dragway used to hold a big Stocker meet during the weekend prior to the NHRA Nationals. Drawing the biggest names in the nation, I guarantee there isn't one racer noted on this flyer that Don, referred to here as "Mr. Chevrolet," hadn't beaten. (Photo Courtesy Robert Genat)

A nice shot of the Impala's suspension at work as Don launches off the line at Detroit. Dyno set track records wherever he went. At Cecil County in June, he did the trick, turning an 11.83 while defeating Bud Faubel's 1963 Plymouth in a best-of-five match race. His biggest win with the 1963 came at Daytona, where at the NASCAR Winternationals Don won overall Stock. (Photo Courtesy Robert Genat)

run, a crewman moved the Catalina up the staging lane, preparing for Beswick to take the wheel when he returned from his run. A little-known rule of the day stated that the person who moved the car through the staging lanes had to be the one to race the car. When the car pulled to the line, Beswick hopped in, and he was waved off. Sorry, Farmer, rules are rules and you're disqualified! Don, all set, hit the loud pedal and ran the Bel Air through the quarter. The only problem was, Don failed to wait on the green. Not familiar with the bye run rules on the tree, he left the line after staging. Is it any surprise that when asked about the new start system at the time, he stated he hated it and preferred the flag start.

Don stated the best combination he ever had was the 1962 Bel Air with all the Z11 parts. "It was 421-ci with a .060-over bore and step seal rings. The car was quicker than the 1963 Impala. With the aluminum front end, it was probably close to the same weight." After the Nationals in 1963, Don went back to the Bel Air. He had lent the Bel Air to a gentleman who worked for him, Richard Broome, later of NASCAR, who was racing the car in North Carolina. "It definitely ran better than the '63 and I ran it for the rest of the year." The Impala was sold and, sadly, rolled sometime in 1964. The owner was running the car on a loose, unsanctioned track outside of Atlanta when the incident happened.

> ## Sorry, Farmer, rules are rules and you're disqualified!

At the end of June, NASCAR held its Dixie 400 race in Atlanta, and while attending Don met up with his old friend Troy Ruttman. Ruttman had won Indy back in 1952 and was in Atlanta making laps in his Mercury. It was through Ruttman that Don received word that the people at Mercury were interested in talking to him. Don made tracks for Detroit and by the end of the year he had a signed deal with the manufacturer.

Induction for the limited-run Z11 cars was based upon twin Carter AFB carbs on a two-piece aluminum intake manifold. The cowl induction was a great innovation that I'm sure worked better than the hood scoop that Dyno trialed. The Impala drew its fresh cool air from the voids in the inner headlight buckets. The distributor was an aftermarket Spalding Flame Thrower. (Photo Courtesy Robert Genat)

By Don's own admission, the 1963 wasn't as quick as his 1962 Bel Air and accordingly wasn't raced as frequently. After the 1963 Nationals, Don went back to driving the Bel Air. It's believed that 57 of these Z11 Impalas were built; all were non-SS models. (Photo Courtesy Robert Genat)

"Fast Eddie" Schartman

Fast Eddie Schartman recalls it was 1962 when he first met Don. "I was working as a line mechanic at Cleveland's Jackshaw Chevrolet. They sponsored my '62 Chevy and they had a good connection with Chevrolet. Don came up from Atlanta to pick up parts and we became friends. Don offered me a job to come work for him in Atlanta and build engines for him." Schartman moved down in 1963. When the Mercury deal came along in 1964, he started driving Dyno's 1962 Chevy Bel Air. With Don's blessing, Schartman tore into the Bel Air, pulling the body off the chassis and cutting weight from it. Schartman figures that he removed a total of 500 to 600 pounds from the car. With a Z11 427 for power, the Chevy terrorized the South, running 10-second times.

"I was racing three to four times a week earning up to 300 bucks a match, plus a couple hundred in appearance money. Don and I had a deal that we split the winnings fifty-fifty." The Chevy retained Nicholson's name on the flanks, which wasn't appreciated by his new bosses at Mercury. "They wanted me out of the Chevy, so I told them, 'Well then, give me a car.'"

When Nicholson received his Comet hardtop in the spring of 1964, Schartman got the wagon. "Then they wanted me out of the wagon because they weren't selling 427-powered wagons." Schartman won Mr. Stock Eliminator at the 1965 NASCAR winter meet, but he grew tired of working for someone else and handing over half of his winnings. He struck a deal with Mercury in 1965 that saw him driving Dyno's Wedge-powered Comet.

Schartman moved back to Cleveland in 1965, and even though he butted heads regularly with Don on the track, they remained friends. When the flip-top Comets appeared in 1966, Schartman was the only one who could keep pace with Don. During 1968 and 1969, Schartman ran a pair of Cougar Funny Cars before turning to Pro Stock in 1970. By the mid-1970s, he had become disenchanted with the sport and retired.

Jackshaw Chevrolet in Cleveland sponsored Ed Schartman's Z11 Impala. It was while working there that Schartman and Don got to know each other. Don went to Cleveland to pick up parts that Chevrolet supplied. (Photo Courtesy Robert Genat)

Don lets loose with the 427 Impala at Detroit. If that wheelbase looks a little shuffled, it just may be. A common trick used by many back in the day was to slide the body as far back on the chassis mounts as they could to get as much weight on the narrow slicks as possible. (Photo Courtesy Robert Genat)

MERCURY RISING (1964–1965)

At the 1964 NHRA Winternationals, it took a holeshot by Ronnie Sox in the Factory Stock final to defeat Don. Fresh cool air was fed to the Holley-equipped 427 by ram tubes plumbed through the inner headlight cavities. The rear-opening bubble scoop was meant to expel hot underhood air. (Photo Courtesy Randy Hernandez)

When General Motors pulled out of racing in 1963, it stated publicly that the company was falling back to its 1957 AMA ban on involvement and support of all forms of motorsports. Other sources state that it had more to do with the fact the Justice Department was breathing down GM's neck. GM's new car sales held approximately 57 percent of the market; there was a genuine possibility that the Sherman Antitrust Act would be invoked, thus splitting up the corporation. It seems that racing, even though it was a small percent of overall sales, was hurting General Motors rather than helping it. Whatever the reason for the exit, when it came to drag racing, guys who had enjoyed factory support, including Dave Strickler, Sox & Martin, and Don Nicholson, began to look elsewhere by the end of the season. With Dyno Don's reputation, there was no way that he was going to be left dangling in the breeze.

1964

In stepped Fran Hernandez and Lincoln-Mercury. The manufacturer first entered the world of drag racing in 1964, and the timing couldn't have been better for both Don and Sox & Martin, whose names were on contracts by the end of November 1963. Working with a limited budget, Hernandez, Mercury's

Performance and Evaluation manager, had Dearborn Steel Tubing build 11 drag race–only 427 high-rise–powered Comet Calientes. In such a limited number, the cars were destined to run NHRA A/FX. Two prototypes were initially built; one was a station wagon that went to Don and the other was a hardtop that some reports suggest went to the team of Sox & Martin. Success back in 1962 with his Chevy II wagon showed Don the advantage of running a wagon. The added rear weight and shorter wheelbase of the Comet wagon (109.5 versus the hardtop's 114 inches) helped plant the narrow 10-inch tires. Don retained the prototype wagon. As Mercury's Al Turner recalls, it was a handful, "It was a bit of a monster, more temperamental than the hardtop."

The highly modified 427s featured twin 780-cfm Holley carbs, cross-bolt mains, and a steel crank.

Forged pistons helped squeeze out a high-octane 14:1 compression and gases flowed through valves measuring 2.19 and 1.73 inches. As with the near-identical 427 Ford Thunderbolts, horsepower was pegged at 425. Following the similar build pattern as the Thunderbolt, modifications to fit the engine to the Comet included trimming the shock towers and relocating the upper control arm mounting points. To conform to rules of the day, it was necessary to retain the stock track width. To do so, upper and lower control arms were modified. Because a short upper arm can produce some drastic camber changes when the front end rises during acceleration, Don chose to use standard Comet upper and lower control arms (moving the lower pivot point out) in conjunction with offset rims to retain the stock track width. To lighten the

In 1964, Lincoln-Mercury would go drag racing, building 10 of the 427 Comet hardtops and this lone wagon for Don. When Don arrived home from his visit to Lincoln-Mercury, he surprised everyone by rolling up the drive in a company-provided baby blue Mercury Monterey. Though appreciative of the car, Don's wife's first impression wasn't the greatest. She thought it was ugly. (Photo Courtesy Robert Genat)

Ed Schartman probably put more runs on the wagon than Don did. Here, at New York's Dover Dragstrip in October, Ed match races the Hemi Honker Dodge of Bud Faubel from Chambersburg, Pennsylvania. The Honker's 10.80 times were no match for the Comet's wheel-standing 10.60s. (Photo Courtesy doverdragstrip.com)

Comets, the fenders, hood, doors, and front bumper were all made of fiberglass. The interior was stripped of the heater, radio, underlay, sound deadener, and radio.

Don modified his Marauder wagon further by blueprinting the 427 and adding a Crane cam and springs. Jardine headers replaced the factory exhaust and was said to be worth 3 mph on the top end. This boosted horsepower to the 500 range. A Hays clutch inside a RC protective bellhousing filled the space in front of the BorgWarner T10 transmission. Aiding gear changes was a Hurst shifter. To make room for the big M&H slicks, the wheel tubs were hammered out and the leaf springs were narrowed. Don also used offset shims to center the 31-spline 9-inch rear end in the wheelwell. The wagon had what one might call a "semi-active" rear suspension with specially designed track bars and shocks. Autolite's John Horseman created the shocks; they were designed with what he called a "blow-out valve." When the clutch was let out, the rear end locked up like a solid rear axle. The Autolites initially held solid, then the valve would pop and the shock went back to normal. Horseman compared the shocks to what we see on today's Pro Stock cars.

According to Mercury's Al Turner, "We had to go 3/16 inch on the inner wall tube so they wouldn't split it with the valve." Horseman made about five sets of these shocks before they finally got what they needed, and Don tested all of them. To cut down on drag and reduce roll resistance, the front brake adjusters were backed off, lightweight bearing grease was used, and tire pressure was maximized. These were all modifications Don had made to previous cars. To help gain additional front-end travel, the upper shock bushings were removed. Dyno Don took the wagon out to Houston on December 8, where he was also match racing his 1962 Chevy against Arnie Beswick.

On the wagon's maiden voyage, straight off the trailer, it recorded a 12.08 time.

Don recalled taking the wagon to the AHRA Winter Nationals (February 7–9) at Bee Line in Arizona and being protested by the Mopar set, who screamed that the short wheelbase of Dyno's wagon gave him an unfair weight advantage. The AHRA agreed. Mercury's Al Turner protested, stating he had a verbal agreement with AHRA president Jim Tice that the wagon could run, but Don was tossed. In response, Turner pulled all the Mercurys from the race. Dyno Don debuted his Comet coupe within months, and even before the car was lettered, he had reset the A/FX record with an 11.21 at Baltimore. As Dyno told drag race historian Charlie Morris, "I guess the Mopar guys should have quit while they were ahead."

The Cleveland-based Bellino brothers, Mike and Rocky, took class at the 1964 NHRA Winternationals after Don tweaked their Chevy. Ed Schartman was employed at Jackshaw Chevrolet before moving south to join Don at Nalley Chevrolet. By the time the Bellinos won class, Don was already with Mercury. (Photo Courtesy Thomas Nagy)

Ed Schartman took over driving the Comet wagon in the spring of 1964. His biggest win in the car came at the NASCAR Winternationals in February 1965. There, he survived a 50+ car Super Stock field to beat the Dodge of Keenan O'Connell in the final with an 11.16 time. (Photo Courtesy doverdragstrip.com)

Prior to the NHRA Winternationals a week later, the Comets were tested at Long Beach, where they were said to have run 11.0 times. At the Winternationals, Don's wagon set low ET with an 11.44 and he faced Ronnie Sox in the Factory Stock final. Although Nicholson ran the quicker 11.47, it was Sox for the win with a holeshot, 11.49.

With no more than a handful of NHRA and AHRA national events scheduled in 1964, match racing was where a serious drag racer could shine. And Don did shine; he lost only 2 of 76 races he entered. The wagon left fans gasping as it yanked the front wheels 6 inches to a foot off the ground as Don powered through the gears. This was something you just didn't see a door car doing, let alone a station wagon. No competitor was safe when it came to Don and his wagon. On April 5, he strolled into Detroit, where he laid waste to the factory team of the Golden Commandos. Don beat them in their own backyard, taking the five-rounder in three. In the process, he lowered the track record, which the Commandos had just set, from an 11.62 to an 11.54. On May 3,

Dyno faced the GTO of Arnie Beswick at York US-30 for a night match. At the time, Beswick was at the top of his game, having put together quite the string of victories with his blown Pontiac GTO. The thing with Beswick was that you never knew whether he was going to run the blower. He'd say no blower then show up with one. On this night, Don laid Beswick to waste, blower and all, with a best of 11.18 at 126.22 mph.

While Don was tearing it up with his Marauder wagon, hired hand Ed Schartman took the reins of Dyno's much-modified 1962 Chevy. He was winning his share of matches and splitting the gross with Dyno. Schartman took the Chevy up to Detroit in April for a match against the Grand Spaulding Dodge driven by Pat Minick. Fan anticipation grew as the racers performed the pre-race ritual of laying down the traction-inducing rosin and performing their burnouts. With each driver ready, they staged side by side and waited on the green. Schartman got the jump and never looked back, banging through the gears to take the first round over Minick's Stage III

At Indy in 1964, Don laid waste to Tom Grove in the Melrose Missile as he marched on to the class final. Don turned full-time racer in 1964 and racked up 80,000 miles on the road. The miles paid off, because Don's win percent was greater than 97, having won 74 battles. Bite was by M&H. (Photo Courtesy Randy Hernandez)

Don's record of 74 match races with just two reported losses helped establish Mercury's drag race reputation in 1964. Don stated that one of the reasons they put him in the coupe was "because everybody on the Mercury team started complaining about the station wagon because I had the quicker car." (Photo Courtesy Forrest Bond)

426 with a close 11.86 to a 12.02. Round two saw Minick take a holeshot lead, but he was unable to hang on to it. Schartman drove around him with an 11.70. He made it a clean sweep, taking the third round with an 11.87 clocking. He'd bring the Chevy back for a single run and burn through the rosin to turn a phenomenal 11.50.

Dyno debuted the hardtop Comet in May and approximately six weeks later, the Marauder wagon was shipped to Hawaii for a brief tropical vacation. Mercury's Al Turner arranged the trip at the request of Jim Pflueger, proprietor of Hawaii Raceway Park. Pflueger wanted the "name" car and a driver for the July 4 grand opening

of the track. The name driver hired to run the car that day was Jack Chrisman. The wagon stayed in Hawaii for approximately two months and was campaigned during that time by Earl "Safari" Char. Upon the car's return to the mainland, Dyno's Chevy (that Schartman had been running) was regulated to the sidelines when Schartman took over driving the wagon. Rechristened the *Ugly Duckling,* Schartman ran the wagon as late as the spring of 1965 before taking the reins of Don's Wedge-powered Comet. Dyno unveiled his SOHC Comet Caliente at Cecil County on May 16, where he butted heads with Phil Bonner's Wedge-powered Falcon. Don took the

The first week out with the Caliente, Don set the A/FX elapsed time record at Cecil County with an 11.21. Blocked-out inner headlights initially ran ducting to the twin Holley carbs. (Photo Courtesy Forrest Bond)

Don takes a break to pose proudly with his Caliente. His wife, Patty, designed the Crane Cams logo, which is still in use today. The front wheels are rare Howards. Don's helper and tuner at the time was the well-liked Linton Parker. (Photo Courtesy Randy Hernandez)

match in three rounds. The Comet recorded a best of 11.16 at 128.22 mph. Don returned for a solo run after the match and with the help of a little rosin, set the track record with a 10.94 at 128.89. It seems a stretch, but reports from the day state that the Comet lifted the wheels in all four gears.

Dyno took a hard final-round loss to the Comet of Bill Shrewsberry at the Fremont *Hot Rod* magazine drags before hauling back to Cecil County where, on July 26, he defeated both Sox & Martin and Dave Strickler in the same evening. It took Dyno all three rounds to dispose of Ronnie Sox. In the middle stance Sox took the win with a track Factory Experimental record of 10.98. Don took the final round, erasing Sox's track record with a 10.96. The win gave Don the opportunity to face Dave Strickler in the Jenkins-tuned Hemi-powered *Dodge Boys* car. Strickler warmed up the big hemi with runs of 11.04 and 11.07. Come race time, Don put it to the Dodge in the first heat with an 11.05 while Dave faltered, missing the 2-3 shift. In the second, Don took a holeshot lead to win the match with an 11.15 at 125.69 mph to Strickler's 11.11 at 125.97. For all his success in 1964, Don enjoyed the fruits of Ford and Mercury through 1970. Although Chrysler failed in its attempt to lure Don from Lincoln-Mercury in 1964, it did manage to land Sox & Martin at the end of the season. As told by Mercury's Al Turner, Sox & Martin wanted two cars just like Don had and the company refused. Heading back to North Carolina from Detroit, Buddy Martin stopped in Atlanta to confer with Don. It was from Dyno's shop that Martin placed his initial call to Chrysler.

York US-30 found it could easily fill its seats by hosting four-wide match races, something track manager Bill Holz did on a regular basis. For an August 22 match, he lined up the Comets of Dyno Don and Ronnie Sox, as well as the hemi cars of Bud Faubel and Dick Landy (Landy was on an eastern tour with his S/SA Dodge). Dyno proved to be unbeatable, setting a new track record with a 10.97 during a warm-up run and taking the three-round match. In the first round, Don was left flat on the line as the flagman failed to notice his "not ready" signal. Bud Faubel crossed the line first with an 11.11 followed by Sox who knocked out an 11.34. In the second, Don was the first out of the gate at the drop of the flag. His 3-foot wheelie yielded to no one and he sailed through the top-end lights with Faubel hot on his heels followed by Sox and Landy. Round three proved to be a repeat of two with Don showing all three the way home.

At the Nationals, the Comet broke against eventual class winner, Dave Strickler, whose Jenkins Competition–prepared Dodge can be seen to the left in this photo. Per NHRA A/FX rules, the M&H piecrust slicks were a maximum 10 inches wide. (Photo Courtesy Robert Genat)

A rarely seen bird's-eye view of the Comet taken on Labor Day weekend. Don's 11.05 national record, noted on the quarter panel, came in July at Pennsylvania's famed York US-30. (Photo Courtesy Robert Genat)

In September, Cecil County played host to what may have been the biggest match-race bash of the season, the first *Cars* magazine Super Stock Invitational. Thirty of the nation's quickest Super Stock and Factory Experimental cars ran heads up. The only rules were that all cars must weigh a minimum of 3,200 pounds and run a maximum of 427 ci. Leading the way were the Ramchargers, who showed up with both their A/FX and the S/SA cars. Both were in the 10s with the S/SA car running the first round's low ET of 10.92. Bud Faubel was also on hand with two cars. However, it seemed that all eyes were on Don and his Comet, which rattled off 10-second runs of its own. Action opened up with the Ramchargers making

Chrysler Partnership

Dyno in a Mopar? Never you say? Well, it almost happened in 1965. Chrysler contacted Don late in 1964 with an offer of a Hemi car along with a salary. There was no room in Mercury's meager budget to pay a salary but it did tip Don off to the Single Overhead-Cam (SOHC) engine that was just around the corner. It sounded like fun times ahead for Don and that was enough to convince him to stick around. The icing on the cake was the Lincoln Continental that Mercury provided for Don's wife, Patty, to get around in. This wasn't the only time Chrysler came knocking in Don's career, hoping to win him over. Prior to the 1970 season, it was Don who approached Chrysler looking for a deal. Don had talked to Ford late in 1969 hoping the manufacturer would step up for 1970 and provide him with both a Funny Car and a heads-up door car. Ford balked at the idea of dishing out two cars because it just wasn't in their budget. Therefore, Don, looking to have his desires met, went shopping elsewhere. A deal with Dodge came very close to being inked but it fell through thanks to last-minute disagreements.

headway with both of their cars, until they had to face each other in the quarter-final action. There, the S/SA car eliminated the FX car, running 10.87 at 129.68 to a 10.99 at 126.93. In the semifinals, the Ramchargers' S/SA Dodge fell to Dyno's Comet.

To make the final round, Don defeated Phil Bonner's *Georgia Peach* Falcon in the third with a 10.87 at 127.11 mph to an 11.10 at 123.98. In the final go, Faubel's *Honker* made its first-ever 10-second pass, running a 10.99 at 126.40 mph, but it wasn't enough as Don's Comet recorded a 10.75 at 127.65 for the win, and low ET of the meet. Part of Don's winnings included a Chrysler Hemi engine. Finishing second in standings were the Ramchargers, who received a 427 Ford. I wonder if the pair made a trade.

The *Ugly Duckling* wagon was sold to Steve Bagwell, and its demise came when a clutch explosion tore up the car. The damage was so severe that Bagwell stripped the car and buried the remains. The Comet hardtop was sold to Matt Fenton, who continued to campaign the car through 1965 with Ivan Jordan behind the wheel. The history of the car is something like this: It's believed that Benny Jerman purchased the Comet directly from Fenton and then sold it to Paul Bednarik in 1980. When Bednarik purchased the car, it had been sitting beside Jerman's shop in Maryland for a number of years. The car was pretty rough and cut up; its rear suspension had been moved forward 10 inches. However, it retained a number of the "good" parts, including fiberglass fenders, hood, glass doors, decklid, rear end, and ladder bars. In the mid-1980s, Bednarik traded the car to Brent Hajek, who had the car restored, replacing floorboards, trunk pan, taillight panel, and so on. Today, the Comet remains in Brent's possession.

Running a match in Georgia around the time of the 1964 NHRA Nationals, the wagon is caught catching air as Schartman burns through the rosin. Note the later fiberglass hood, minus the teardrop scoop. Schartman's biggest win in the wagon came at the NASCAR Winternationals at Daytona Beach in February 1965, where he survived a 50+-car Super Stock field to beat Keenan O'Connell's Dodge in the final with an 11.16 time. (Photo Courtesy Randy Hernandez)

Ed Schartman ran the wagon well into 1965. Note Schartman's use of Don's secondhand Chevy hauler. When Don received his Ford hauler, he also received a Lincoln Town Car for his wife, Patty. Even mechanic Tom "Snake" Jones got in on the act, using a red Comet Cyclone as a daily driver. (Photo Courtesy Randy Hernandez)

SOHC It To Me

To think, if it weren't for the Chrysler Hemi, there just may never have been the single overhead-cam 427. If it weren't for NASCAR president Bill France's reneging on his approval of the SOHC, drag racing would have never enjoyed the benefits. Why was the engine built in the first place? Chrysler won the NASCAR crown in 1964 and Ford followed in its footsteps with the conventional 427 high-riser engine. Not willing to settle for second place, Ford responded by building the exotic Hemi-headed SOHC engine, an engine that went from the drawing board to completion in 90 days.

To keep costs of the Cammer to a minimum, the engineer team, led by Norm Faustyn, built the engine using the existing 427 high-riser as its base. To handle the increased power of the twin-cam top end, the bottom end saw a beefing up that consisted of cross-bolted mains, an improved oil system, cross-drilled forged crank, and forged pistons swinging from forged rods. The cast-iron Cammer heads featured gargantuan 2.25-inch hollow stem intake valves and 1.90-inch sodium-filled exhaust valves. To rotate the twin cams, Ford went the less expensive route of running a gear-driven chain that, when laid out, measured 6 feet long. Although it was cheaper, the chain wasn't nearly as effective as the gear drive that Top Fuel ace Pete Robinson later developed. Cast-iron rockers mounted on hardened steel shafts actuated the valves. Valve lash adjustment on the early Cammers was by lash adjusters; the later design saw this changed to adjusting screws. The void FE block's cam space was filled with a dummy shaft that operated the oil pump and dual-point distributor. A separate chain ran the shaft off the crank. Covering the maze of gears and chain was a two-piece aluminum cover with removal access covers. Topping the heads were a pair of magnesium covers.

In 1966, Pete Robinson won the Top Fuel world championship with the SOHC engine. By the end of the decade, Top Fuel Cammers were producing in the neighborhood of 2,000 hp. The Cammer was only produced from 1965 into 1967, and by the time the decade closed, parts were becoming scarce, even for the top pros. This, in conjunction with prohibited cost, made the engine all but obsolete.

The NASCAR version of the SOHC 427 featured a single 4-barrel and was rated at 616 hp at 7,000 rpm and 515 ft-lbs of torque at 3,800. The twin 4-barrel dragstrip Cammer was rated at 657 hp at 7,500 and 575 ft-lbs at 4,200. To think, if you had approximately $2,500 to spare during the mid-1960s, you could walk into your local Ford or Mercury parts dealer and walk out with your own Cammer. (Author's Collection)

This photo was shot in March 1965 at Lassiter Mountain Dragstrip in Birmingham, Alabama, one of the many "outlaw" tracks that dotted the nation. Schartman was in the process of defeating Bill Jacobs's Kid Goat, a Hemi-powered Dart, in a three-round match. The Black Widow Car Club developed Lassiter in 1958; dynamite was used to blast a flat surface out of the hillside. (Photo Courtesy Randy Hernandez)

This is how the top runners traversed the country in 1965. Don went nearly unde-feated in 1965 and earned the title of "Match Race King." That Chevy truck didn't last long into the season; Don received a Ford F350 tow rig. (Photo Courtesy Nicholson Family Collection)

Don's promising debut at the 1965 NHRA Winternationals went down the tubes with a broken axle. No issues at the follow-ing Springnationals, where he did walk away with class hon-ors. Don tried both M&H Race Masters and Goodyears to aid traction. Rear-gear choices were 4.71 or 4.88. (Photo Courtesy Randy Hernandez)

1965

With the introduction of Ford's SOHC 427 in the 1965 Comet, the continuation of Don's 90-percent win record was ensured. As with the 427 high-riser in the 1964-model Comet, the Cammer was no easy fit into the 1965. To garner the needed additional space for the Cammer, Detroit Steel Tubing cut the shock towers loose and rotated them 180 degrees outward, which removed them from the engine bay. In addition, the upper control arm mounts were moved outward the width of the frame. Further suspension mods included lengthening the spindles to raise the front 2 inches. To maintain proper front-end geometry, the lower control arms were moved outward 2 inches and also lowered 2 inches. Once the reworking was complete, DST had gained an additional 8 inches of much needed space.

As the advertisements of the day stated, the Comets wailed and, initially, no other Factory Experimental match racer could touch them. Dyno brought his Comet to the Yellow River Dragstrip in Covington, Georgia, on February 21 to face Phil Bonner's SOHC Mustang. As invincible as these two factory hot rods appeared, both cars broke in the first round of the planned three-round match race. While Dyno was heading for second gear, he destroyed the Top Loader. Bonner coasted across the finish line after breaking the rear end. The cars returned for round two after an extended delay while repairs were made. Leaving the line side by side, the two cars remained that way until half-track when Dyno inched

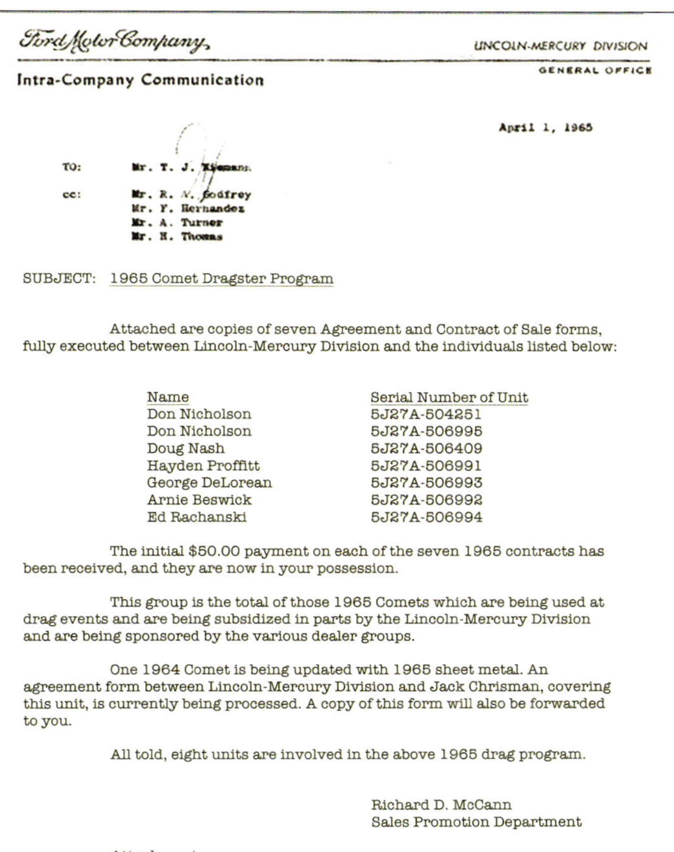

Ford Motor Company,   LINCOLN-MERCURY DIVISION
                                                              GENERAL OFFICE
Intra-Company Communication

April 1, 1965

TO: Mr. T. J. Ziemann.

cc: Mr. R. N. Godfrey
         Mr. F. Hernandez
         Mr. A. Turner
         Mr. N. Thomas

SUBJECT: 1965 Comet Dragster Program

Attached are copies of seven Agreement and Contract of Sale forms, fully executed between Lincoln-Mercury Division and the individuals listed below:

Name	Serial Number of Unit
Don Nicholson	5J27A-504251
Don Nicholson	5J27A-506995
Doug Nash	5J27A-506409
Hayden Proffitt	5J27A-506991
George DeLorean	5J27A-506993
Arnie Beswick	5J27A-506992
Ed Rachanski	5J27A-506994

The initial $50.00 payment on each of the seven 1965 contracts has been received, and they are now in your possession.

This group is the total of those 1965 Comets which are being used at drag events and are being subsidized in parts by the Lincoln-Mercury Division and are being sponsored by the various dealer groups.

One 1964 Comet is being updated with 1965 sheet metal. An agreement form between Lincoln-Mercury Division and Jack Chrisman, covering this unit, is currently being processed. A copy of this form will also be forwarded to you.

All told, eight units are involved in the above 1965 drag program.

Richard D. McCann
Sales Promotion Department

Attachments

As documentation shows, Dyno was allotted two Comets in 1965. Ed Schartman drove the second car, which was powered by a 427 Wedge. Don left Ed to his own devises and he did pretty well. Additional Wedge-powered Comets were built, though the exact number is unclear. (Photo Courtesy Randy Hernandez)

At the 1965 NHRA Winternationals, Don was looking good, setting low ET with a 10.89 before breaking in the first round of eliminations against Bill Lawton's Mustang. In May at Cecil County, Don took the record from Gas Ronda (10.87) by recording a 10.56. Dyno held the record for the next six months. (Photo Courtesy Ray Kobe / Golden Commandos Collection)

Yeah, she's a tight fit. Don stated that the Cammer was initially slower than the Wedge. "I tore it down and cut about .100 off the block to get the compression up, and degreed the cams." The car picked up a couple tenths and 4 mph. The Holleys pictured gave way to Webers. The radiator is a standard 289 piece. (Photo ©TEN: The Enthusiast Network. All Rights Reserved.)

Peering through the lightweight, fiberglass door, you can see that the interior featured just the bare necessities. Bucket seats were also fiberglass. A 10,000-rpm Sun tach mounts in plain view on the dash. To speed along gear changes, the Top Loader had the teeth cut off the second, third, and fourth synchro rings. (Photo ©TEN: The Enthusiast Network. All Rights Reserved.)

Hard off the Gainesville start line charge Don and Sox during this spring 1965 match. Both cars were capable of 10-second times. In short order, both were sporting injectors and running 9s. (Author's Collection)

ahead, gaining a foot by the finish line, and taking the win with a 10.54. The deciding final round saw Dyno once again crossing the line first, taking the win by a car length with a 10.52.

What gave Don and the Comet the upper hand, even over his Ford counterparts, were the aftermarket Crane cams run by Mercury. Ford couldn't understand why Mercury was thrashing the Ford cars on the track, going so far as accusing Al Turner of stealing its speed secrets. According to Turner, "They told the guys at the engineering group not to talk to me." Unlike Mercury, which had been running special Cranes since 1964, Ford was running factory grinds in its 427. As good as the SOHC was, initial issues saw the engine going through bearings. According to Turner, reducing crankshaft diameter solved the problem.

"We went down to the same size journal as the hemis and ran their bearings. It took Ford longer to figure it out," said Turner. To run the Chrysler bearings, not only did the

Certificate of Performance

NATIONAL

CLASS RECORD

authorized by

NATIONAL HOT ROD ASSOCIATION

This certifies that DON NICHOLSON

a contestant in a National Record Run Event, did establish an official National quarter-mile acceleration record in A/FACTORY EXPERIMENTAL class during the period of official record runs, having been electronically timed by the CHRONDEK TIMING SYSTEM at a speed of 130.05 MPH, with an ELAPSED TIME of ---- seconds. This National record shall remain in effect until such time as it is officially exceeded at an NHRA Record Run Event, or until it is otherwise declared invalid by the NHRA.

Established at PHENIX DRAGWAY   Date APRIL 10   , 19 65

NATIONAL HOT ROD ASSOCIATION
DEDICATED TO SAFETY

NATIONAL HOT ROD ASSOCIATION

Certified by: Jack Hart

Through the years, Don set and reset a countless number of mile-per-hour and elapsed-time records. The first one he captured in 1965 was the mile-per-hour mark, which the Melrose Missile *had held for the previous nine months. (Photo Courtesy Nicholson Family Collection)*

Ed Schartman would wheel Don's Wedge-powered Comet through 1965. Running A/FX, Fast Eddie is seen here at Bristol, home of the NHRA Springnationals. The Comet was good for legal mid-10 second times and lower 10s with a stroked match race motor. Today, the Comet is in the collection of Brent Hajek. (Author's Collection)

At Carlsbad in February 1965, Don took a three-car match over the Comets of Jack Chrisman and Hayden Proffitt with a best of 10.68. His "Outstanding Performance" trophy is just one of a countless number he took home in 1965. (Photo Courtesy Nicholson Family Collection)

In a 1965 poll conducted by **Drag Racing** magazine, Don was ranked number-one fan favorite and dragstrip draw. He repeated in 1966 and 1967. In addition, Super Stock & Drag Illustrated *magazine* voted him driver of the year in 1965. And it's no wonder; he had just five losses on the season. Note the powder rosin laid out. Burning through the rosin made for super bite and crowd-pleasing wheels-up launches. (Photo Courtesy Randy Hernandez)

When Ford-Mercury refused to allow its team drivers to face the radically altered–wheelbase Mopars, Don went against the manufacturer's wishes and tore into his Comet, altering the wheelbase and dropping weight by swapping in a straight-axle front suspension. There was little the manufacturer would or could do about it, because Don was their numero uno. (Photo Courtesy Phil Bonner Jr.)

By late in the season, little remained of the Comet's interior; all it had were a tachometer, gauges, shifter, and a single seat. More difficult to see is the parachute ring and the gas pedal with toe strap. Note the lack of side windows and rear window. In addition, vent holes were drilled in the trunklid and the taillights were removed. (Photo Courtesy Nicholson Family Collection)

crank have to be turned down to size but also width. This gave the Cammer a slight stroke. Turner states that they went to Fred Carrillo and got six sets of corresponding aluminum connecting rods that cost him no more than a pair of decals on the car. "It would have taken engineering six months and $250,000 dollars to get them. I got them in a week." The aluminum rods cushioned the blow between strokes and made life easier on the bearings. According to comments made by Earl Wade, because of rod stretch, head clearance ran .006 to .0065 inch. On the main bearings, Don ran .005-inch clearance. This was necessary because the crank flexed a lot. Any tighter and they'd spit out bearings.

Looking for more of an advantage over the competition, Don installed four 58-mm two-throat Webers on the Cammer just before meeting the Ramchargers on May 16 for a match race at Martin, Michigan. Don hoped to extract a little revenge after a rare loss to the Detroit-based team the previous season. To ensure a level playing field, track owner John Griven had each car weighed in at 3,200 pounds. In addition, the fuel tanks were drained and topped up with local fuel. After weigh-in and prior to the five-round match, the Ramchargers' Jim Thornton and crew were spied changing slicks. Suspicion got the best of track officials, who decided that the tires needed weighing. The slicks taken off the car were weighed, and then the slicks on the car were pulled and weighed. The discrepancy was approximately 300 pounds. A little investigation showed the heavier tires had been filled with water! Once the M&Hs were reinstalled, Thornton

> ## In 1965, Mercury was telling us not to race those 'funny' cars. But Mercury wasn't paying us a salary.

was forced to run with the water-filled slicks in the trunk. No doubt the extra weight had an effect on the outcome of the five-round match. Don won it in three with a best of 10.57 at 131 mph. What's the old adage? Winners never cheat, cheaters never win? So they say.

In July, Don decided to go the full funny route with his Comet to take on the radically altered–wheelbase Mopars head-to-head. Going back to early in the year,

Altered doesn't begin to describe Don's Comet, seen here running Ford boss Dick Brannan at Indy. The Comet's modified wheelbase measured 110 inches, 4 inches shorter than stock. Fabricated 2 x 3 traction bars measuring 28 inches long, and a pair of Air-Lift bags helped to plant those 10-inch Goodyears. Don coaxed a best of 9.10 at 150 out of the Comet while winning a match race against Ronnie Sox at Tampa Dragway on November 28. (Photo ©TEN: The Enthusiast Network. All Rights Reserved.)

At the NHRA Nationals in 1965, Don and other "exhibition stockers" were forced to run Gas or Altered. Don's Comet fell into B/A, where it failed to advance. To meet class requirements, Don was required to add a headrest, fuel shut-off, and a throttle-return toe strap to the gas pedal, as well as wear a fire suit. Just a couple months before, on July 10, the Comet became the first to run a 9-second time when Don recorded a 9.91 at 137.40 mph while winning a match race against Bud Faubel at York US-30. (Photo Courtesy Forrest Bond)

Ford refused to allow its factory teams to run against the funny Mopars and Mercury drivers had little choice but to toe the line. The rumor at the time was that if they refused, Ford would cut off their parts supply. Don, seeing his match-race bookings dwindling, took matters into his own hands. As relayed by author Bob McClurg in his book, *Diggers, Funnies, Gassers & Altereds*, Don stated, "In 1965, Mercury was telling us not to race those 'funny' cars. But Mercury wasn't paying us a salary. I couldn't afford NOT to go out there and race!" After getting beaten by Ronnie Sox twice in a 24-hour period, once at Jacksonville and again at Tampa, Don tore into his Comet, sliding the rear wheels forward 10 inches and modifying Hilborn injectors to mount onto his Weber intake manifold. Being the manufacturer's biggest draw, there was little that Ford or Mercury could or would do about Don going against its edict. Was Ronnie Sox worried about the Comet that Don was about to unleash? Apparently not. "Let him waste his time building his funny Comet

. . . because I'll just build up a Plymouth twice as funny as his," Sox stated.

Before another Sox and Don showdown came a four-car bash at Bill Holz's York US-30 on July 10. Billed as the nation's first funny car showdown, it was a planned five rounder that featured Don, Tom Sturm's *Just 4 Chevy Lovers* Chevelle, Bud Faubel in the mid-engine *Cotton Picker* Dart wagon, which was initially campaigned by NASCAR hold-out Cotton Owens. The fourth car was California's Dick Landy and his Dodge. Landy was enjoying his second trip east and had really been cleaning house. Lining up four wide on the York strip, the first run saw Faubel jump to an early lead and hang on with a 10.10 victory, just ahead of Don's 10.14, Sturm's 10.49, and Landy's off pace 10.56. Round two was a write-off due to foul starts. Round three saw Faubel again take the win with a 10.09 to Don's 10.11. Landy picked up the pace slightly, hitting 10.46 followed by Sturm's 10.56. Don took round four with a 10.12 while Faubel followed with a 10.16 followed

A late-season outing at the famed Lions Dragstrip shows the Comet in full altered mode. Don later stated that after he altered the wheelbase, the car became one the "squirreliest" cars he ever drove. The home-fabricated scoop helped "ram" air to the injector tubes. (Photo Courtesy Randy Hernandez)

The Comet was almost a full funny by July 1965, with altered wheelbase, nitro, and injectors. A straight-axle front came shortly after this photo was taken. Tom "Snake" Jones (right) pulled wrenches for Don in 1965. Jones really made the rounds, having later worked alongside early Funny Car pilots Roger Lindamood and Jay Howell, among others.

This is where Tony Conover discovered Dyno's old Comet in 1986, buried in a cluttered garage in Van Nuys. Most of the good parts were still intact. (Photo Courtesy Irwin Kroiz)

by Landy and Sturm. With no chance of winning the match, Landy and Sturm sat out the final round. Faubel and Don lined up before the track curfew kicked in for one final, *mano-a-mano* battle. With the ambers off and a go on green, it was Don out first. The cool night air couldn't have agreed more with the Comet as it blazed the clocks with a 9.91 at 137.40 mph, becoming the first Comet in the nation to break into the 9s. Faubel, hot on Don's heels ran a 10.03 at 134. Happy with the win, *Drag News* reported that Don's key goal was to shut down the Mopar of Landy, which had been grabbing headlines with his string of East Coast victories.

Don hauled the Comet south, this time to Richmond, Virginia, for the much-anticipated rematch with Ronnie Sox. The best-of-five battle proved to be a match of errors. Rain, which washed out the ET clocks, was the first race delay. With the weather clearing and the track dry, the pair lined up for the first match, which proved to be no match at all. Sox's *Paper Tiger* blew its hemi and Don sailed to an easy 137.92-mph victory.

With the *Paper Tiger* out of commission, it was agreed that Sox would run the team's second car, the carbureted *Paper Tiger Too*. To help even things up, Don agreed to run gas through his Cammer rather than the usual 30-percent

Back when old race cars weren't worth much, someone performed some major surgery on the Comet. Although it is hardly recognizable, plenty of telltale signs pointed to this being Dyno's original Comet. (Photo Courtesy Irwin Kroiz)

This was the first time an unblown door car had cracked 150 mph.

load. A warm-up run by each car showed them to be a pretty equal paring, with Comet hitting a 133.80 and the Plymouth a 133.81. Round two was a bust for Don when he had issues getting the Hurst into second gear. Round three went to Don after Ronnie proved to be a little too excited and fouled. Shortly after the match, Don swapped out the coil spring front suspension for a much lighter Woody Gilmore straight axle.

Don clashed with Detroit's Ramchargers one more time before the end of the season. In November, the pair butted heads in a historic best-of-five battle at Capitol Raceway in Maryland. Once again, Don proved why he was considered to be the best after taking the match in four. In three of the rounds, Don's driving skills shone through as he won them on holeshots. His best time of the match was a 9.36 at a record 150.10 mph. At the time, it was reported in the *Drag News* and *Super Stock & Drag Illustrated* (*SS&DI*) that this was the first time an unblown door car had cracked 150 mph.

Dyno sold the Comet to Pete Gates for a cool $5,500 shortly before the August 1966 Super Stock Nationals. Part of the deal was that Gates received all the guidance he'd ever need from Dyno and tuner Earl Wade. Still getting used to the car, Gates shared driving duties with Don until Gates was comfortable behind the wheel. By the time the Super Stock Nationals rolled around, Gates felt ready. To the surprise of many, "Pete the unknown" proceeded to clean house. He steamrolled through the 2,700-pound fuel class during Friday night's action. In the final, he defeated wily veteran Del Heinelt in *Seaton's Shaker* Chevelle with a 9.07 at 150.85 mph. Gates improved on those times Saturday night when he took Bob Harrop's Dodge with an 8.97 at 152.54, and then defeated Bud Faubel for class with a 9.09. A dispute kept Gates from Sunday's class elimination but he returned for handicap Super Eliminator where he survived five rounds and beat Eddie Schartman in the final.

Today, the Comet, or what remained of it after years of modifications, survives thanks to the efforts of Tony Conover and Dick Bridges. Conover discovered the car in 1986 in Van Nuys, California. "It looked like the Comet had been raced into the 1980s and was pretty rough. At some point the previous owner had decided to chop the roof." Thankfully, most of the good parts were still there: the straight axle, glass fenders, hood, 9-inch rear end, and ladder bar suspension. Thanks to the extraordinary efforts of Conover and Bridges, among others, this historic piece survives.

DYNO SOARS (1966–1968)

Don's return to Irwindale with a new Comet shell went much more smoothly. The total weight of the Comet came in at just a hair more than 1,700 pounds. Although the car looks "factory," the only OEM parts on the body were the grille and taillights. (Photo Courtesy Forrest Bond)

One has to look back to 1966 to see when the flip-top Funny Car first appeared. Lincoln-Mercury led the way with these new-style match racers. Reviewing the company's "Program Appropriation Request," dated August 17, 1965, Fran Hernandez requested $330,000 to build one "featherweight" supercharged Comet roadster "that might be fiberglass." In addition, three lightweight match-race Comets were also proposed, all powered by the SOHC 427. As we know now, a change of plans saw four featherweight funnies built. Once again, Dyno was leading the charge for Mercury, as he would through 1968.

1966

It was a banner year for Mercury and its Comet. *Super Stock & Drag Illustrated* (*SS&DI*) named the Comet the Performance Car of the Year, Indy chose the car to pace the 500, and the manufacturer set the match-race world on fire when it introduced the revolutionary flip-top Funny Car. It was a great year for Dyno, who manned one of the new Funny Cars, recording a phenomenal 98-percent win record that helped earn him a spot on the *Hot Rod* magazine Top 10 list and saw him named Funny Car driver of the year by *SS&DI*.

Yup, the body was light, but not that light. The complete Plastigage epoxy shell weighed in at 225 pounds. Paul Shedlik of Wayne, Michigan, applied the orange paint and topped it with gold Murano pearl. Shedlik was a paint and body man at Dearborn Steel Tube before going to work at Ford's design studio. When word reached him regarding the forthcoming flip-top Comets, he opened his own shop with Lincoln-Mercury as a main client. (Photo Courtesy Randy Hernandez)

1966 Comet Eliminator I

Regarding the birth of the flip-top Comet Funny Car, Al Turner recalls sitting in Chrisman's southern California garage one night in 1964 with Chrisman and Gene Mooneyham. They were sharing a laugh and discussing Chrysler's altered wheelbase cars when he said, "What if we set the engine back 25 percent like Mooneyham's, with a tube chassis and a fiberglass body on it? We would kick their ass!" That was the beginning of the whole thing. The following year, Chrisman returned with his rebuilt Comet, carrying a Cammer and set back 25 percent. The funny Comets of 1966 were a natural progression.

Not to lose sight of the fact that it was all about selling cars, Lincoln-Mercury general manager Paul Lorenz let Fran Hernandez and Turner know that

Don stated that the 1966 Comet "was the most fun car of them all." And it's no wonder, with a track record of only 3 losses in 80 races. The only time the car lost was when it broke. (Photo Courtesy Randy Hernandez)

According to Mercury's Al Turner, Logghe had a flexible chassis that it used for dirt track cars; it was the basis for the Comet chassis. At this point of construction, the tinwork, interior trim, and transmission had yet to be installed. (Photo Courtesy Robert Genat)

"if the cars are going to look like the altered-wheelbase Chryslers and not the cars we are selling then we're not going to be in drag racing." To showcase his idea, Turner built a scale model using balsa wood for a chassis with a Mattel body on top. He presented it to management, telling them that this is what they planned to build. With a green light from Lorenz, work got under way. The lucky recipients of the four flip-top Comets were Jack Chrisman, the newly formed team of Roy Steffey and Ed Schartman, the Colorado-based team of Kenz & Leslie, and Dyno Don, of course.

While the Logghe brothers (Ron and Gene) went about building the 116-inch-wheelbase chassis, Plastigage of Jackson, Michigan, received a Mercury design plug to form the bodies. The initial plan for the Comets was to have complete lift-off bodies that would be pinned to the chassis. However, when the bodies returned from Plastigage they were heavier than expected. At that point, it was Ron Logghe's idea to hinge the bodies at the rear, thus creating the flip-up design. According to Al Turner, the Logghes were sworn to secrecy regarding the chassis design and guaranteed Mercury an exclusive one-year deal that prevented them from building and selling the design to others.

When it came to the Cammers, Chrisman ran a GMC blower on top of his while the remainder of cars ran Hilborn injectors. Dyno tested the first Comet at West Palm Beach, Florida, with a 4-speed but found shifting too cumbersome. Between missed gears and over-revving, the 4-speed just wasn't going to work in the new car.

The Yellow River Dragstrip really wasn't much of a track. Don ran numerous hair-raising match races on outlaw tracks such as this. This photo appears to have been taken in the spring, because Don has not yet switched to the Jardine "weed burner" headers. (Photo Courtesy Wayne Langford)

The unique flip-up Comet, the first of its kind, drew all kinds of attention. Here, an engulfed Dallas TV announcer describes the potency of the injected single overhead-cam 427. I can hear him now, "Astounding as it may sound, folks, this engine produces enough torque to effectively alter the speed at which the earth rotates." (Photo Courtesy Connell Miller)

A beefed-up C6 automatic was swapped in before testing was completed and Dyno never ran the 4-speed in competition. Unconfirmed reports state that two bodies may have been lost during testing. Apparently, high-speed air pressure may have been an issue.

Don debuted his *Eliminator I* Comet at the AHRA Winter Nationals held at Irwindale in February. The debut was nothing short of spectacular, and not in a good way. On its first hard pass, the body blew off as the car approached the traps, leaving Don exposed to the elements at close to 150 mph. It was reported that wind pressure had pushed in the body-retaining latch, causing it to come up. On other Comets, the latch was reversed to prevent reoccurrence. What became of the damaged body? Factory reps had the remains hauled to the far side of the pits and burned.

Contrary to what many might believe, the men of Ford and Mercury racing never shared information with each other. Their racing divisions were serious rivals, in the same sense as Ford versus Chevy, for example. Says Turner, "There was no love lost between Ford and Mercury. Ford's Charlie Gray felt that I should share information with him. I told him, 'You don't share your paycheck with me.'" By mid-1966, the Comets had really stepped it up, thanks in large part to the .700-lift Crane cams they were now using. Even though Ford had told its racers they couldn't use anything but Ford parts, you can be sure that there were a few who failed to adhere to the rules. The Cranes were crafted with 4340 steel because the factory cams were all flexing. Turner paid Harvey Crane $3,000 for the masters and kept them out of Ford's reach. Schartman got the first .700-lift cams in mid-1966; apparently

It must have felt like Christmas all over again to Don when he was handed the keys to the rig and Comet. When looking for the roots of today's flip-up Funny Car, you need to look no further than Don's 1966 Comet. Don's was the first built and the first to debut. (Photo Courtesy Nicholson Family Collection)

While testing in Florida, it's believed that the Comet lost at least one body. Numerous changes came out of these tests, including a switch from a 4-speed to C6 transmission. The Comet ran full side windows early on. (Photo Courtesy Randy Hernandez)

The 427 featured Jardine headers, Hilborn injectors, Crane cams, and a Mallory ignition. The engine was set back 24 percent of stock wheelbase. Initial testing was done with a 4-speed but positioning made it nearly impossible for Don to shift the transmission. (Photo Courtesy Randy Hernandez)

In its day, the rear suspension of the Comet was a work of art. Watt's linkage controlled the 9-inch rear while Kelsey-Hayes disc brakes helped bring the Comet to a stop. The rear gears varied but 4:11 usually filled the bill. Coil-overs were adjustable and said to be drag racing firsts. (Photo Courtesy Randy Hernandez)

Logghe supplied the coil-over shocks, which were tuned to each corner of the chassis. The suspension allowed for 5 inches of travel. The chrome-moly straight axle had 21 degrees of caster and Logghe spindles mount on Halibrand rims. (Photo Courtesy Randy Hernandez)

From a safety perspective, yesterday's chassis just doesn't hold a candle to today's Funny Car. Al Bergler did the necessary tinwork. Note the offset driver's position and 4-speed shifter. (Photo Courtesy Randy Hernandez)

Don didn't know this. Don approached Turner stating, "His car's going a quarter of a second quicker. Schartman ain't that damn smart!"

In a match race that was considered nothing short of earth-shattering, Dyno faced Eddie Schartman at Martin US-131 and recorded the first 7-second pass for Funny Cars. It was a best-of-three race held Saturday, September 17 in front of more than 4,000 lucky spectators. In the cool 56-degree fall air, Dyno's Comet defeated Schartman in two straight and clocked a best of 7.96 at 171.75 mph. A few misguided souls have accused Don of running the highly explosive, performance-enhancing hydrazine to record the record time, but he flat-out denied it then and later in an interview with John Jodauga of the *National Dragster*. "The only time we used it was at the 1966 Nationals where we had to run Ed Schartman for the XS class final. Our engine was going away and Earl and I thought we'd try it that one time because we had nothing to lose. It didn't make our combination respond so we never tried it again," Dyno stated.

By October 1966, Don and other Funny Car drivers were pushing for a return to pump gas, as they felt the move made the Funny Cars safer and it lowered operating costs. Their stance was that many drivers were finding it necessary to run nitro at a costly 100 percent to remain competitive. Moreover, many teams were experimenting with hydrazine. It was said that as little as 2-percent hydrazine added to the nitro increased horsepower by as much as 15 percent. If it was handled carelessly, a racer could see his engine go off like a grenade.

1967

Don started the new season right where he ended the previous one. He opened with class wins with the 1966 car at the AHRA Winter Nationals and the NHRA Winternationals as well as Bakersfield. The Cammer's newfound power was said to come by way of a larger Hilborn 175 fuel pump that had been added to the combination in 1966. It was an idea picked up from Don Garlits and was said to be worth an additional 200 hp.

At the AHRA Winter Nationals, Don qualified the injected Comet for the 16-car Unlimited Fuel category with a leading 8.54. The run was made with a fresh

The 8-Second Wonder

In a comparison of how well the new Comet performed versus the previous year's match racers, Don met up with Jim Thornton in the Ramchargers' 1965 Plymouth at Georgia's Atlanta Speed Shop Dragway in April for a best-of-three. As requested by Julius Hughes and Frank Brumby, the track owners, the cars ran the first round right off their ramp trucks to avoid breaking during warm-up runs. After a coin toss to decide lanes, the drivers performed the ritual of burning through the rosin to make the track nice and sticky. Both cars were ready to rip; it's just too bad the timing equipment wasn't ready. A malfunctioning tree had Thornton leaving early without tripping the foul light. As the cars passed the tree, Thornton had the lead. Because of the faulty equipment, no times were recorded but by the time the cars cleared the traps, the winner was obvious. Don had the Dodge by a good car length. Before the start of round two, time was taken to repair the faulty lights. With burnouts complete, the crowd, which turned out to be the track's second largest of the season, was on its feet in anticipation. Both cars were out by the time the green bulb glowed. Thornton and the candy-striped Dodge were across the line first, taking the win with a 9.05. Round three saw Thornton firing the stubborn hemi with the help of Don's crew. Once again, both cars were lined up and raring to go; they left at the first hint of green. On the top end, it was Don. The track announcer, Harold Springs, could hardly contain his emotions, broadcasting Don's astounding time of 8.68 at 156.68 mph.

The Comet's debut at the AHRA Winter Nationals at Irwindale didn't go quite as planned. On the car's first hard pass, the body blew off as Don approached the traps. The shell came to rest just outside the guardrail. It's difficult to make out, but what is visible in the first shot is mostly the parachute. The object, or cloud, visible over the guardrail to the right is the car's body just after impact. The Ford-Mercury people in attendance had guys pick the remains and walk it across the strip to an area behind the pits where it was burned, away from prying eyes (and lenses). Don escaped with little more than a bump on the head where the fleeing body struck his helmet. (Photo Courtesy Forrest Bond)

During the 1960s, drag racing was evolving at a dizzying pace. In two short years, it went from Stockers to flip-up Funny Cars. Leading the way was Dyno and his line of Mercury Comets. By the end of 1966, Don held the ET and/or the mile-per-hour record at more than a half-dozen tracks. According to compiled records, Don competed in 80 races during the year and lost just 3. (Photo Courtesy Ken Gunning)

Cammer and a new set of M&H slicks that necessitated a little bodywork by Don and a hacksaw. The qualifying time wasn't bad, especially when you consider a freshly paved track and a sandy top end that made the pass a little dicey.

The following day, Don added a new Art Carr convertor and turned an 8.57 prior to Sunday's eliminations. Leaving no stone unturned, Don did a quick inspection of the lanes before the eliminations. By sticking his foot in the staging beams, Don discovered that he could raise his foot 1½ inches in the left lane before tripping the clocks. The right lane yielded only a 1/4-inch before tripping the lights. It's the little things that make a difference and even though the variation in beams may seem minimal, it could mean the difference between a green light and a red light. Choosing the left lane no doubt helped Don make it to the final round, where he faced Mercury rival, Ed Schartman. Don dropped opponents including Don Gay's blown *Infinity II* GTO in the semis while Schartman eliminated the Lenarth & Wolford *Secret Weapon* Jeep. Although Don had lost to Schartman at both Indy and the world finals in 1966 because of a tired mill, it wasn't the case on this day. With a clean start for both drivers, the pair buzzed the track with no clear leader until the win light flashed in Don's lane. An 8.26 at 171.75 mph by Dyno dropped Fast

The sketch that launched the career of John Jodauga. When John began his first semester at the Art Center College of Design in 1966, he had the opportunity to do some freelance illustrations for Drag Racing magazine. One of his first assignments was to do a drawing that would be mounted in a Perma-plaque and presented to Don as the "Driver of the Year" for the outstanding results shown by the Eliminator Funny Car. The sketch was in his portfolio when he first met NHRA president Wally Parks in early summer 1967. Parks liked the style and commissioned him to do the program covers for the 1967 Nationals and 1968 Winternationals. (Photo Courtesy John Jodauga)

Eddie, who turned an 8.48 at 169.69 mph.

At Pomona for the NHRA meet, Don dominated Supercharged Experimental Stock, qualifying with an 8.39 at 171.42 mph. In the final, he polished off Roger Wolford's Jeep with an 8.56 at 170.45. At Sacramento for the

Earl Wade looks on as Dyno "preps" the track prior to a match at Kansas against Larry Reyes in the Kingfish Barracuda. After a three-year absence as chief tuner, Wade rejoined Don in the summer of 1965. (Photo Courtesy Jim Marlett)

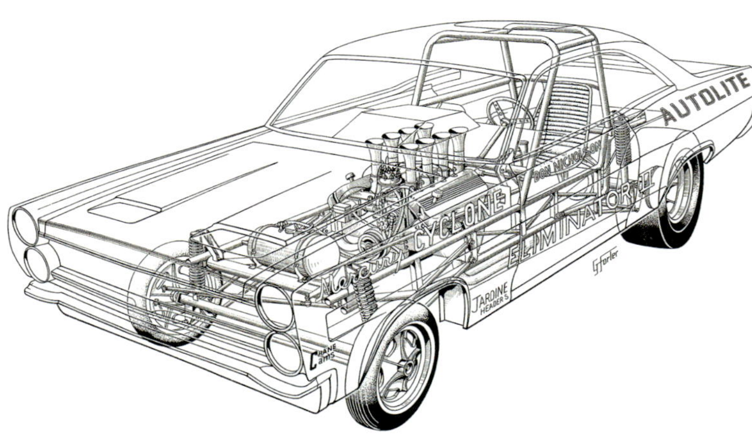

*This **Eliminator II** cutaway comes courtesy of Tom West and shows the simplicity, by today's standards, of the early Funny Car. The injectors shown here gave way soon enough to a Pete Robinson 6-71 blower. (Photo Courtesy Tom West Collection)*

Hunting was something Don enjoyed but rarely had the time for. When a family member asked if he'd be interested in joining in a hunting trip to Palmdale later in 1967, Don jumped at the chance and bagged himself a few wascally wabbits. (Photo Courtesy Nicholson Family Collection)

Bakersfield meet, Don dominated the 2,000-pound category, winning the eliminator both days with a best of 8.21 at 172 mph.

Dyno's 1966 Comet was destroyed at Cecil County in early 1967 during a show in which Don caught air on the top end, went off the track, and ended up in a swampy area. Tommy Grove was in the opposing lane that night.

"I was slowing after going through the traps and Don just flew by me. After bringing my car to a halt, I jumped out and was the first to reach him. He was pretty banged up but okay. The car, by the looks of it, was pretty much destroyed."

Al Turner stated that after testing the Comet in

> **I was slowing after going through the traps and Don just flew by me.**

the Ford wind tunnel, a front air dam was mounted; it added an additional 350 pounds of downforce at speed. "Don chose to remove the air dam when he ran at Cecil, which led to the crash. He ended up in the hospital and I told his wife Patty that I didn't feel sorry for him. He knew what would happen."

1967 *Comet* Eliminator II

The new Comet appeared similar to the 1966, but it had a number of upgrades. For openers, the new Logghe chassis featured a four-point roll cage compared to the previous year's roll bar, which made it a safer ride. In addition, the engine was located 5 inches farther rearward for improved traction. Body-wise, the shell sat lower on the chassis and things such as the drip rail moldings were removed to improve stability at increased speeds. Weight-wise, the body was said to be approximately 50 pounds lighter but the weight savings came from chassis refinements. Regarding the injected Cammer, little had changed initially from 1966; Earl Wade pulled the wrenches and, later, Jim Campbell assisted with the tuning. A C6 automatic with a 3,000-stall Art Carr convertor sat between the Cammer and the 9-inch rear that carried 3.89 gears. Transferring the power to the track were 11.75x16–inch Goodyears.

One of the more satisfying victories of Don's 1967 season came at the *Drag News* Invitational held at Atco, New Jersey, late in June. Always one of the more popular independent races, the mid-week race drew more than 6,000 fans and the biggest names in Funny Car: Bruce Larson, Hubert Platt, Jungle Jim, Cecil Yother, and Ed Schartman, to name a few. And wouldn't you know it, the final boiled down to the nation's two fastest cars, the Comets of Don and Schartman. First up, though, was round action, in which Dyno defeated Texas's favorite son, Roy Gay, in the *Infinity II* GTO in the first with an 8.33 at 148.76 mph. Meanwhile, Schartman faced the blown Chevy II of Jungle Jim and dropped him with an 8.28 at 168.86 versus an 8.39 at 162.72 mph. Dyno's second-round opponent was the *USA-1* Chevelle of Bruce Larson. At a

distinct disadvantage against the SOHC Comet, Larson "tipped the can," hoping for a miracle. It proved to be no contest as Larson's 8.90 couldn't come close to Dyno, who unleashed an 8.11. Steve Bovan's West Coast–Chevy Camaro failed just as miserably against Schartman, who recorded an 8.48 to take the decisive win. Going into the final, the fan favorites were split pretty even, but the upper hand was given to Don, having run the quicker

Here Don demonstrates the in and out of the flip-top Comet. Mercury suggested the cardinal red paint and the Halibrand wheels set it off nicely. The wheelbase measures 116 inches, just as it was on the stockers. (Photo Courtesy Steve Reyes)

Don's 1967 Comet had a much cleaner body, built with aerodynamics in mind. Not only was it lower than the 1966 car, the 1967 also featured such subtleties as no drip rails and flush-mounted glass. The grille remained a factory-cast part. This photo was shot during early tests in Michigan. (Photo Courtesy Randy Hernandez)

This was the top-of-the-line Funny Car setup in 1967. Along with the new car, Don also received a new hauler and a Lincoln Continental. Even though the truck lasted him two years, Don received a new Lincoln annually. In 1969, he received a gold Lincoln Mark 3 that was said to be the first off the production line. (Photo Courtesy Rod Short)

times. The two Comets left side by side; it was anybody's race most of the way. However, through the lights it was Dyno for the win with a new track record, 8.03 at 172.41 to Schartman's 8.27 at 166 mph.

On July 7, Don revisited the 7-second zone, recording a 7.99 at 178 mph at Lakeland, Tennessee. Shortly afterward, the floodgates opened and most of the top Funny Cars began running 7-second times, simply by replacing their injectors with blowers. Doug Thorley stunned the troops with a 7.86 clocking later in July and a 7.69 while winning Indy on Labor Day weekend.

A couple weeks later, Dyno chose to trial a blown engine, borrowing the SOHC 427 from Atlanta neighbor, Pete Robinson's AA/Fuel Dragster for a three-round match at Delaware's Delmar Dragway against Thorley. Robinson was on hand turning wrenches for Don. Never having tried the blown combination, Don took the car out for a trial run. The first pass was incomplete as the C6 transmission in the Comet succumbed to the increased power. With a new transmission in place, the pair lined up for the first round. On the green it was Thorley out front as Dyno's Comet went airborne. Don kept his foot on it before letting up in high gear as the front end came up once again. Thorley's win came in 8-flat at 178.21 mph. Back for round two, the Comet was now carrying an extra 150 pounds of ballast up front. It was a clean start for both cars and was looking good before Thorley got out of shape, nearly crossing the Comet's path. Don popped the chute early and took the win with a 7.98 at 166.66 mph. For safety's sake, all parties decided not to run a third round because it was late and the dark had set in.

Speaking of safety, late in 1967, Don was still pushing for some Funny Car guidelines from fellow racers and the sanctioning bodies. In an open letter to the trade papers, he suggested no nitro, straight alcohol with blowers, a minimum weight of 2,200 pounds, stock appearing bodies, and a maximum of 430 ci. Don's concerns have been well documented, as he genuinely feared experiencing a Funny Car fire. He lasted another year before giving up on the category.

Pappy Hart at Lion's Drag Strip outdid himself on November 4 when his third annual East versus West match bash drew a reported 12,800 fans. Match combatants came from all across the nation and included such heavyweights as Jim Liberman, Butch Leal, Dick Harrell, Roger Lindamood, Tommy Grove, Terry Hedrick, Kelly

Don's whole outfit, from car to clothes, was meticulous. Note the front-mounted distributor running off a dummy camshaft. At Car Craft's inaugural All Star Banquet on Labor Day weekend, Don took home the award for Fuel Driver. (Photo Courtesy Nicholson Family Collection)

The Comet went through one repaint after the body collapsed on the front wheels during an early-season match down south. Paul Shedlik painted it and Paul Hatton did the lettering. Full side glass and white accent pinstriping were added. The opening in the windshield was added when Don went the blower route mid-season. (Photo Courtesy Nicholson Family Collection)

Back home for the holidays in sunny California, Don capitalized by winning the Western Funny Car Nationals at Fontana during the first weekend of January 1968. There, he set low ET with an 8.01 and defeated Ray Alley's Barracuda in the final with an 8.08 to take home the $2,000 prize money. (Photo Courtesy Tom West Collection)

Don saw a banner year in 1967; he recorded 78 victories and just 2 losses. In the first seven years of Don's career, he had made the cover of car magazines 15 times and was featured in more than 40 articles. In addition, he had appeared in front of more than 4.3 million spectators in 350 cities in 43 different states. (Photo Courtesy Nicholson Family Collection)

Chadwick, and the Comets of Jack Chrisman, Ed Schartman, and Don. Expectations were especially high regarding the three Comets. In the first, Chrisman advanced after overcoming the 8.02 holeshot by Terry Hedrick in *Seaton's Shaker* Corvair with an 8.09. Schartman's day ended early after tossing a blower against Butch Leal.

I wonder what Mercury would have thought of this, a Chevy towing the Eliminator II *with the crew all onboard. Surprisingly, they were usually pretty cool with it. Sometimes, Don's friends wanted the honor of towing the cars, and he was happy to oblige. Making others' days was something Don thoroughly enjoyed. (Photo Courtesy Nicholson Family Collection)*

Dyno and his Comet debuted with a "retuned" Pete Robinson blower in place of the Hilborn injectors to eliminate Jungle Jim with an 8.30.

The highlight of the second round was Dyno defeating Leal. Don, always a fan favorite, brought a roar of cheers from the crowd when he cranked a 7.92 at 179.28 mph to Leal's 8.05 at 177.10. Chrisman, in the other remaining Comet, lost a sure one when he fouled to Don Sappington and his *Candid Camaro*.

The final East versus West match ran at 11 p.m. with Don facing Tommy Grove in his blown SOHC Ford Charger Mustang. Grove, having previously run a 7.98, was fair competition for Don and it was a good race. After heating the tires to their satisfaction, each driver crept into the staging beams. With the flames of spent fuel bellowing from the weed burners, the two cars exploded off the line on the last yellow. It was Don through the lights by inches with a 7.97 at 174.08 mph. Grove's 8.10 at 167.59 mph may have been good enough on another day, against another opponent, but it was no match for the match-race king.

1968

Don started the season driving the Comet at the AHRA Winter Nationals, where he set low ET with a

After failing to register his Comet Funny Car in time for the 1967 Nationals, Don hitched a ride in Frank Chick's Dick Brannan Ford–sponsored SS/B Fairlane. His low 11-second time put him at the head of class before a flat tire ended his day. Just visible in the photo is Bob Price's SS/C 1967 Comet on the left. (Photo ©TEN: The Enthusiast Network. All Rights Reserved.)

The 11.75x16 Goodyears find the traction at the famed Lions more than adequate as they dig in, lifting the front wheels off the track. Crewman Jim Campbell is standing at the rear of the Comet, Earl Wade to the right. Don surrounded himself with the best and always gave credit where it was due. (Photo Courtesy Steve Reyes)

7.63. The dreaded transmission ills, so prevalent during the early days of Funny Car, saw him fail to make the final-round call. That left Gene Snow to face the fill-in, and eventual winner, Jim Liberman. At the NHRA winter meet, the Ford/Mercury team drivers were forced into Holman-Moody-Stroppe–prepared Cobra Jet–powered Mustangs. Not your run-of-the-mill pony cars, the six Mustangs (in total) were specially prepared to run rough-shod through Stock and Super Stock. The cars featured a long list of modifications, including a high-flow aluminum intake manifold, tube headers, a three-point roll bar, blue streak slicks on Cragar S/S rims, and a battery that was relocated to the trunk. Don's Mustang recorded sub–record times of 11.62 at 119.70 mph during early testing.

Dyno Don's 1967 Comet shell was put out to pasture after giving up its Logghe chassis to the new Cougar. Seen here at Pete Gates's shop, where the body switch was made, the shell was sold and raced under the name **Suddenly**, but what became of it has never been determined. (Photo Courtesy Nicholson Family Collection)

It's difficult to detect here, but the engine in the Comet was 5 inches farther back in the chassis than it was in the 1966 Comet. The move was meant to improve traction. The slight tail spoiler was a mid-season addition and intended to improve high-speed stability. The unlettered Corvair in the far lane belongs to "Rapid" Ronnie Runyan. (Photo Courtesy Tom West Collection)

At the Winter Nationals, the Mustang fell into SS/EA, and fall it did. It was a one-race car for Don, who failed to make it out of class after the 428 spun a bearing. Repairs were made to the car and it passed to the new owner, Tom Safford. Safford, who had actually solidified the purchase of the car a week before the winter meet, gave the Mustang a fancy paint job and christened it *Super Snake*. He ran the car a few seasons with partners Norm Nevins and Marcel Cloutier and won a number of Division 7 races. The Mustang survives today; Don Allen restored it to Dyno Don likeness.

What just may have been Don's last outing in the Comet was also his last race in southern California before heading back to Atlanta. It was a 30-car show at Irwindale early in March, featuring Steve Bovan's blown Camaro, Charlie Allen's Dart, Ray Alley's Barracuda, and Stone, Woods & Cook's Mustang, among others. Don warmed up the Comet with a 7.88, slightly off his own track record of 7.81. Don automatically made the show based on previous race results. In the first round, he eliminated the new *Flying Dutchman* Charger of Al Vanderwoude with an 8.09. In round two, the Comet squeezed by Lew Arrington's *Brutus II* Firebird, barely with an 8-flat at 159.49 mph to Arrington's 8.03 at 163.68. Don's final-round opponent, Ronnie Runyan and his *Blue Hell* Corvair, were suffering through transmission issues and offered little resistance to Don, who took the win with a 7.88 at 162.54.

Not long after the meet, Don's crew chief Earl Wade left. He joined up with Dick Bourgeois. The pair campaigned a Doug Thorley Corvair after Thorley took a factory deal with AMC. Replacing Wade was Frank Oglesby, who had turned wrenches for Arnie Beswick and others.

The First Cougar F/C

Dyno Don campaigned two different Cougar Funny Cars in 1968. The first car was previously campaigned by the team of Maynard Rupp and Roy Steffey during 1967

Ford, having merged its racing program with Mercury's late in 1967, had most of the factory drivers in Cobra Jet Mustangs at the 1968 Winternationals. Running SS/EA, Don failed to make class runoffs after the Cobra Jet spun a bearing. The Mustang was a one-race car for Don and had been sold to new owners a week before the Winternationals. (Author's Collection)

with sponsorship from Andy Granatelli's *STP.* Granatelli gave the pair $25,000 dollars to build and run the Cougar for one year. The contract between Granatelli and the pair stipulated that at the end of the year, the pair had to return to him a complete running car. Rupp and Steffey built the car at Logghe Chassis and, according to Steffey, it was the first Cougar Funny Car built.

It was better and lighter than the standard (Logghe) cars. Helping to keep the weight in check was a lightweight fiberglass body laid up by Marv Eldridge at Fiberglass Trends. A .030-inch aluminum bulkhead and flooring were added over top of the 117-inch wheelbase chassis. The SOHC featured Crane 612A cams and Hilborn injection. Helping the fuel feed, the fuel nozzles were relocated lower than usual, thus preventing interruption of the butterfly valve when they were in the wide-open position. An Art Carr–prepped C6 was behind the Cammer. The pair debuted the Cougar at the NHRA Springnationals, where they turned promising 8.20 times. As the season progressed, they did well match racing but found major event wins elusive. At the end of the season, the car was returned to Granatelli and then sold to Don early in 1968.

Both Dyno Don and Mercury teammate Ed Schartman unveiled their Cougar Funny Cars in May, with Dyno recording a 7.85 during his first outing early in the month against Terry Hedrick in *Seaton's Shaker.* Along with the new car came a new sponsor. Don had picked up Coca-Cola; his was the first car to be sponsored by the soft drink manufacturer. Schartman and Don faced each other July 7 in a match race at Milan. It was a five-round

Sports Service Inc. issued up to nine different "Wild and Groovy" wall posters for sale in 1968, and Dyno's first Cougar Funny Car was one of the featured cars. Advertisements for the posters could be found in a number of car magazines. A bargain at $1.50 each, no doubt the 19 x 25-inch posters are valuable collector's items today. (Author's Collection)

The Rupp & Steffey 1967 Cougar became Dyno's ride in 1968. This was the first Cougar Funny Car built. Don't you love the stock appearance? The taillights were factory Lincoln-Mercury parts. (Photo Courtesy Forrest Bond)

The Cougar's Fiberglass Trends body covered a Roy Steffey–Logghe chassis and Al Bergler tin. Backing the Nicholson/Wade Cammer was an Art Carr C6. The Hilborn injectors were fed a 90-percent fuel blend through 56A nozzles. (Photo Courtesy Nicholson Family Collection)

match that saw Don come out on top in three. In the process, Don set the all-time miles-per-hour and elapsed-time records for Funny Cars when he recorded an astounding 7.48 at 185.86 mph.

Tragedy struck the Nicholson camp in July while en route to Detroit after the Super Stock Nationals. Crewmen Jim Campbell and Wally English were hauling the Cougar north, taking the Pennsylvania Turnpike in a heavy fog when they rear-ended a stopped semitruck. English, who was riding shotgun, was killed in the collision. Needless to say, Don was devastated. When it came to his crew, you weren't just a part of the team, you were

The candy Cougar looked its best during a match at Milan during the summer of 1968. Paul Shedlik applied the candy red and pearl gold paint using a model no. 60, full-size automotive Paasche air brush. A veiling head was used to get the web effect of the pearl. (Photo Courtesy Mike Cochran)

Helping Don maintain the Cougar through 1968 were Jim Campbell and Pete Williams, who took over when Earl Wade left to join up with his old partner, Dick Bourgeois. Previously, Campbell was with Pete Gates, tuning his Comet. The rear tires on the Funny Car had grown to 14x16 by 1968, nothing like today's 17.78-inch width. (Photo Courtesy Nicholson Family Collection)

Don's Cammers used only the best parts and it showed in the cars' performance. A Mallory mag ignition lit the fire. Safety-conscious Don made use of a Stahl-Moroso shut-off, set at 9,000 rpm. Helping hold the 1,000+-hp mill together was a Milodon bottom-end support. The two tanks up front hold fuel and water. (Photo Courtesy Michael Pottie)

Here at Milan during the summer of 1968, Don takes on one of the day's finest, Larry Reyes, in the Super 'Cuda. Don set the Funny Car world on its ear in July at the same track when he ran a 7.48 at 185.86 mph in defeating Eddie Schartman's Cougar. (Photo Courtesy Mike Cochran)

welcomed as part of the Nicholson family. Don really liked Wally and had pegged him to drive the rarely seen *Eliminator Jr.* Super Stock Cougar.

In the crash, the Funny Car was torn from the ramp truck and was damaged extensively. The chassis was repaired and a new body installed prior to the car joining Mercury's Streep Scene exhibition. The Cougar was later sold to Syd Foster, who raced it under the name *King Cou-gar.* A blower explosion eventually destroyed the body. Today, the *STP* Logghe chassis survives under a Jim Barillaro–restored 1967 Jack Chrisman Cyclone body.

The Second Cougar F/C

A new Cougar body was procured from Fiberglass Ltd. and mounted to the stage 1 Logghe chassis of Don's 1967 Comet by Kar Kraft, a specialty firm used almost

Although the Cougar's chassis was parallel to the track, the body featured a nose-down rake that helped ensure the car remained glued to the track. Twin Simpson drag chutes and rear Airheart disc brakes brought the Cougar to a safe halt from its usual 190-mph runs. (Photo Courtesy Michael Pottie)

exclusively by Ford through 1970. The new car was completed and ready for a match at Milan on August 25 against Terry Hedrick. Hedrick had just come off a win at the AHRA Nationals, where he turned a 7.65. Don took the Milan match in three and, in the process, lowered the track record with a 7.39.

At the NHRA Nationals, the Experimental Stock Funny Cars were placed in Super Eliminator. After taking S/XS class, Don marched to the category final by defeating the A/FD of Yancey-Camp, the *Comp Coupe* of Al Bergler, and the Supercharged Gasser of K. S. Pittman; he turned low ET for the Funnies with a 7.84. In the final, Don faced the AA/C Ford of Paul Stage, who had been given a slight handicap start, a handicap Don failed to make up. Don recorded another 7.80 time, but it wasn't enough to catch Stage's 7.91.

Looking at the Indy entry list from 1968, Don had three cars preregistered to run at the Nationals: Entry number 877, the *Eliminator* Cougar Funny Car; entry number 878, the *Eliminator Jr.* SS/FA Cobra Jet Cougar; and entry number 879, the *Eliminator II* 1967 Comet, which, for obvious reasons, was not available. Don relinquished the Funny Car seat for good after a match race in October at Piedmont, where he ran a best of 7.32. Frank Oglesby took over and was in the seat for a match-race win at New Bern, South Carolina, against Shirl Greer's

Like Humpty Dumpty, the wrecked Cougar Funny Car body couldn't be put back together again. A new body found its way onto the repaired chassis and the car then made the rounds as part of the Streep Scene display. The Cougar was later sold to Louisiana's Sidney Foster. (Photo Courtesy Nicholson Family Collection)

New Tension on November 3.

Don hired Oglesby with the intention of putting him behind the wheel of the Cougar. As Oglesby recalls, "Don ran maybe two more races after the Nationals before I took over." Don, having grown weary of the fires and blower explosions so prevalent in the early Funny Cars, wanted out of the "hot seat."

Making use of Pete Gates's shop in Warren, Michigan, the new Cougar body was mounted to the existing 1967 Comet chassis. Don had the rear suspension on the Logghe chassis set up so that he could run four shock absorbers (if necessary), adjustables, or 50/50s. Don's theory was, "On a slick track you run (the suspension) looser to get more lift. On a good-biting track you need more control so you tighten it up." (Photo Courtesy Nicholson Family Collection)

Such were the days before Funny Car Eliminator. Don vacated the Experimental Stock (Funny Car) Cougar shortly after playing runner-up in Super Eliminator at the Nationals to Paul Stage in 1968. Stage had just come off an Eliminator win at the Springnationals. (Photo ©TEN: The Enthusiast Network. All Rights Reserved.)

The Eliminator Jr.

Another one-race-only car for Don was the Pfeiffer Lincoln-Mercury–sponsored SS/FA Cougar. Ford brought Don and the Michigan-based dealer together in 1968. Dan Pfeiffer paid Don directly to run the name and display his car when he was in the area. The Cobra Jet–powered Cougar was to race at the NHRA Nationals but made only a pass or two due to a mix-up in the technical papers that Ford had provided to the sanctioning body. According to a *Petersen* magazine article published at the time, the minimum weight of the car should have been 200 pounds more than what it was. Interestingly, Ford's paperwork showed that this was the difference in weight between the 428 and the 390. Checking the specifications of the two engines today, one can see the weight of the two are the same. Therefore, for the second year in a row, Don was stuck watching the Nationals from the sidelines. When talking about the rarity of the *Eliminator Jr.*, Cougar historian Royce Freeman, the current owner of Don's daily-driver 1968 CJ Cougar, states that, "tops, there were maybe 10 of those [XR-7] GTs built." Dan Pfeiffer recalls that the dealer sold two of them. A few people have searched relentlessly for the *Eliminator Jr.*, but its whereabouts remain a mystery.

Pfeiffer Lincoln-Mercury in Grand Rapids, Michigan, sponsored the Eliminator Jr. *Directly across the road from the Pfeiffer dealership on 28th Street was another performance dealer, Berger Chevrolet. Pfeiffer recalls the days when the road wasn't so busy and the two dealers street-raced each other up the road with the loser having to buy lunch. Paul Shedlik applied the paint which mimicked Don's Funny Car. (Photo Courtesy Nicholson Family Collection)*

Why so many blower explosions? When it came to the Ford Cammer, Oglesby put it down to this: "On the Fords, it related to the fact one cam ran ahead of the other. As per Ford, you set the passenger-side cam with 7 degrees advance; at about 7,000 rpm, they were supposedly about even (the chain picked up the slack). The problem with that is that the port velocity is different on one side than the other and if you didn't wind it tight enough, or if you short-shifted one of the gears, it confused itself, went lean on one side, and blew the blower off. To solve that, we went to Germany and had a high-tensile chain made that wouldn't stretch so much (probably a couple links removed as well). We never told anybody."

For Oglesby, it solved the blower explosion issue. However, you could never do anything about the weak

Frank Oglesby gained experience behind the wheel of Dyno Don's Cougar before taking off on a successful Funny Car career of his own. How popular was the Eliminator*? If handouts are any measure, Frank recalls giving out 20,000 of them in 1968 alone. (Photo Courtesy Tom West Collection)*

Frank Oglesby had great success running Dyno Don's Cougar through 1969. He impressed Ford enough that in 1970, when he debuted his own Funny Car, the manufacturer gave him a parts deal. This photo was shot on the return road at Detroit on April 20, 1969, during a popular Funny Car show. (Photo Courtesy John Gacioch)

From any angle, at any speed, Don's Cougar looked great. Paul Shedlik was responsible for the paint on all of Don's Funny Cars, from the 1966 Comet through to this, his final Funny Car. Paul Hatton laid on the stripes and lettering. Pete Seaton's blown big-block Chevy–powered Corvair (driven by Terry Hedrick) was Don's competition on this gorgeous Milan day. (Photo Courtesy Mike Cochran)

block. The weakness was due to a lack of material in the bottom end, which led to cracking. The SOHC engines were built using the standard 427 block, so they retained the holes where the camshaft was supposed to go. The blocks cracked between the empty camshaft holes and the main webs.

The Cammer had "about" 1,000 more useful RPM than the Chrysler Hemi and could rev up to between 10,000 and 10,200 rpm. The Cougar didn't have a tachometer, which left Oglesby to shift by the seat of his pants. Oglesby remembers the C6 transmission being a bigger pain than the Cammer and that he had to travel with a few spares. "We had more transmissions than engine parts." The quickest Oglesby recalls the car running was a 7.24 at 195 mph, "and it handled great!" A 90-percent load of nitro and low compression got it done. Oglesby adds with a chuckle, "We had no problems with it, outside of running over the odd part." Not bad at all considering that the car ran 93 match races in 1968, as well as some NHRA dates.

Goes to show the level of Don's popularity when hotels and motels welcomed his arrival to town. Heading into Tulsa for the World Finals in 1968, racers and fans alike were greeted by the Holiday Inn's show of appreciation. Don had won the Car Craft magazine Funny Car driver of the year award. (Photo Courtesy Nicholson Family Collection)

One match that many folks wish they could forget took place during an eight-car show at Georgia's Yellow River Dragstrip on March 2, 1969. Twelve spectators were killed and 40 others injured during a match between Oglesby in the *Eliminator* and the Camaro of Huston Platt. Oglesby didn't see the incident because it happened behind him. One of Dyno's crew was standing behind the Cougar and taped the race. Oglesby recalls viewing the tape afterward at Ted Turner's Channel 17.

It was a narrow track with little more than chicken wire fencing and guardrails that didn't even run the length of the track. Oglesby was in the left lane and got the jump on Platt. Even though the tape didn't show the whole crash sequence, it did show that Platt crossed about 5 feet over into Oglesby's lane. The back end slid around so that the Camaro was pointing back into its own lane. Apparently, Platt pulled the chute, which caught a fan that, witnesses state, had reached over the

fence to retrieve a beer. The weight of the spectator tangled in the chute pulled the Camaro off track and into the crowd. The car eventually came to rest on the track, but in many pieces. Platt came away from the crash without injury, but he was later treated for shock.

The incident became a legal mess and everyone but Dyno Don and Oglesby were sued. Recalled Oglesby, "Sponsors including Coca-Cola were sued. The owner, Shug Campbell, was cleaned out, but most of what he owned was in his wife's name." The track never reopened after the crash and the so-called "outlaw" tracks began to disappear shortly after.

At the end of the 1969 season, the Cougar was sold to a gentleman in Cleveland, Ohio. It's said that the new owner had other plans for the car, which led to him cutting up and scrapping the body. The Logghe chassis was narrowed because plans called for a Pinto body. It was a pretty sad ending for Dyno Don's final Funny Car.

Frank Oglesby first proved himself as a wrench man before establishing himself as a top-notch driver. Dyno's old crewman, Pete Williams, worked alongside Oglesby through the beginning of 1969 before Oglesby hired on Kenny Wilt and longtime friend Larry Nalley. (Photo Courtesy Michael Pottie Collection)

Driver/Tuner Frank Oglesby

Frank Oglesby had been kicking around organized drag racing for 10 years before hooking up with Don in 1968. Oglesby was raised in rural Illinois and moved to Chicago, where he got involved in running the Indiana-based Bubble Buster Top Fuel car. He spent a couple years in the Marine Corps before going to work for Mr. Norm's, tuning its blown Dodge. A stint with Arnie Beswick and his Pontiacs followed. Oglesby recalls that Beswick's Mystery Tornado GTO was always losing to Don's Comet so they stripped Beswick's Tempest of approximately 600 pounds and added the blower. "At least then we could keep up with Don."

After a brief stop in Tennessee, tuning the Kingfish Barracuda for Bill Taylor, Don hired Oglesby on. Recalled Oglesby, "Don hired me to take over driving the Funny Car, although I was a little reluctant at first, as I had heard that story before from Mr. Norm's, Beswick, and Taylor." Oglesby had driven for Beswick a few times but he was just too good of a "nitro tuner" and was never given the opportunity to drive regularly.

Oglesby was Don's crew chief on the Cougar through October 1968 and took over driving when Don headed back West. For 1969, Oglesby was left to his own devices and saw Don maybe a half-dozen times through the year. After recording an 85-percent win for the year, Oglesby moved on at the end of the season to run his own car.

"I was driving, repairing, and maintaining the Cougar myself, so it made sense." Ford offered Oglesby a parts deal and he did the rest. "I questioned whether I did the right thing, as getting bookings under Frank Oglesby were a lot harder to find than booking as Dyno Don's *Eliminator*. But then I only had to make half the amount of money as I wasn't splitting it." Oglesby had a tremendous year with his Quarterhorse Mustang in 1970, running as quick as anyone. He ran a number of nitro Funny Cars under the name before landing a two-year deal in 1979 with the Coca-Cola brand, Mello Yello. In 1982, Oglesby took his first retirement from drag racing to run his engine shop. He returned in 1988 to take one last kick at the can, running a Jet F/C, before retiring for good.

Coming at you is Frank Oglesby who was both a natural tuner and driver. The Eliminators Cammer featured a Pete Robinson 6-71 blower and Hilborn injectors. Don's final season in the Funny Car saw him win the Car Craft magazine driver of the year award. (Photo Courtesy Steve Reyes)

Frank Oglesby took full reins of the Eliminator Cougar shortly after the Nationals in 1967. At his first national event, the 1969 NHRA Winternationals, he failed to make rounds with the car. The Eliminator name, first used by Don in 1966, appeared in 1969 flanking Mercury's top-of-the-line Cougar muscle car. (Photo Courtesy Lou Hart)

HEADS UP (1969–1973)

The old Jerry Harvey Mustang was an instant winner for Don. Mid-10-second times from the "beast" earned Don the Modified crown at the 1969 NHRA Springnationals. Before the close of the season, the Mustang cranked mid-9-second match-race times. (Photo ©TEN: The Enthusiast Network. All Rights Reserved.)

It was Don's fear of catching fire that made him vacate the Funny Car. Around that time, Don stated, "I actually enjoy going 8.50 or so and about a 160, but the only thing I like about the Funny we know today is the fact I'm not in one." With the growing popularity of heads-up factory iron, Don's return to the door cars was a welcome sight. Match-race pay-outs for the top stockers were reaching upward of $1,000 for a three-round match by the late 1960s, a fee that closely rivaled what Don was paid running the Funny Car. Taking into consideration the cost comparison between running a Funny Car versus a door car and you can see that, financially, the move

was a no-brainer. Don's previous experience with the Cammer paid dividends when the NHRA birthed the Pro Stock category in 1970. It made him the leading Ford racer in the nation, a title that he carried well into the coming decade.

1969 and 1970

Don's transition back to the door cars in 1969 was made easier by the purchase of the proven SOHC-powered Mustang of Jerry Harvey. The car was one of a dozen built in 1965 by Holman-Moody in North Carolina at Ford's request. The initial intent

When Don's daughter asked him in 1969 why he bought the Mustang, he told her, "Because it's a beast." She said, "We had the Mustang and Super Cat Cougar at home and we called them Beauty and the Beast." The Beast started out as a 1965 Mustang and had previously won Street Eliminator at the 1966 NHRA Winternationals for Jerry Harvey, turning an 11.51. (Photo Courtesy Curt Vogt)

was for the car to dominate the popular A/FX class. This particular Mustang of Don's has quite the history. It was built as a Ford test mule before being passed on to Len Richter, who ran it under the Bob Ford banner as *Pegasus*. A broken axle at the 1965 NHRA Winternationals saw Richter play runner-up in Factory Stock to the Tasca Ford Mustang driven by Bill Lawton.

Holman-Moody updated the Mustang in 1966 and then it passed to Jerry Harvey. Harvey painted it champagne gold and named it the *Quiet One II*. Hubert Platt had a short stint in the car during 1968, driving it long enough to set the A/MP class record at Indy with a 10.75. Don purchased the Mustang late in the year and continued to race it in Modified, as well as money-generating match races. The car required little tweaking by Don. However, as Wade recalled, "The car took a week to clean off all the dirt and grease and oil. Harvey didn't take real care of it."

Running A/MP at the NHRA Springnationals, Don earned his first NHRA national event category win since the 1962 Winternationals by taking Street Eliminator. The Street Eliminator category was a real mixed bag, consisting of Gassers, Sport Production cars, Street Roadsters, and Modified Production cars. Don got a taste of each as he battled his way to a

The Mustang engine bay was wall-to-wall Cammer with no room to spare. Don ran the Holman-Moody plumbed ram air before switching to a different intake manifold setup. The gauge by the cowl monitors the fuel pressure. (Photo Courtesy Curt Vogt)

final-round appearance against the C & W Motor Parts–sponsored B/SR of Ralph Smiderle. Don had an easy go of it in rounds one and two, getting by the broken Gassers of Mitch Mitchell, the "World's Fastest Hippie," and the *Mr. Crude* Anglia of Canadian Ralph Hope.

If things could have gotten any easier for Don,

they did in the third when a coin toss gave him a bye. In round four, Don faced the crowd favorite Bo Laws and his D/SP Corvette. Having the slower-class car, Laws was given a handicap start over Don and led the race most of the way. Don caught the Corvette on the top end, passing Laws with a 10.57 at 112.07 mph. Smiderle himself received a bye in the semis to earn his place in the final. The white Roadster took a .07 handicap start, but by the time they reached the tree, Don was on him. With a no break out rule in place for the final run, Don let it all hang out and took the win with a record ET of 10.49 at 120.96 while Smiderle trailed with a 10.649 at 127.47. Don followed up by taking A/MP class at Indy in September, where he lowered the class record with a 10.40 time.

Dyno sold the Mustang late in the season and, believe it or not, a street racer in New York bought it. Brooklyn resident Tab Talmadge (which was apparently an alias) became the lucky owner. Talmadge, who reportedly made his riches dealing drugs and running numbers, offered Don a sum of money he just couldn't refuse. All indications are that the Mustang was the first bona fide 9-second street racer in New York. Talmadge, it's said, earned more than a million dollars street racing the Mustang, and it's easy to see how when you consider the wagers placed ran as high as $150,000 per race.

In the mid-1980s, enthusiast Curt Vogt went looking for the Mustang and discovered it resting in the bowels of Brooklyn. Vogt had invested approximately a year of his time, dealing with the less than scrupulous types of New York City and chasing leads to come up with the holy grail of Dyno Mustangs. It took a lot of persuading and $11,000

The remains of Dyno Don's Mustang, just as it was found in 1986. The new owner's initial plan was to drive the car on the street, and he installed a Wedge engine where the Cammer once sat. Apart from the missing engine, all the key parts were present, including the "FORD" parachute discovered in the trunk. (Photo Courtesy Curt Vogt)

for Vogt to finally convince the owner to sell. On top of it, Vogt paid out a finder's fee of $5,000 to the gentleman who led him to the car. Resting in a musty old garage, the Mustang was, for the most part, complete. The SOHC mill was long gone and gray primer covered the familiar gold and blue paint. Vogt had the Mustang restored to Dyno Don likeness by the Super Stang Shop in Lyons, New York. The missing Cammer and drivetrain parts came courtesy of Vogt's own Cobra Automotive in Connecticut. Vogt sold the Mustang to Don Snyder in 1991, and today it remains a key piece in his fine collection of cars.

Don poses proudly with his Mustang during a break at Indy in 1969. As seen in this photo, the ram air tubing has been replaced with short velocity stacks. In addition, the intake manifold has been swapped for a rare factory high-rise and, accordingly, the fiberglass hood has been modified for clearance. By the end of 1969, the Mustang was recording mid nine times. (Photo Courtesy Curt Vogt)

The stripped Mustang shell reveals the amount of modifications made for drag racing. Note the cut out inner fenders and radiator support. The original upper shock mount, tow bar brackets, and four-point roll bar are also visible. (Photo Courtesy Curt Vogt)

Although the interior of the Mustang showed years of neglect when it was discovered, it remained pretty much as Don ran it, 27 years earlier. It's as primitive as it can be. Note the parachute ring dangling at the door. (Photo Courtesy Curt Vogt)

Kar Kraft Cougar

In the fall of 1968, Ford's Bunkie Knudsen commissioned the firm Kar Kraft to build a limited number of Boss 429 Mustangs. In total, 859 cars were built for 1969 with another 500 and change built for 1970. Lincoln-Mercury's head of performance, Emil Loeffler, got on the wagon when he requested two Boss Cougars to be built, one for Dyno Don and one for Eddie Schart-man. Ford's Matt McLaughlin did him one better when he initially approved 50 of these lethal beasts to be built for dragstrip use only. Sadly, however, the build never went beyond two prototypes and the two cars built for Don and Schartman. With 20 orders in hand, the build order for the 50 was canceled. The reason why is speculation only. A good possibility may have been because of the changing muscle car climate. By 1969, performance

Don ran this SOHC Cougar for approximately six months in 1969. At one point, he referred to it as the worst car he ever had. Realizing the rarity of the car years later, he wished he still had it. Seen here at New England, the Cougar averaged 10 teen times. The tires are Goodyears on Mickey Thompson rims. Shocks were 90/10 up front and 50/50 out back. Ladder bars are HMS parts. Note the lack of front brakes. The car originally came off the assembly line with drum brakes, which gave way to Airheart discs. All were ditched to save weight. (Photo Courtesy Paul Wasilewski)

was becoming a bad word, sales were down, and insurance companies were socking it to those reckless Baby Boomers.

Just like the Mustang, the Boss 429 was not an easy fit in the Cougar's tight engine bay. To make the transplant possible, it was necessary for Kar Kraft to modify the shock towers for additional space. With the two cars completed in April, Schartman's stayed in the Michigan area and was prepared for its car clinic debut in January 1970; Don's was shipped to Holman-Moody & Stroppe (HMS) in Long Beach, sans 429, for some additional drag race prep. HMS garnered additional room in the engine bay by incorporating a right-hand drive Australian Falcon steering box. Mounted on the outside of the left frame rail, the change gained approximately 6 more inches of much-needed space.

Don received a Boss 429 engine before the car arrived on the West Coast. Once received, the engine was hauled over to the Autolite dyno facility where Art Chrisman made some pulls. Earl Wade thrashed on the engine, getting Crane Cams involved and having them cut various bump sticks for trial. The final decision to run the Cammer came after the Boss showed to be down on power, approximately 50 hp down when compared to the Cammer. Don, wanting to get the car out match racing, butted heads with Mercury's Al Turner about using the Cammer. Don won out, reasoning that he wanted to win races and it wasn't going to happen with the Boss 429.

The Cougar arrived at HMS sporting Wimbledon White paint. Somewhere along the line it received a two-piece fiberglass front-end, glass doors, and dashboard from Contemporary Fiberglass prior to being painted candy tangerine. Lexan windows helped to bring the weight down as did an aluminum grille that replaced the factory cast-iron part. Sponsorship came by way of Pfeiffer Lincoln-Mercury in Grand Rapids. Dan Pfeiffer prided himself on being a performance-oriented dealership along the lines of Nickey Chevrolet and Mr. Norm's, both in Chicago. Looking back, Pfeiffer felt the dealership lost money on the sponsorship. While on display in the dealer's showroom, the Cougar was stolen one night and returned to the lot with a blown engine. As part of

Earl Wade prepped the proven Cammer that featured goods from Mickey Thompson, Milodon, and Crane. Titanium bolts were used throughout. The twin 660-cfm Holley center-squirt carburetors mount atop stacked spacers and a rare factory 2 x 4 aluminum intake. (Photo ©TEN: The Enthusiast Network. All Rights Reserved.)

Back in 1969, the Cougar Eliminator made a good street rat but not so much a drag car. Don stated that as good as the car looked, "it was just the wrong balance." The scooped hood gives this away as an early photo. (Photo ©TEN: The Enthusiast Network. All Rights Reserved.)

the sponsor deal, Pfeiffer provided Don with a Colony Park station wagon, a car Earl Wade rolled into a ditch one night in Texas. To top it all off, the Pfeiffer name was misspelled on the car ("ie" instead of "ei").

Don started booking match-race dates for the Cougar in April 1969, before even receiving the car. Before the Cammer from the Mustang was installed, it was freshened with Mickey Thompson rods and pistons that squeezed out 12.5:1 compression. A pair of Crane cams with a reported .605 lift worked with Crane springs, allowing the engine to buzz to 9,000 rpm. Different carburetors were tried, including twin Holley 780s. The spent fuel then exited through a set of Jardine headers. A Schiefer clutch transmitted power through a slick-shifted Top Loader that housed a 2.36 first gear. Out back, gears of Don's choice, either 4.57 or 4.86 filled the 9-inch center.

Debut times for the 2,950-pound car were 10.19 at 137.76 mph. The best time found for the Cougar was a 9.99 at 138 mph, recorded during a match race at Thompson, Ohio, in September. In later interviews, Don made it clear he didn't care much for the Cougar and described it at one point as "a real turkey." He said, "It was too heavy and just not the right balance."

Randy Payne took over the car in 1970 and had no better luck with it. He failed to "get it together" at the

From any angle, the restyled 1969 Cougar looked appealing. Though not Don's quickest car, trust that plenty of competitors did catch the rear view. Don later eliminated the trunk-mounted spoiler. The side stripes were unique to this car and differed from production models. (Photo ©TEN: The Enthusiast Network. All Rights Reserved.)

The Cougar was a car that Don purchased from Ford for $1 in April 1969. Kar Kraft built it with a Boss 429; it took some serious discussion with his Mercury boss before Don was allowed to run a SOHC 427 in the car. The idea was that Don ran the proven Cammer while he developed the Boss 429, which never quite worked out. (Photo Courtesy Ed Meyer)

NHRA World Finals. That year saw Don borrow the Cammer for his Maverick. It didn't help, as Don failed to make the field. Payne drove the Cougar for a brief spell, but it soon disappeared from the scene. The car passed through a few owners over the years, and received extensive mods before Ed Meyer purchased what was left of it in 1992 and restored it. The restoration was extensive; the floorboards and part of the firewall had to be replaced. Records show that this is the only Boss 429 Cougar remaining.

In match-race competition, Don continued to roll over the competition. In August, Cecil County ran the first annual Mr. USA Super Stock race that featured Jenkins, Sox, Chick DeNinno, Sam Auxier, and Steve Kanuika in the Jungle Jim–sponsored Camaro. Don chose to run the Harvey Mustang rather than the 200-pound-heavier Cougar, and he couldn't have made a wiser decision. Competition was tough with Ronnie Sox setting the pace, becoming the third person in the 9s behind Jenkins and Dyno Don. First round action got underway with Don dropping the Charger of DeNinno with a 9.90. Don battled his way to the final after defeating Auxier's tunnel port Mustang in the second with an unreal 9.86 at 139.31 mph for top MPH of the meet. Don's final round opponent was Grumpy Jenkins, who defeated Malcolm Durham's Camaro in the first with a 10.08, then ran a 9.89 in the second to overcome a holeshot by Sox.

The final was one for the books. After building fan anticipation, sweeping in the rosin, and performing a

Super Cat Cougar

The Don Nicholson Super Cat Cougar project was chronicled in the March and April 1969 issues of *Car Craft* magazine. It was a build sponsored by Lincoln-Mercury and soft drink manufacturer Coca-Cola, which eventually gave it away as the grand prize in its "Coca-Cola National Thirst Eliminator Program."

Powering the Cougar was a Dyno Don–prepped 428. *Car Craft* initially drag tested the Cougar and managed a stone stock best of 13.93 at 102 mph. It was at this point that Don got involved in the project. Bolting on a set of wild Jardine pipes and a pair of Lakewood track bars, he managed a 13.46 at 105 mph. The 428 was then pulled, blueprinted, and reassembled to NHRA F/S specs. A Hurst shifter and Schiefer clutch were added as well as 90/10 shocks up front, 50/50s out back, and 4.56 gears stuffed into the 9-inch rear.

Once it was buttoned up, Don tested the 3,600-pound Cat at Irwindale. With a pair of 9.50 Goodyears in place and open headers, the Cougar managed a best of 12.78 at 109.35 mph, .05 shy of NHRA's ET record and almost a mile per hour quicker than the existing record. Quite impressive considering that the car was halfheartedly prepared and was running approximately 200 pounds over legal class weight.

Once Don was done wringing out the Super Cat, it made the rounds of the show circuit and promo events before being turned over to Coca-Cola and given away. The story goes that the young man who won the car lacked the necessary funds to cover taxes and was forced to sell it. Over the years, the Cougar passed through a few hands and eventually ended up with a blown engine. In 1998, it was discovered in a Florida carport, ravaged by the elements. Rescued, the car was turned over to Performance Restorations in Mundelein, Illinois, which brought it back to its former glory. The Cougar was sold at auction in 2003, fetching a cool $140,000 dollars.

Don warms the Super Cat Cougar during a Car Craft *magazine test session at Irwindale. The prep of the car was featured in the magazine in a two-part series during spring 1969. Sponsored by Lincoln-Mercury and Coca-Cola, the car was given away to a sweepstakes winner in Coca-Cola's Thirst Eliminator contest. (Photo ©TEN: The Enthusiast Network. All Rights Reserved.)*

Under the lights of the Pan Pacific Auto Show, Don poses proudly with the Car Craft *magazine Super Cat Cougar he helped prepare. The Cat survives today and has gone through a quality restoration. (Photo Courtesy Nicholson Family Collection)*

How Streep It Is

Streep is a combination of the words *street* and *strip* and dreamed up by the good folks in Lincoln-Mercury's advertising department. The manufacturer used the word to help promote its line of 1969 performance cars. Throughout the year, Streep Scene exhibits were shown at select dealerships and at major car shows. As a Mercury team player, Don attended up to 25 of these exhibits, dishing out tech tips, answering questions, and generally promoting the Mercury line of cars. Part of the $250,000 exhibit was the slot car drag strip. It was a pretty cool setup for its day, a full diorama with a

Don's not-so-fierce competition here at the Streep Scene slot car drags is Edwina "Winkie" Louise. Winkie had worked for PURE Oil as Miss Firebird through 1968, having replaced Linda Vaughn when she went to Hurst in 1965. (Photo Courtesy Nicholson Family Collection)

The slot car display pitted the two Cougars of Ed Schartman and Don against each other. Participants took a seat and, when the tree came down, hit the gas. They shifted through the gears that actually controlled the cars. Miss a shift or fail to power shift and the car slowed. At the end of "eliminations," the winner could face Don himself. (Photo Courtesy Nicholson Family Collection)

At the 46th Annual Auto Show, held at the Pan Pacific Auditorium, Richard Nicholson checks out the cockpit of the display Cougar. Note the door cut into the body. Those attending the show were given the opportunity to have a seat in the Cougar and take a ride down the quarter-mile, through the help of a display screen. (Photo Courtesy Nicholson Family Collection)

Because of its limited budget, Mercury never had a clinic program per se. The closest it came was in 1969 when it loaded up two rigs and hit select shows, events, and dealerships with its Streep Scene promotion. Don was a goodhearted soul who happily participated at a good number of these shows. He eagerly promoted Mercury's performance offerings and doled out helpful tips to street rats and budding drag racers. (Photo Courtesy Nicholson Family Collection)

How Streep It Is (Continued)

working Christmas tree and all. The exhibit also included a "Streep Simulator" that enabled the audience to experience how it felt to make a 190-mph pass in Don's *Eliminator* Funny Car. Adding to the authenticity at many shows was the voice of drag racing, Jon Lundberg, on the PA. A factory Cougar *Eliminator* as well as the Dyno Don–prepped Super Cat were on display at most shows.

When it came to rowing a 4-speed, Don should be ranked as one of the best. Here he's about to give the Hurst in the Super Cat Cougar a workout. (Photo ©TEN: The Enthusiast Network. All Rights Reserved.)

Dyno's Maverick was rushed into action and debuted at the AHRA Winter Nationals wearing a coat of primer. Unable to get the mechanical bugs hammered out, Don fell in the first round, hitting a redlight against the Camaro of Dick Arons. Don was paid a hefty sum by the AHRA to appear at its events. (Photo ©TEN: The Enthusiast Network. All Rights Reserved.)

number of burnouts, the pair was ready. On the green it was Don out first, and all the way! Through the traps, Dyno took the win with a 9.88 at 138.46 mph to Jenkins's quicker but later 9.77 at 138.67. As Earl Wade was noted to say, with complete satisfaction, "We came to win and beat Jenkins as well."

The First Maverick

To make the quickly approaching AHRA and NHRA winter meets, Dyno Don picked up a plain 6-cylinder, three-on-the-tree Maverick from Foulger Ford in Monrovia. A tree fell on the car and damaged it, so the dealer gave it to Don. Often referred to as the seven-day wonder, the Maverick was immediately hauled to M & S Welding in Azusa, where its transformation began. Mike Hoag, half owner in M & S, recalls that the Maverick arrived Friday at around 10 a.m. By 3:30 p.m., with the help of partner Sherman Gunn, Don, Earl Wade, Bob Mandel, and Steve Fleming, the car was stripped.

"Little finesse was used in tearing the car down. We just got in there with a pair of dykes and cut wires and everything went in the trash. Nothing was saved." Once it was stripped, Wade and Mandel flew back to Atlanta to fetch the SOHC engine and transmission from the heads-up Cougar. In the meantime, the M & S crew went to work making room for the new mill. A dummy block

Yes, it's been a while since Pro Stock cars looked this stock. These pros are lined up at OCIR in February 1970 for the U.S. Pro Stock Championship. A foul start in the final saw Don's seven-day wonder play runner-up to the Camaro of Grumpy Jenkins. (Photo Courtesy Nicholson Family Collection)

was positioned in the engine bay to determine where they would have clearance issues. A cylinder head was slipped into place, but when it came to the valve cover, there was no room. Drawing a centerline parallel to the shock centerline, the tower was shaved, or "sculpted" down to the upper A arm to gain the needed space.

By contrast, at the NHRA winter meet, the Maverick looked downright mean with its flashy coat of paint. Dyno Don's Maverick was the first to run a 9-second time when the SOHC car recorded a 9.93 at OCIR prior to the NHRA Winternationals in 1970. Note the rear-opening scoop initially run on the Maverick. (Photo ©TEN: The Enthusiast Network. All Rights Reserved.)

Don runs the Maverick over the scales at OCIR during the Pro Stock Championship in February 1970. Evidence of the front suspension modifications, to make room for the Cammer, can be seen by the outward location of the wheels. Recognize anyone else in the photo? Buddy Martin for one. (Photo Courtesy Brian Kennedy)

According to Hoag, it was pretty basic. "We cut out as little as possible, no more than absolutely necessary to maintain integrity." M & S added 4130 steel supports running from the shock towers to the firewall, which was secured with pull pins. Further changes to the front suspension included moving the control arms out a couple of inches. Everything, including factory joints, was gas welded. One of the biggest issues that the crew at M & S ran into was the clutch linkage. A lot of work went into setting it up because there was just no room.

When it came to weight reduction, A&A provided fiberglass fenders, hood, and a decklid. Mike Hoag had a working theory at the time when it came to building cars: "If you could take 1 pound off for $10 from the center of the door forward it was worth it. From the center of the door back, removing 1 pound was only worth $3. We removed something like 10 pounds from the crossmember alone. We actually weighed what we cut out and yup, it was worth it."

Don and Wade were continuously going through the Cammer, looking for more power. The Crane Cams now were running .700 lift. ForgedTrue pistons machined by Wade swung on Mickey Thompson 6.7 rods. From experience, Don ran "loose" bearings on the bottom end to keep the Cammer alive. Oil pressure could be a problem. Dan Nowak, one of Don's crew during the early 1970s, recalls, "In the pits, we'd raise the rear wheels off the

Can you believe that this was the face of Pro Stock at the beginning of 1970? Protecting Don was a three-point Lakewood bar and a four-point harness. The bench seat gave way soon enough to a pair of lightweight Berry Plexiglas buckets. (Photo Courtesy Nicholson Family Collection)

Yup, she's a tight fit. The Cammer was pulled from the Cougar and with a little (or a lot) of elbow grease and contouring, installed in the Maverick. These images were shot at OCIR during the Pro Stock Championship in February 1970. Visible here are the necessary mods made to the shock towers and the fabricated tower supports. Take a closer look at the stacked spacers under the Holleys. (Photo Courtesy Nicholson Family Collection)

ground and fire the car to get the oil warmed. Don had an oil pressure gauge under the dash and glancing at it, I saw it was peaked at 120 psi. He'd come back to the pits after a run and it would read 10 to 20 psi."

When it came to feeding fuel to the Cammer, carburetor choice varied but, more times than not, worked-over twin Holleys 660 center-squirts filled the bill. The carbs were mounted on spacers bolted to a factory single-plane aluminum intake manifold. In short order, this intake gave way to a fabricated independent runner manifold. Fuel was fed via a pair of Conelec 257 trunk-mounted pumps. Backing the Cammer was a Hays clutch in a Lakewood scatter shield and a choice of Top Loader transmissions. Don tried anything from a 2.36 first gear to a rare NASCAR 2.54 box as well as a 2.78 first gearbox that was whipped up by Doug Nash. Nash machined off the 2.78 gear from the small-block's small input shaft, removed the 2.36 from the large input shaft, and pressed it onto the 2.78. Unlike today, when racers rent tracks, back in 1970 this kind of experimentation usually took place at match races.

The Dana third member under the Maverick usually carried 5.13 gears and was bolted to leaf springs provided by Holman-Moody. Traction came by way of fabricated 2 x 3 ladder bars, twin Mr. Gasket shocks per side, and 13-inch Goodyears. With the drivetrain in place, the Maverick was hauled to Jerry Jardine for headers. When

the car returned to M & S on the morning of the seventh day, it was sporting a fresh coat of primer paint. As Mike Hoag remembers, for whatever reason, Don did not want the car to remain white. The morning was spent wrapping up odds and ends before Don and crew headed to Arizona for the AHRA race. Hoag recalled that when it came to the build, Don paid for everything himself. Nothing came from Ford that he was aware of.

While others headed east for the Gatornationals after the NHRA winter meet, Dyno headed north to Fremont for the February 15 Northern Nationals. In the final, Dyno took the win against Bill Bagshaw with a 10.04 at 138.46 to the Bandit's 10.17 at 135.98 mph. Don was the first to set both ends of the NHRA Pro Stock record, doing so at Atco, New Jersey, in September 1970 at 9.81 at 139.31 mph. (Photo Courtesy James Handy)

Through 1970 and 1971, Don and his Mavericks were one of the few real threats to Chrysler's domination. At the NHRA Springnationals in 1970, Don played runner-up to the Plymouth of Sox & Martin. (Photo Courtesy Brian Kennedy)

Considering the potency of the Cammer, its not surprising Don broke a number of Dana 60 rear ends. He solved the problem by annealing the gears. The first year of Pro Stock with the Maverick was said to be quite a learning curve for Don and company. (Photo Courtesy Robert Nielsen)

The car's debut at the AHRA Winter Nationals proved to be less than spectacular. During qualifying, the Cammer went south, leaving Don and crew to do some serious thrashing. Repairs were made in time for eliminations only to see Don redlight against Dick Arons in the first round. At the NHRA winter meet, the Maverick, now sporting new colorful Carney paint, fared no better. After qualifying in the middle of the 32-car pack with a 10.47 at 128.95 mph, it was time for more repairs to the Cammer. Don and crew replaced a rod and returned Sunday to face the hemi 'Cuda of Don Grotheer in the first round. Grotheer put away the hastily repaired Maverick, running a 10.26 to Dyno Don's 10.41.

Although the new season got off to a slow start, by mid-year Dyno and the Maverick were clicking. Through the summer, the car had no problem when it came to winning matches. Don won the AHRA Eighth-Mile Drags at St. Louis. He followed it up by taking King of Kings meet at Capitol Raceways on July 1, where he defeated Ronnie Sox in the final with a low ET of the meet, 9.74 at 140.18 mph. Through June and into July, Dyno Don was winning every week and seemed to have Sox & Martin's number. Days after beating Sox, Don defeated Herb McCandless in the team's destroked Duster at Phenix City, Alabama. "Mr. 4 Speed" didn't stand a chance, running a 10.12 to Don's 9.96. Don's time was a new track record and the first 9-second Pro Stock pass at Phenix City. Closing the month, Dyno once again defeated Sox, this time at Lakeland in Tennessee.

Don and Ford's first Pro Stock national event win came at the AHRA Grand-American race at Epping's New England Dragway on August 2. The AHRA had been running a heads-up Pro Stock–style category since 1968, referring to it as Super Stock. In no way should the AHRA category be confused with NHRA's handicap Super Stock. The Epping race was the 7th of 10 AHRA Grand-American

At the NHRA Nationals in 1970, Don and his Maverick set low ET with a 9.90 but were unable to get around the Duster of Arlen Vanke in the semifinals. Vanke fell in the final to Herb McCandless. (Photo Courtesy Brian Kennedy)

At the Super Stock Nationals in 1970, Don qualified the Maverick 9th in the 16-car field with a 10.15. Here, the easygoing Dyno Don shares a laugh with Ed Schartman while taking a break. Mechanical issues kept Don from the winner's circle this year. (Photo Courtesy Michael Mihalko)

races held in 1970 and, as expected, all of the top names in the heads-up category were present.

At the race, 29 national records were set, starting with Don whose Maverick ran a 138.46 to set the Super Stock mile-per-hour mark. First-round action got underway with Dyno Don running a 10.04 on a single after opponent Bob Gaudreau broke. Dyno faced Jim Little in the second, getting out in front, and staying there with an easy 10.62. In the semis, Don eliminated Bill Hielscher decisively with a 9.98 at 138.88 mph to Hielscher's 10.54 at 129.87. In the final, Don faced Ronnie Sox in the Sox & Martin Duster. Sox ran a 10.17 in the semis against the debuting Duster of Ed Miller, which managed a tremendous holeshot on Ronnie but trailed in the end with a 10.24. To the spectators' delight, the two finalists performed a half-dozen smoking burnouts in search of optimal traction. The feat worked out for Don; he buried Sox with a crowd-pleasing 9.88.

Dyno Don made it two AHRA National event wins in a row after towing into Bristol on August 29 and taking home the gold. Don opened up by defeating Gene Cromer in the first with a 10.11 before facing and eliminating favorite, Don Carlton in the *Motown Missile* in the second with a 10.24. Don's 137.19 mph on the run stood as top speed of the meet. Carlton and the trick *Missile* trailed with a 10.35 at 132.74. In the semis, Don took care of Dick Humbert in Bill Stepp's Challenger with a 10.16 at 137.19 to a 10.26 at 134.93. Facing Don in the final was a familiar name: Herb McCandless in the Sox & Martin Duster. To make it to the final round, McCandless had defeated Ed Miller in the semifinals with a 10.15 at

135.95 to Miller's 10.21 at 134.12. And in the final go, it was Don out first and all the way. Dyno defeated McCandless with the low ET of the meet, 10.07 at 136.77 to McCandless's 10.17 at 135.33.

Even though he failed in his attempt to win the NHRA Nationals in September, Dyno Don did lead the pack by setting low ET and top speed of the meet with a 9.90 at 139.00 mph. He lasted until the third round, when a scored cylinder saw the Cammer losing power and Don fell to eventual runner-up, Arlen Vanke, turning a 10.05 to a Vanke's 10.04. The same month, Don set both ends of the Pro Stock record at Atco, New Jersey, with a 9.81 and 139.31.

If that hood scoop on the first Maverick appears a tad over the 7-inch NHRA height rule, it was. What made it acceptable was the fact that the height of the opening was within the 7-inch rule. The tunnel-rammed Cammer needed the space. (Photo Courtesy Nicholson Family Collection)

Don closed the season second in the AHRA Super Stock points standings behind, you guessed it, Ronnie Sox. Not bad results from a car that was built in just seven days. To hired driver Ken Dondero, the seven days showed. Don hired Dondero late in 1971 and didn't think much of the car, which by the time he came on board, was showing its age.

"If M & S built the first car, I don't think they would admit to it. The second Maverick was much nicer."

What little Ford factory support there was disappeared after October 1970, as new president Lee Iacocca refocused the company's attention on economy and turned his back on performance. With no factory support and only sponsorship from Jardine and Mr. Gasket, Don had to have been proud of his mid-season success. His Maverick had become such a threat that competitors such as Jenkins and Sox were pushing the NHRA to ban the Cammer. In a four-way match at New York's Nationals Speedway in the fall, Dyno Don faced Sox, Hielscher, and Leroy Palarchio in the Ramchargers' Challenger. Dyno took all three rounds and defeated Sox twice, running times of 9.79, 9.76, 9.73, and 9.68. Thanks in large part to Dyno Don and Wade's years of experience with the Cammer; when everything was clicking the car was nearly unbeatable.

It wasn't so much breakage early on that prevented Dyno Don from putting up consistent numbers, it was

Ford's nearly unbreakable Top Loader transmission was slick-shifted with the help of Doug Nash. Don bragged that he never missed a shift with it. The rear transmission mount was a solid steel piece. (Photo Courtesy Nicholson Family Collection)

Running AHRA Super Stock at Lions late in 1970, the Maverick appeared with its two new "lightened" doors. Note that the scoop has been modified. Gone are the Foulger Ford and Mickey Thompson stickers. Against the fence (right) is crewman Dave McGrane. (Photo Courtesy Michael Pottie)

Appearing in fresh candy red paint at the 1971 NHRA Winternationals, Don drove the first Maverick to a semifinals appearance before falling to the Duster of Arlen Vanke. New car bugs kept the debuting second Maverick out of the show. (Photo Courtesy James Handy)

Some say the Maverick never looked any better. I don't know about that, though the candy paint did look good. Don would have better luck with this car, qualifying it while failing to qualify the new car. Times in the 9.60s would be realized before this car was retired. (Photo Courtesy Nicholson Family Collection)

his struggle to make the car react the same each time out. Dave McGrane had said, "The first Maverick hooked up too hard or not enough, it was inconsistent and took a full season to sort. A lot was learned the first year." One of the biggest improvements, it's said, was found when Don switched to a 55-pound flywheel. "Consistency improved and the car would *really* leave."

1971

Don opened the 1971 season by winning AHRA's first Grand-American race of the season, which was held at Lions over the January 9 weekend. Don waded through the 16-car field to meet and defeat Bill Bag-shaw in the final with a 9.81 at 139.98 mph to a 9.89 at 139.31 mph. After qualifying with a 9.76, second only to the 9.71 recorded by Bob Lambeck's Dart, Don was a picture of consistency, recording times of 9.85, 9.84, and 9.83. On top of it, the aging Maverick set top speed of the meet with a 139.96. In a *SS&DI* magazine interview, Don stated that he felt he was at a distinct disadvantage with the first Maverick because it was built by the rules. Compared to some of his competitors' cars that saw engine locations and firewalls moving about and bodies and parts being acid dipped, the Maverick was nearly stock across the board. Save for a few holes in the firewall that needed plugging, the Maverick never had issues with tech inspection.

There was a push in the early days of Pro Stock to ban the SOHC Ford. It seems those in the Chevy and Mopar camps complained that it wasn't a production engine, but more than likely, it was actually the fact that Dyno Don was coming on strong. At St. Louis in June 1970, Don won the AHRA Seventh Annual Eighth-Mile Championship drags with a best elapsed time of 6.46. (Photo Courtesy Fred Von Sholly)

Something old, something new. Don had both Mavericks at the NHRA Winternationals in 1971, relying on the older car (left) after the new ride failed to qualify. The solid candy paint on the old car hid acid-dipped doors, which were added late in 1970. (Photo ©TEN: The Enthusiast Network. All Rights Reserved.)

At the NHRA winter meet, Don arrived with his two Mavericks in tow. With the new car sidelined, the old car advanced to the second round with a 9.99 before falling to the Dodge Demon of John Petrie. Don left the new Maverick at home for the upcoming Gatornationals, instead relying, momentarily at least, on the proven car. It was a quick trip to Florida for Don, as he failed to get around Arlen Vanke in the first round. Turning his attention to the new car, the seven-day wonder was put to pasture behind Don's Atlanta home after the Gators, where it sat until Marty Furlipa of Lodi, New Jersey, purchased it. Marty operated the company East Coast Export, which sold race cars and parts to Sweden. In 1975, the Maverick was sold and shipped to Lars Flodman, who resided just outside of Stockholm. How long Flodman raced the Maverick is unknown. Whether the car even survives today is also unknown.

The first couple seasons of Pro Stock were lean times for Ford, and many times Don's was the only one to qualify. Twin Holley Dominators sit atop one of two different intakes Don ran on the second Maverick. The combination seen here was used to win the Summernationals in 1971, breaking Chrysler's stranglehold on NHRA Pro Stock. (Photo Courtesy Nicholson Family Collection)

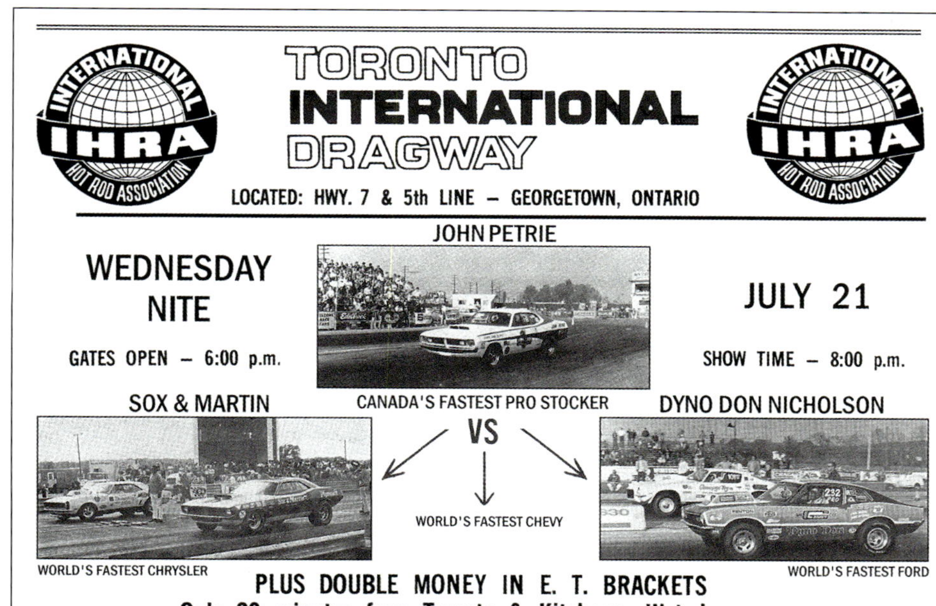

Regardless of the track, regardless of the country, Dyno's Maverick was capable of defeating the leading Mopars anywhere, any time. At Toronto International in Georgetown, Ontario, Don came out on top in this three-car show. (Photo Courtesy Robin McQueen)

The Second Maverick

Dyno was back at M & S late in 1970 to have them build the second Maverick. This car took a little longer than the first, spending close to a month under construction. Unlike the first "showroom" Maverick, this one started out as a body in white and was acid dipped. To strengthen the body without adding weight, the main panels and roof were sprayed with expandable foam. Mods followed a route similar to that of the first Maverick. The key differences were a six-point roll cage and frame connectors that tied the unibody together. As the current owner of the car, Doug Kenney will attest that the Maverick retained its original floorboards. The Cammer saw some upgrades in the form of General Kinetic cams, Holley 1150 Dominator carbs, and a new Independent runner–intake manifold. Don and Wade had worked in conjunction with Edelbrock through the latter half of 1970 to ensure the new intake setup worked. Supposedly, only a few of these intake manifolds were built. The first one, which Don used, was based on a modified Hilborn injector base and an existing Chrysler hemi top.

Doug Nash was called on to slick shift the Top Loader transmission, which was quite the process. Nash's first step was to machine off the synchronizer gears. He then made a synchronizer ring out of steel with large cog teeth, as opposed to the small ones that were on the factory gear. This ring was heat-treated and pressed into place on the gear. An associate of Nash's, Jack Schick, made a

The interior of the 1971 Maverick houses the bare necessities to get the job done. Don's sponsor Mr. Gasket supplied the vertical gate shifter to control the Doug Nash slick-shifted transmission, the first used in Pro Stock competition. Missing from the photo is the shifter-mounted cable that controlled ignition retard. Ken Dondero recalls the tachometer regularly spinning to 8,500 to 9,000 rpm. The dashboard is fiberglass. Today, the Maverick remains one of the finest examples of an unrestored drag car. (Photo Courtesy Geoff Stunkard)

fixture to hold the gear in place. The fixture was designed so that ice water ran through it to keep the temperature down while he heli-arced spots along the ring to fix it in place. It was a time-consuming process, as this had to done for every gear in the case. The sliders were then machined on a Bridgeport, removing two teeth, leaving one, and removing the next two and so on. Everything was then de-burred and the transmission reassembled. Don's prowess with a 4-speed should never be under-rated. He was one of the best and really liked the Nash Pro Shift setup. He stated that he had not missed a gear since he had Nash go through the transmission.

Tied to the Mr. Gasket shifter was an ignition spark retard cable that really helped the top-end charge. Primitive in design, the cable was clamped to the distributor, and when Don shifted from second to third, it pulled on the cable. The Cammer ran 50 degrees lead and when Don hit third the cable pulled it back to 48. Out back, the proven setup was a Dana rear perched on multi-leaf springs and fabricated ladder bars to help with bite. The famed West Coast painter, Molly, in La Habra was called on to get the Maverick looking show worthy. Don had the car completed just days before its disappointing NHRA Winternationals debut.

With bugs being worked out, Don played runner-up to the 'Cuda of Sox & Martin at the cars' next showing, the NHRA Springnationals, running a 9.78 to Ronnie Sox's 9.70. Don followed with a win at the seventh annual Super Stock Nationals in May. Fifty cars showed for the 16-car field, and leading the way were Don Carlton's *Mopar Missile* and Dyno Don's Maverick, each with a string of 9.70 times. First-round winners included Carlton, Dyno Don, Grumpy Jenkins, Wally Booth, Don

Don hauled the seven-day wonder to Florida for the Gatornationals in 1971 only to fall in the first round to Arlen Vanke, turning a 9.88. Interesting to note is that the old Maverick is sporting the signal lights from the new car, which stayed home in Atlanta during the trip. (Photo Courtesy Steve Reyes)

Here at OCIR, Don warms the Firestone Drag 500s on the Maverick prior to a run. Helping to get the power to the ground is an M & S ladder-bar suspension and Mr. Gasket shocks. The Maverick carried NHRA Division 2 competition number through 1971 and Division 7 number into 1972. (Photo Courtesy Steve Delgadillo/Lou Hart Collection)

Grotheer, Mike Fons, Bill Stiles, and Wayne Gapp. It was Stiles who surprised many when he eliminated the favored Carlton in round two. Dyno Don, meanwhile, advanced after defeating the Demon of Bob Riffle, setting low ET of the meet in the process with a 9.75 at 141.28 mph.

In the semifinals, the 1970 Camaro of Jenkins took an easy one over Gapp's Maverick, which got out of shape coming off the line. In the other semi pairing, Dyno Don ran a bumper up on Fons to take the win with a 9.83 to Fons's 9.87. So, in the final, it was the Chevy of Jenkins versus Dyno Don's quicker Ford battling for the payout of almost $9,000. Don had close to 2/10th up on Jenkins and it showed in the final. Getting the jump off the line, Don maintained a fender length lead all the way to take the Camaro with a 9.76 at 141.06 to Jenkins's 9.97 at 139.75.

It was Don who finally broke Chrysler's 18-month stranglehold on NHRA Pro Stock. After Grumpy Jenkins won the category's first two events, it became an all-Chrysler show dominated by the cars of Sox & Martin. Dyno earned his and Ford's first NHRA Pro Stock title when he defeated the Dodge Challenger of Mike Fons at the Summernationals in New Jersey. It was no easy feat for Don, who qualified the Maverick down the pack with a 9.85, .29 behind number-one qualifier, Don Carlton. During trials, the Maverick rotated an axle tube in the

Dana while pulling a chassis-twisting wheelstand. A late night session saw the tube brought back into alignment and welded. By the time Sunday's eliminations rolled around, Don and his trusty crew of Earl Wade and Dave McGrane had found another 2/10ths in the Cammer and opened up with a first-round win over the Camaro of Ron Hutter, recording a 9.68.

The round-two matchup between Don and Jenkins had the fans on their feet. Jenkins in the last Chevy remaining fell to the Maverick as his 9.86 was no match for Don's 9.64. In the closet race of the weekend, Don faced Carlton's *Missile* in the third and came out on top with a 9.66 to Carlton's 9.67. The next car to fall to the Maverick was the 'Cuda of Canadian John Petrie, who came up short to Don's 9.72. Fons, who had eliminated Landy's Dodge in the semifinals with a 9.61, gave Don a good run for the money. After a coin toss for lane choice and the usual prerace burnouts, the pair got off to a good clean start. On the big end, the Maverick recorded a 9.63 at 141.73 mph to stop the Rod Shop Challengers 9.68 at 142.63.

Don won his second AHRA Grand-American race of the season in September; he defeated the Camaro of Joe Satmary at Marion, Ohio, with a 9.77 at 141.37 mph. Satmary, with the lone Chevy in the 16-car field, had defeated the Carmen Rotonda–driven Challenger in the semis with a 10-flat, while Dyno Don eliminated Wayne

Yeahhhh, baby! Smoke 'em if you got 'em. Don resorted to Funny Car–style burnouts to harness the power of the Cammer. Current owner of the Maverick, Doug Kenney, found numerous holes on the underside of the hood and, when he asked Earl Wade about it, he was told: "We were changing scoops weekly to try and find extra power." The Maverick survives with the scoop seen in this photo. (Photo Courtesy Tom West Collection)

Cecil County, Maryland, track manager Ron McNeal touted the strip as the traction capitol of the nation. It seems Don had no qualms with that as the Cammer's 700 horses easily planted the nearly 3,000-pound Maverick up on its wheelie bars. The plate between the taillights was a parachute mount. The AHRA allowed a Pro Stocker to run without front brakes, as long as it had a chute. (Photo Courtesy Fred Von Sholly)

Don worked hand-in-hand with Edelbrock in the development of the Cammer's independent runner manifold. Dyno Don tried out the intake for the first time at the 1970 NHRA Springnationals. Fuel starvation issues saw Don fall to Ronnie Sox in the third round. The manifold's plenum was an existing Edelbrock part for a big-block Chevy TR-1X. A Mallory magneto and coil sparked the Champion plugs. (Photo Courtesy Nicholson Family Collection)

Gapp's Boss 429 Maverick with a 9.78. In the final, Satmary overpowered the slicks and lost the race in a cloud of tire smoke, turning a 10.02 through the lights.

Don ended the season by winning Holley's Winner Circle Points Championship. According to Holley, the highly select group consisted of nationally known professional drag racers receiving direct sponsorship and support from the aftermarket manufacturer. Dyno accumulated 90 points, 40 ahead of runner-up, the Kimball brothers. Participants included racers from each division, including Butch Leal, Wally Booth, Bill Jenkins, and Barrie Poole.

By the end of 1971, the NHRA had agreed to weight breaks for the small–cubic-inch compacts, allowing the Pintos, Vegas, and Gremlins to compete against the big-block–powered cars in 1972. However, Don wasn't through with the Maverick just yet. At the 1972 NHRA Winternationals, he qualified fifth at 9.734 at 140.84 mph. A disastrous run on Friday ended with extensive damage to the engine, clutch, and transmission, forcing Don and his crew to spend Saturday morning making repairs. Bandaged back together, the Maverick ran a 9.85 in round one to defeat the Wedge-powered Comet of Barrie Poole. Quite the feat considering that Dyno Don's Cammer was only running on seven cylinders! In the second round, Dyno lost fire, wiping out what little hope

he had of advancing the crippled Maverick. Waiting in the wings was Don's own mini-Pro Stock. His Pinto never made it to the Winternationals due to delays at the paint shop, which put off its final construction.

At the AHRA Winter Nationals at Bee Line, Don trialed one of Doug Nash's early 5-speed transmissions in the Maverick. This was the first Pro Stocker to use the new, slick Nash piece. At the meet, the Maverick ran the low ET and top speed with a 9.60 at 143.08 mph. Don was to race Lynn Harrison in round 1 (Harrison was substituting for Dick Landy), but the Maverick lost oil pressure after the initial burnout and was shut off.

The quickly evolving world of early 1970s Pro Stock had made the Maverick obsolete, and by the end of 1972, it had run its last race for Don. The car was sold to Robert Rashid in Michigan, who blew up the Cammer the first time at the track. Earl Wade rebuilt the engine for Rashid, and the car was raced sparingly before going into storage for the next couple of decades. Rick Hamilton became the next owner, who then sold it to Wayne Jeffers. Jeffers passed away and his girlfriend ran it through Mecum auctions, where it failed to meet reserve. This allowed current owner, Doug Kenney, to buy the car privately. Somehow, the Maverick remained intact all these years and is a prime example of how Pro Stock used to be.

The second Maverick was retired shortly after being driven by Ken Dondero at Indy in 1972. Dondero made it to the semifinals, where he fell to eventual category winner, Ray Allen. Dondero's opponent here is the Camaro of Don Lorentzen. (Photo Courtesy Tom Schiltz)

It didn't matter, California to Pennsylvania, from coast to coast Don's Maverick was the most! At Pennsylvania's Sunset Dragstrip in June 1971, Don won the PDA's Fourth Annual eighth-mile Pro Stock Nationals. In the process, he set the track record with a 6.23 at 122 mph while defeating Dick Landy in the final. A month later at Union Grove, Don ran Pro Stock's quickest time ever of 9.39. Hey, check out the STP shirt on the kid on the left. Too cool! (Photo Courtesy Larry Knapp)

Dyno Don and Dave McGrane perform maintenance on the Maverick during a break in action during 1971. The 1150 Holley Dominators sit on a fabricated intake, made up of Hilborn and Chrysler parts. The induction setup helped the Maverick realize 9.30 times. That's a rare aluminum Ford radiator in front of the Cammer. Don's Maverick would be the last Cammer-powered car to win a national event. (Author's Collection)

Dyno In a Rambler?

According to previous interviews with Bob Swain, head of performance at American Motors, the company came close to signing Don to a deal in late 1971. AMC was just stepping into Pro Stock and was looking for an established name to run its program. After being left high and dry by Ford when the manufacturer pulled out of racing, Don showed interest and, in no time, hammered out a deal with AMC. With everything but signatures on the dotted line, Don made one final request. He wanted AMC to provide his wife, Patty, with a Lincoln Continental. AMC, eager to make the deal, agreed and a new contract was written up. At the last minute though, Don had a change of heart, stating that he just couldn't desert his loyal fans by switching. Eventually, the manufacturer signed Wally Booth and Ford-Mercury fans everywhere let out a collective sigh of relief.

1972

It wasn't going to be a good year in NHRA Pro Stock for anyone who wasn't named Bill Jenkins. The NHRA was looking for a way to level the field in Pro Stock and found the answer when Jenkins presented NHRA executive director Jack Hart the idea of small-block–powered compacts. Jenkins pushed the idea from a marketing perspective; the buying public was purchasing small cars and, by racing the same, the crowds would pour in. The NHRA agreed and new rules and weight breaks would be written for the 1972 season.

As Jenkins noted in the book *Grumpy's Toys: The Authorized History of Grumpy Jenkins' Cars*, "Jack Hart didn't flinch when I presented the weight breaks to him." Yes, you read it right; Jenkins wrote the NHRA weight breaks for 1972. The breaks worked out favorably for the small cars, especially the Vega and were as follows: Wedge-engine cars would be required to carry 6.75 pounds per cubic inch; inclined-valve engines, 7.0 pounds; and all others, specifically Ford's

At the IHRA Nationals in August 1972, Don in the Pinto faced off against his hired driver, Ken Dondero in the Maverick. Don made it to the finals where he fell to the Duster of Sox & Martin. (Photo Courtesy Todd Wingerter)

Kendig carbs sponsored the Pinto, but Don never used the "variable venturi" 1,250-cfm carbs in competition. The carbs' performance did not meet that of the proven Holleys. Don had George Cerney paint this car. (Photo Courtesy Brian Beattie)

SOHC and Chrysler's Hemi, would be required to carry 7.25 pounds per cubic inch. Do the math and it's easy to see that Chevy had a distinct advantage.

When it came to AHRA Pro Stock, where things were a little more balanced, Dyno Don ruled. There he would parlay two national event wins and two runner-up finishes into his first ever World Championship. All with his own small-block–powered compact.

Sometime in the latter half of 1971, Ford's performance boss, Charlie Gray Jr., commissioned Don to have five Pro Stock Pintos built. As Ford racer Barrie Poole, a close friend of Don's, recalls, "Don arranged for Tom Smith's Wolverine Chassis to build the five cars. Tom was taking longer than expected, so I was asked by Ford to lend Smith a hand to ensure the mule car got done on schedule. I more or less played gofer, chasing parts, and helping out where I could." The mule car became the car Poole drove out of Sandy Elliot's dealership in Chatham, Ontario. Wolverine built four of the five Pintos with M & S Race Cars building Don's. Financially, the Pinto was an obvious beneficial move for Don. As he mentioned in a period interview, "I could build a competitive small-block for what it costs to repair the SOHC Ford."

The Pinto's Runabout

Between February 1972 and February 1974, a total of three different Pintos ran under Don's umbrella. The first debuted at the 1972 NHRA Gatornationals in March. Although the car ran promising 9.60 times during mid-week testing, when it came to race day, Don failed to qualify the car due to what was reported as electrical issues. At the same race, Ken Dondero qualified the Maverick in the number-two position behind Grumpy Jenkins's Vega with a 9.46. Dondero survived until the semifinals, when he fell to eventual winner, Don Carlton, whose *Motown Missile* nipped him running a 9.54 to a 9.55. As a consolation to Don, his misfiring Pinto did manage to take home the Best Engineered Car Award.

"Dyno Don" Nicholson's Pro Stock Pinto — "Best Engineered Car" at 1972 NHRA Gatornationals

Lawce Bros. & Gunn AA/Altered — "Best Engineered Car" at 1971 NHRA World Finals

Mike Hoag and Sherman Gunn of M & S Race Cars helped turn Don into a Pro Stock winner by prepping both his Mavericks and his Pintos. Their construction technique and attention to detail helped earn the company a pair of Best Engineered Car awards. (Author's Collection)

Come 1972, revised NHRA rules allowed for small-block–powered compacts, and it was Dyno and his Cleveland Pinto leading the Ford charge. Chrysler, not happy unless it was winning, pulled its team drivers mid-season in protest of what it perceived as less-than-favorable weight breaks. Bob Lambeck, a strong independent, marched on before turning to Super Stock the following season. (Photo Courtesy Nicholson Family Collection)

The First Pinto . . .

The first Pinto was received at M & S Race Cars as a body in white. An acid dip at Areochem in Orange, California, removed approximately 80 pounds of excess weight before a 1¼ x 2–inch square tube chassis went under the car from the firewall back. As per NHRA rules, factory-original frame rails were required from the firewall forward. The factory front rails were tied together by a removable, and slightly lowered, fabricated crossmember. An eight-point roll cage was installed that helped protect Don in case of a rollover and tied the car together front to back. A & A Fiberglass supplied the

Supporting the Dana rear end were fabricated ladder bars and multi-leaf springs. Unbreakable axles came from Summers Brothers. As you can see, when it came to the Jardine headers, there wasn't a lot of ground clearance. (Photo Courtesy Nicholson Family Collection)

Giving Don a bit of running start on the small-block was the fact that a fair amount of development was done as early as 1969 through Ford's SCCA program. The tach-drive distributor is by Mallory. Note the fire wall location in this early 1972 photo compared to later photos. (Photo Courtesy Nicholson Family Collection)

A reasonably stock front suspension made use of a Pinto rack, lowered front crossmember, and Airheart disc brakes. Also visible here is the Weaver oil pump. Don trialed the dry-sump system, hoping that it would cure the bearing issue he was having with the Cleveland. It didn't. (Photo ©TEN: The Enthusiast Network. All Rights Reserved.)

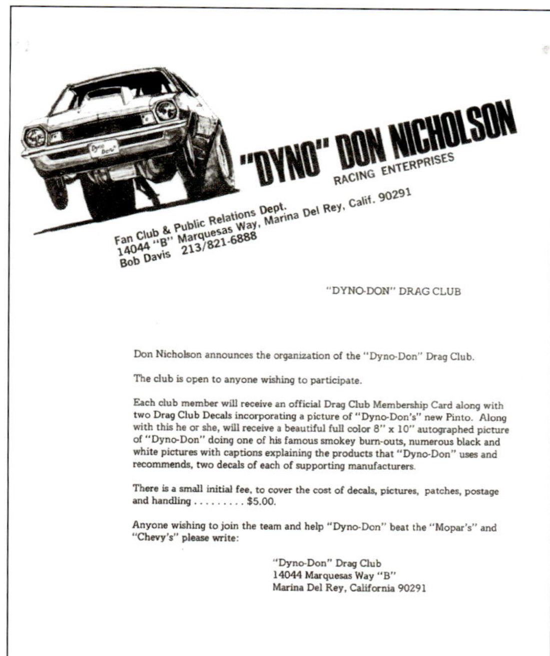

Back in 1973, $5 would have gotten you membership into the Dyno Don Drag Club, which was Don's fan club. The club actually dates back to the Funny Car days of the 1960s. I wonder how many contributed to help Don defeat the Mopars and Chevys. The contact, Bob Davis, worked for Hooker headers and prided himself as being a PR man. (Author's Collection)

lightweight fenders, hood, and dashboard. At the rear of the car, five leaf springs per side carried a 9-inch rear end, which was later replaced by a Dana. Helping to plant the 12- to 13-inch Firestone Drag 500s were M & S–fabricated ladder bars. The rear-end width was said to be 37 inches from backing plate to backing plate. Summers Brothers axles with full floating hubs allowed removal of the axles without removing the wheels. Bringing the Pinto to a stop from 140+ mph runs were disc brakes at all four corners made up of parts from Airheart and Loc. Up front, the brakes mounted on lowered spindles, which helped get the car out of the air. A Mr. Gasket shifter moved the Doug Nash 4-speed from gear to gear, helped along by a Hays clutch and 50-pound flywheel.

By late 1971, dyno pulls were being made on the Cleveland at Edelbrock, where a fabricated short-tube manifold was developed. Topping the manifold for Don was a choice of either 660 cfm or 4500 Holleys. Even though Willard Kendig sponsored Don through 1972, the man's unique carburetors were never used in competition, as they failed to put up the numbers to match the Holleys.

When it came to the heads, to improve the less-than-ideal sharp angle of the exhaust ports, Don made use of port plates to raise the ports 1¼ inches. To incorporate the rectangular aluminum plate, a 1⅜-inch-wide slice was cut from the length of the head. Airflow Research (and later Mullen) performed additional work on the heads that included using titanium intake valves, steel Donovan exhausts valves, and a Jomar girdle. The girdle helped eliminate flex when the Cleveland buzzed to 9,000 rpm. A General Kinetics roller cam with .614 lift and 332 duration was used. With the use of a torque plate developed by Don, the block was opened up a maximum .030 over.

Following the lead of the NASCAR boys, Don ran full-skirt Venolia pistons. This seemed to lessen any issue regarding cracking in the cylinders. The pistons were gas ported and carried a .043 top ring and a modified low tension Speed-Pro oil ring. Compression came in at over 12:1. A Weaver dry sump oil system was trialed early on because Don struggled to keep bearings in the Cleveland. The issue proved to be twofold; the issues were connected to factory design but both were corrected soon enough. One issue was the externally balanced Cleveland crank. The cast part worked fine on a daily driver but not so in a high-RPM Pro Stock mill. The crank "whipped around in the block" and in Don's case, took out the number-2 and number-4 bearings. It was machinist Bill Coon who "enlightened" Don. Coon had previously worked with Doug Nash and solved bearing issues he had been having with the crank in his 289-powered *Bronco Buster* match racer. Coon eliminated the flex, or whipping, issue by internally balancing the crank and assembly. Problem solved. Issue two related to the bottom end that was starved for oil thanks to a flawed factory design. Unlike the earlier 289–302 that was designed with three oil galleys, cost-saving measures saw the Cleveland designed with just two. The problem with the Cleveland design lies in the fact the main galley runs front to rear through the right side of the block and opens up to each lifter bore. Pull the lifters on a Cleveland and you can see large egg-shaped oil holes that intersect with the main galley. These holes are too large and flood the top end, starving the main and rod journals at high RPM.

Dan Nowak describes how the issue was discovered and how it was rectified: "In 1973, we had just swapped in another engine (using the shop of Mr. Rod in Michigan). The intake was off and I was priming the engine using a speed handle in the distributor hole. In no time at all, the oil was oozing out the lifter holes and had half-filled the valley. Once the problem area was discovered, we tried running oil lines to the main caps. We found that it didn't work after we split a bearing cap after just one race." Don solved the problem by having Bill Coon sleeve the lifter bores and drill them out with a hole of approximately 1/16-inch. Why 1/16th? Apparently, it was a number Don just threw out; he wanted the hole big enough that debris wouldn't get caught up. Helping to keep the Cleveland alive was the necessary high oil pressure. Don ran 50-weight Pennzoil in the Pinto, just as he had in the Mavericks.

En route to capturing the 1972 AHRA World Championship, Don grabbed his first national event win of

Showing off its well-tuned suspension, Don's Pinto rides the wheelie bars during a clean launch at Old Bridge Township Raceway. It's difficult to distinguish here but the quarter panels were bowed out for additional tire clearance. The rear bumper has been narrowed. (Photo Courtesy Brian Beattie)

Although Don failed to qualify for the NHRA World Finals held at Amarillo, Ken Dondero did, and the decision was made to compete with the steadily improving Pinto. In the final, Dondero's off-pace 9.93 wasn't enough against Jenkins's 9.78. (Photo Courtesy Steve Call/Edelbrock Archives)

the season on April 11 at Palm Beach International. There, he defeated number-1 qualifier, Ronnie Sox and his destroked Hemi Duster in the final. The three-round race was a fairly easy go for Don; his only real battle came in the first round. There, he defeated Dave Atkins in Bill Hielscher's Camaro with a 9.58 at 143.31 mph to the Chevy's 10.00 at 138.46. That's as tough as Don's day got. In round two, while Sox received a bye, Don was faced with running the Vega of Grumpy Jenkins. According to the AHRA publication, *Drag World*, it wasn't much of a race. "The Grump stopped a few yards off the starting line, revved it up a couple of times, and then hurried on his way." Don took the win with a 10.47 time. In the final, Sox fouled out, wasting a fine 9.51 at 144.46 mph to give Don the win. Don, catching Sox's redlight, took it easy with a 10.16 at 70.64 mph.

Don continued on his march to the championship by playing runner-up at a couple of AHRA races in August. On August 6, he fell to the Demon of Herb McCandless at the Gateway Nationals in St. Louis and on August 27, he lost another close one to the Vega of Jim Hayter at the Grand-American race at Olathe, Kansas. To lock up the World Championship, Don defeated Dick Landy at Fremont on October 8. However, this was not before eliminating unknown Gene Gate in the first round with a 9.66 at 144 mph, the Duster of Bob Lambeck in the second with a 9.591 to a trailing 9.83, and Larry Huff's Challenger in the third with 9.553 at 143.54 mph to a 9.675 at 144.23. In what proved to be an anticlimactic final, Landy broke on the line and

At OCIR on November 15, the front panels of the Pinto were munched after taking a hard right into the guard-rail off a burnout. Repairs were made in time for the Supernationals a few days later. Don arrived on Saturday just in time for a qualifying run but broke on the line. He had another shot at it on Sunday morning but the transmission broke going into fourth gear. It was after the World finals, October 22, that Don had the engine and firewall relocated to take advantage of the revised 1973 NHRA rules. These new rules were first run at the Supernationals. (Photo Courtesy Pete Quinn)

Ken Dondero

Ken Dondero had a way with a 4-speed stick that was the envy of many pros. Dondero started making a name for himself in the early 1960s, drag racing a 1952 Chevy Gasser in northern California. In short order, he had friends asking him to drive their cars, which led to an early partnership with Carl Beattie. The pair campaigned an E/Gas 1955 Chevy and terrorized strips such as Vacaville and Half Moon Bay. Dondero hooked up with Bob Panella in 1967, and in 1969 took Super Eliminator in Panella's blown B/GS Anglia at the NHRA Winternationals. This early success led to driving stints with Pro Stock legends Dick Landy, Dyno Don, Bill Jenkins, and Gapp & Roush, among others.

Dondero made hundreds of trips down the track in Pro Stock and won a couple AHRA World Championships in the process. He hooked up with Landy in 1971 but found him to be too demanding. It wasn't a difficult decision to jump ship when Don came calling in 1972. Not only did the pair share similar personalities, they even looked alike. Cheryl Dondero recalled that on more than one occasion people mistook Ken for Don. "Ken just played along and let the person walk away none the wiser."

After successful 1972 and 1973 seasons running two cars, Dyno Don, like everyone else, felt the burn of the early 1970s fuel crunch and made the decision to cut back his operations. He suggested to Dondero that he take up Jenkins's offer to drive for him, which he did.

Dondero, having earned his reputation banging gears, never lost a step when the Lenco planetary transmission came into vogue, as proven by the two AHRA Championships he won with Jenkins. Dondero dominated the two years, winning 9 of 11 races in 1975 and 11 of 13 in 1976. Ongoing friction between Jenkins's two drivers, Dondero and Larry Lombardo, boiled over. At the end of 1976, Dondero had had his fill of what he perceived to be Lombardo's petty jealousy and moved on. He did a stint with Gapp & Roush in 1977 and another with Landy in 1980 before taking a premature retirement.

In 1981, Ken owned and operated Dondero Tires in Costa Mesa and was living comfortably on Balboa Island. He had a couple of Harleys and enjoyed the open road. In 1983, he got wind that Jenkins's operation was up for sale and talked his old friend Bob Panella into going drag racing once again. Dondero sold his tire shop to Pete Vaniderstine and hit the road with the Panella Camaro in 1984.

Showing he still had what it took, Dondero closed the season at number 7 in NHRA Pro Stock. He retired from drag racing for good in 1986 and lived between Balboa and Tulare, where he purchased and operated Ken's Auto & Tire. In his spare time, what little he had of it, he enjoyed traveling and restoring muscle cars. His daughter adds, "He loved working and running his shops. He always said how lucky he was, doing what he loved."

Dondero's Pinto (seen here) at Ohio's Edgewater seems to find the traction more than adequate, thanks in part to the twin strips of rosin. Economics saw Don cut back operations in 1974, and he said good-bye to both Dondero and the Pinto. (Photo Courtesy Bob Martin)

United States Racing Team

Feeding off of Pro Stock's popularity was Al Carpenter's United States Racing Team circuit, which ran from 1972 into 1974. The whole idea behind the program was to raise awareness and gain sponsorship to help ease the increasing financial burden that the car owners were facing. Carpenter had listened to Joe Satmary vent after his Camaro bowed out early at the Nationals in 1971. Satmary was upset when he discovered that his measly winnings didn't come close to covering his expenses for the weekend. Carpenter put forth to other racers the idea of a circuit and, shortly after Indy, they held their first meeting. Along with Satmary, Jenkins, Sox & Martin, and Landy were believed to be the first to ante up the $1,000 buy-in. It took Buddy Martin to persuade Dyno Don to sign up. Don had been making his own arrangements from day one and felt he was doing all right on his own.

The circuit consisted of eight events the first season, featuring 16 Pro Stocks with 4 each from Chevy, Ford, Plymouth, and Dodge. The Chevy players included: Bill Jenkins, Dave Strickler, Bill Blanding, and Wally Booth. Booth, who signed on while campaigning a Camaro, switched alliances late in 1971 and built an AMC in 1972. He remained on the Chevy team. The Ford team consisted of Dyno Don, Eddie Schartman, Gapp & Roush, and Hubert Platt. For Plymouth, it was Sox & Martin, Arlen Vanke, Don Grotheer, and Ronnie Lyles. The Dodge team consisted of Don Carlton, Dick Landy, Herb McCandless, and Mike Fons. Fill-ins when needed included Ray Allen, Warren Johnson, John Hagen, and Bruce Larson.

Al Carpenter booked the shows at $16,500 a race, plus 50 percent of pit money. Out of that was paid appearance money to the racers as well as a fee to Jon Lundberg, the circuit's hired mouth behind the microphone. Appearance money became a sticking point for some, as it wasn't being doled out evenly. Jenkins, for instance, was always paid a little more. This, in part, contributed to the demise of the circuit before the end of the 1974 season. Approximately a dozen races were held in both 1972 and 1973. The inaugural race took place March 14 at Phenix City, where Don in his Maverick set low ET with a 9.54 and were to face Sox's Duster in the final. A lost clutch during a warm-up burnout saw the Maverick replaced by Eddie Schartman's Comet. Don finished the first season third in points behind the two Sox & Martin cars, driven by Ronnie Sox and Herb McCandless. A pretty good showing, considering he had missed dates due to prior commitments.

The 1972 United States Racing Team proved to be an unqualified success, featuring the biggest names in Pro Stock. Shown here is the program from that first season. In this cover shot, Don is second from the right in the second from bottom row. (Photo Courtesy Terry Gilkes)

The finely tuned chassis of Don's Pinto gains traction at Ohio's National Trail. Shift points came at 8,500 to 9,000 rpm. From 1972 through 2006, National Trail hosted the NHRA Springnationals. Don won it in 1977. (Photo Courtesy Bob Martin)

Dyno Don sailed on through with a wide-open 9.524 at 143.70.

On Labor Day weekend, a number of big name racers bypassed the NHRA Nationals and instead battled for the big-dollar payout of the Don Garlits PRA race at Tulsa. Preferring his chances at Indy, Don had both his Pinto and Maverick in attendance. Ken Dondero drove the Maverick and succeeded in making it to the semifinals; Don also made the semis. That's where the pair's day ended. Don lost on a Rich Mirarcki holeshot, 9.70 to a 9.78, while Dondero ran a 9.70 in falling to eventual category winner, Ray Allen at 9.61. At the World Finals on the weekend of October 20–22, Dondero, driving the red Pinto, played runner-up to Jenkins's dominating Vega.

Revised NHRA Pro Stock rules for 1973 were announced in September. They allowed for an engine setback, as long as the number-1 spark plug was not to the rear of the front spindle centerline. To make room for the new engine location, the rules also allowed for the firewall to be relocated. These modifications were made to Don's Pinto after the World finals and prior to a Pro Stock show at OCIR on November 15. M & S made the changes, which, by the looks of the car's stance, included suspension mods.

The year 1973 was a good one for the Fords with Dyno, Glidden, and Gapp leading the way in Pro Stock. Seen here at Indy, Don held both ends of the class record going in but bowed early and looked on as Bob Glidden won his first national event. (Photo Courtesy Bob Martin)

Another shot from the famed Dragway 42. Although considered illegal, on the rare occasion Don mixed his fuel it was one part aviation gas to four parts Sunoco 260. He mentioned this to his old friend Butch Leal while waiting in the staging lanes at the Gatornationals in Florida and Leal's response was, "Is that it? I run 50/50." (Photo Courtesy Todd Wingerter)

Yes, at one time a crewmember (Bob Mandel in this case) was allowed to hold the car steady in the water box. Don performed burnouts in the box while in third gear. A drop hop or two usually followed the burnout. TravelLite was a failed business venture for Don. Located in Irvine, California, the company manufactured portable lighting products. Don had a deal with Hooker Headers that was said to be worth $5,000 dollars. (Photo Courtesy Bob Martin)

1973

Don raised concerns in 1973 regarding the escalating cost of building and running a Pro Stocker and his fears that the category was evolving into "Funny Stock." He had lived through the evolution of Stockers to Funny Car and wasn't interested in doing it again. Operating on a shoestring budget with no big money from major sponsors, Don was all for regulations that limited construction techniques, thus preventing costs from escalating and killing the category. Some of Dyno Don's ideas included implementing predetermined weight breaks for the match-race Pro Stocks. Dyno Don felt that this killed the need to build exotic lightweight cars.

On the national event front, 1973 got off to a great start for Don and saw him win both the AHRA and NHRA winter meets with the Pinto. The car looked a little different in the New Year with the black side stripe now painted yellow and the old Kendig sponsorship gone. Don invested financially in an Orange County–based lighting company, TravelLite, but when business fell he pulled out. Camera manufacturer Minolta signed on as sponsor at the end of the 1973 season.

At the AHRA Winter Nationals, held January 25–28 at Phoenix, old nemesis Ronnie Sox and his Hemi Duster held the number-1 spot with a 9.17 followed by Wayne Gapp and Dyno Don with times of 9.31 and 9.32, respectively. Prior to eliminations, Sox spun a bearing in the hemi and thrashed to get a replacement engine in before the first round. The loss of Sox's good engine cost him later.

In the first round, Don faced the aging Dodge Challenger of Bill Bagshaw and made quick work of him with a 9.41. In the second round, he raced fellow Ford stalwart, Bob Glidden, for the first time. Glidden recalled the first time he met Don, "I met him during the Supernationals in 1972. I was 21 or 22 years old at my first Pro Stock race. I went by his shop in Orange and he wasn't overly friendly. Even though we never shared ideas, there was never any friction."

It took Don just 9.38 seconds to defeat the up-and-comer Glidden, who had slowed after missing a

Twin Holley Dominator carbs fed the Cleveland the fuel it craved. The intake manifold used fabricated runners on an existing Edelbrock Chrysler top. Note the notch at the base of the windshield for carb clearance and the raised exhaust port plates. Revised rules for 1973 allowed for engine setbacks, as long as the number-1 plug lined up with the spindle centerline. This also allowed for relocation of the firewall. (Photo Courtesy Nicholson Family Collection)

At the 1973 NHRA Gatornationals, Dyno Don defeated the similar Pinto of Gapp & Roush in the final, setting both ends of the record in the process. It was Don's third national event win of the young season. (Photo Courtesy Steve Reyes)

At York US-30 for the 1973 Super Stock Nationals, Dyno came in second to the upstart Vega of Paul Blevins. Yeah, Don was a bit upset. "Good losers don't win races," he was once quoted to say. Here early in the weekend, he goes through weigh-in. (Photo Courtesy Jim Glover)

gear. In the semifinals, Don beat Ronnie Sox with a 9.27, which was good for a new AHRA record. Sox, with his backup engine, just couldn't match his earlier 9 teen times. In the final, a 9.50 at 141.50 mph is all it took for Don to beat Melvin Yow, who was wheeling Bill Stepp's Demon.

Dyno Don joined the other two Dons, Garlits and Schumacher, in winning the pro categories at the NHRA Winternationals. The rain-delayed meet took three weeks to complete and on the second weekend, Don was literally on the outside looking in. He had left his passes in his jacket, which his daughter Cindy took to Big Bear ski resort over the weekend. Don couldn't convince the gatekeeper who he was, arguing with him that if he didn't let him in, he'd miss the race. "Sure and I'm Don Garlits" was the man's retort. A fuming Don was finally let in when he was recognized by NHRA brass.

Dyno's Pinto became the first Pro Stocker to record an 8-second run when he hit an 8.98 in a match at Connecticut in June 1973. The same year, the Pinto held the NHRA ET record for a good six months with a 9.01. (Photo Courtesy Todd Wingerter)

Finally settled in, Don and the now Lenco-equipped Pinto qualified in the 32-car field with a 9.38 at 144.19 mph, .16 behind Don Carlton who recorded a 9.22 in the *Mopar Missile*. In the first round of action, Dyno Don ran 9.45 at 145 mph to defeat the Demon of Canadian Larry Breaux. He defeated Butch Leal's 9.64 in round two with a 9.55, and, in the third, he ran a 9.45 at 145.63 mph to defeat Dick Landy's 9.60 at 145. Don took a bye in the semifinals and held nothing back with a 9.49 at 144.69 mph. In the final, he faced the *Missile* of Don Carlton. In his row to the final, Carlton had defeated Barrie Poole and Bob Lambeck, and had his own bye before defeating the Pinto of Gapp & Roush in the semifinals. Reportedly running one of the rare, NASCAR Clevelands measuring 366 ci, Don recorded a NHRA record, 9.33 at 145.16 mph to sink Carlton, who recorded a 9.60.

At the upcoming Gatornationals, Don qualified sixth with a 9.23 but improved in the first round when he defeated Jerry Miller with a 9.05. In the second, the Pinto recorded low ET of the meet, and a new Pro Stock record, 9.01 at the expense of Don Carlton whose destroked 396-ci Hemi *Missile* lost with a 9.06. As predicted by many, Dyno Don and Wayne Gapp faced off in the final. Gapp and his 351 Pinto had qualified number 1 with a

The bulletproof Dana rear end under the Pinto replaced the Ford 9-inch midway through 1972. New for 1973 were the aluminum Super Trick rims, which dropped a good chunk of the unsprung weight from the car. To make room for the Firestones, the rear wheelwells were stretched 18 inches and steel tubs were installed. (Photo Courtesy Todd Wingerter)

Ronnie Sox met his match in Dyno here at Capitol Raceway in 1973. In total, Don won five national events that year and more than his share of match races, and all on his own dime. As Mike Hoag at M & S recalls, when it came to building the Mavericks and Pintos, Don paid for everything himself. Apparently, Ford nearly broke M & S due to lack of payment for fiberglass parts. Eventually it got its money. (Photo Courtesy Todd Wingerter)

9.02. In the final, Don took a slight holeshot lead and hung on through the lights with a 9.04 at 150 to a 9.03 at 149 mph.

Don ran a number of IHRA national events in 1973, where his success matched his showing in AHRA and NHRA competition. There he played runner-up at the Springnationals and won the All-American Nationals and the Nationals. At all three races, his final round opponent was Don Carlton in the *Mopar Missile* Duster. At the Springnationals in Bristol, Dyno made it to the final

Clutch changes and transmission removal were made easy on the Pinto by removing the tunnel cover. Don relied upon a Schiefer clutch and Mr. Gasket shifter to make it through the gears. Don had previously noted that shifting was all done within the first 6 seconds of each pass. Stewart-Warner gauges and an AutoMeter tach with rev limiter helped keep the Cleveland alive. (Photo Courtesy Nicholson Family Collection)

round only to lose to Carlton on a red light. For Carlton, this win earned him his fifth straight IHRA national event title.

At the IHRA All-American race held in September, also at Bristol, a reported 25,000 fans showed up for the rain-shortened event. To reach the final, Dyno Don and Carlton had to battle through one of the toughest 16-car fields ever gathered. Starting with first-round action, Carlton knocked off the Pinto of Hubert Platt with a 9.15, while Dyno Don took care of the Hornet of Wally Booth with a 9.08. In the second, Carlton defeated Dave Kanners's 9.44 with his second 9.15 clocking. Dyno Don, meanwhile, dropped the *Old Reliable* Vega of Dave Strickler with a 9.09 to a 9.31. In the semifinals, Carlton got by low qualifier (9.02) Melvin Yow in Billy Stepp's Demon. Carlton recorded a 9.22 as mechanical issues saw Yow slow to a 10.01. Dyno Don then had the pleasure of facing the Duster of Sox & Martin. Ronnie Sox made it to the semifinals by defeating his old teammate Herb McCandless with a 9.17. In what has gone into the books as one of the closest Pro Stock races ever, both drivers ran identical 9.16 times. Dyno Don took the win by virtue of a quicker reaction time. The final round couldn't have been much closer; Don took the win over Carlton with a 9.14 at 150 mph to the *Missile*'s 9.16 at 149.

At Lakeland Internationals Raceway in Florida on October 14 for the final IHRA race of the season, Don defeated the Plymouth Duster of Harold Clark, the Vega of Dave Strickler, and the Pinto of Gapp & Roush. In the finals, he turned an 8.96 at 144.50 mph to drop Carlton for the win.

At the 1974 NHRA Winternationals, Don and the well-used Pinto fell to Scott Shafiroff. This was the final national event for the Pinto. Do those fenders look like they're "drooping" to you? (Photo Courtesy Brian Kennedy)

All indications are that Don last raced the Pinto in February 1974. At the NHRA Gatornationals in March, he debuted his first Mustang II. The Pinto hung around for a while, collecting dust, before being sold to Georgia's J. R. Atkins as a roller on Thanksgiving weekend 1976. Over time, Atkins made a number of changes to the car. He modified the roll cage by adding Funny Car–style bars, he replaced the steel doors with fiberglass parts, swapped out the ladder bars for a four-link, replaced the steel wheel tubs with aluminum tubs, and lowered the car. He raced the Pinto into the 1980s with a big-cubic-inch Cleveland, recording a best of 4.90 in the eighth-mile. Alex Polewik purchased the car, minus engine, in 2005, and, at his Midwest Supercars Incorporated shop, he completed a visual restoration. Today, the Pinto resides in Florida as part of Todd Werner's collection.

Both Pintos made an appearance at the NHRA World Finals in 1973. This was the final race for the blue car under Don before being sold and moved to the East Coast. (Photo Courtesy Nicholson Family Collection)

The Second Pinto . . .

The second Pinto, the blue and white car, was one of two cars that Ford commissioned M & S to build in mid-1972. The original idea was for one of the cars to go to Dearborn as an engineer/development vehicle. A change of plans saw both cars heading to the racetrack and running under different dealerships. Foulger Ford in Monrovia, California, received one of the cars, and the other went to Hubert Platt with sponsorship from Paul Harvey Ford in Indianapolis.

Chuck Foulger knew a thing or two about high performance after previously wearing the title of Ford's racing director. He opened his dealership in the mid-1960s in Don's old stomping ground of Monrovia and quickly became *the* West Coast Ford performance

The approachable Dyno Don and his cars always drew the crowds. The Cleveland-powered Pinto would realize a sub record best of 8.83 at 154 mph before Don retired the car early in 1974. (Photo Courtesy Rob Potter)

dealer. Ken Dondero drove the blue-and-white Pinto under the Foulger banner at two races. The first was the 1972 Supernationals, where he qualified number 10 with a 9.60. He failed to make it out of the first round, falling to Barrie Poole's Pinto. For the second, Dondero qualified the car at the rain-delayed 1973 NHRA Winternationals but failed to return the second weekend to continue.

In March, the car went from Foulger to Don and was re-labeled with the Dyno Don name. Even though the Pinto did run additional nationals events, and occasionally the United States Racing Team circuit, it ran mainly to help fulfill match-race dates. As Ford's number-one draw, *Dyno Don* cars were always in demand and generally earned top dollar. Dondero drove the blue-and-white Pinto for the last time at the 1973 Supernationals, where he qualified number 3 with an 8.971 before fouling in the first round against the AMC Hornet of Dave Kanners.

At the end of the season, the car was sold complete to Georgia's Buck Pike, who picked the car up at Don's home in Orange, California. Pike painted the car a navy blue, christened it the *Georgia Cracker*, and terrorized the

South through the summer of 1974. By the end of the summer, Pike had the Pinto up for sale, eventually trading it to Art Gravatt of Melbourne, Florida. According to the Pike family, Gravatt gave up a motorhome, a 1965 Mustang, a trailer, and some cash for the car. At the time of sale, the Pikes were under the impression that Gravatt was going to street race the Pinto. Draglist.com notes Art ran a Pinto in Pro Stock as late as 1978. Whether it was the same car is unknown. Where the car is today is also unknown.

The Final Pinto . . .

Dyno Don's third Pinto was a full tube–chassis car built by M & S. The car ran just one national event under the Dyno Don name and that was the 1974 NHRA Winternationals, where Ken Dondero drove it. As Don himself recalled, the car hooked and left quicker than anything he had ever owned. Due in large part to changing NHRA weight breaks, the Pinto ran only the one race before being replaced. As per NHRA rules of the day, a Cleveland-powered Pinto had to weigh 7.30

Ken Dondero drove Chuck Foulger's M & S Pinto for a couple of races before the Pinto became Dyno's backup car in March 1973. This is believed to be Foulger's final drag race effort. (Photo Courtesy Eric Brooks/Brian Hankins)

Ken Dondero debuted the Pinto at the 1972 season-ending Supernationals. It wasn't until March 1973 that the car received the Dyno Don name. Here Dondero heats the Firestones during a match at Edgewater while a young cousin of his holds the bleach bottle. Extended family often showed up at the races to help out with anything, which included food runs, rosin, and so on. (Photo Courtesy Bob Martin)

Twin Holleys and a Mallory magneto on the Cleveland helped keep Ken Dondero in the thick of things. It's doubtful that Don ever drove this blue-and-white Pinto in competition. Longtime helper Bob Mandel is assisting from the passenger's side while Dondero is seen at the driver's door. (Photo Courtesy Steve Call/Edelbrock Archives)

pounds per cubic inch whereas a longer-wheelbase Mustang II with the same engine had to carry only 7 pounds per cubic inch.

At the Winternationals, Dondero qualified the Pinto fourth with an 8.985 at 152.02 mph but fell in the second to a Scott Shafiroff holeshot. Don qualified his first Pinto in the eighth position with a 9.08 at 150.25 and met his fate at the hands of Shafiroff in the first round.

The Pinto was sold to Bill Bagshaw, minus the engine, months after the winter meet. For power, Bagshaw purchased a Gapp & Roush Cleveland for the car but never installed it before putting the whole works up for sale. A decision to go back to a Ron Butler–built Dart Sport had him calling up Gary Dodd, who had shown an interest in the car when Don first put it on the market. Dodd bought the car in June 1975 and later came back for the engine. From what Dodd recalls, the works cost him between $15,000 and $20,000. Dodd ran the car for a couple seasons, with Earl Wade doing the tuning, before selling it to Vic Sameshima.

Sameshima replaced the Ford mill with a 454-ci Chevy Turbo 400 combination and ran it in Super Gas. Shortly after, the car was wrecked at OCIR when a suspension component broke, sending the Pinto into numerous rollovers before coming to a stop in a tangled heap. The parts that were salvageable were removed from the car and the rest was cut up and literally thrown into a trash bin.

Ken Dondero's biggest win in the Pinto came at the 1973 AHRA Summer Nationals at Dragway 42, where he defeated the Plymouth of Mike Fons in the final. While running with Don, Dondero's competition number was 665 in 1972; in 1973 it was 750. (Photo Courtesy Kevin Johnson)

Ken Dondero ran the new Pinto at the 1974 Winternationals, where he fell in the second round to the Vega of Scott Shafiroff. Dondero was cut loose shortly after. In March, the first Mustang II replaced the Pinto. (Photo Courtesy Alex Polewik Collection)

Shop Kid to Crew Chief

Francis "Dave" McGrane was just one of a number of unsung heroes in the career of Dyno Don. McGrane, a native of Monrovia, California, had an interest in drag racing stoked in 1958 at the age of 12, hanging around the Bourgeois & Wade Speed Shop. Tired of this kid staring in their door every day, the pair eventually put him to work pushing a broom and cleaning parts. McGrane proved to be a quick study, and, a year later, the pair had him helping out porting heads. It was through Wade that McGrane became friends with Dyno Don.

When McGrane turned 16, Dyno Don, who had become a bit of a father figure to him, gave him his old tow car, a 1955 Chevrolet, as a birthday gift. McGrane gained his own dragstrip experience in 1965 by also driving a Comet. He started traveling with Don the following year while still working at the Bourgeois & Wade Speed Shop. Don called McGrane the hardest worker he had ever been associated with. Uncle Sam came calling for Dave in 1967 and shipped him off to Vietnam for all of 1968 and part of 1969. He returned to the Nicholson fold in 1970 and joined the crew on the Maverick. By 1972, McGrane was crew chief for Don and played a big part in developing the 351 Cleveland.

McGrane retired from drag racing in 1975 and went to work for Culver City Ford as a line mechanic. Within a couple years, he caved to his wife's desire to return to her home state of Indiana and moved the family, now consisting of a son and daughter, east in 1977. There, he ended up working for the Power and Light Company as a millwright and retired after 25 years of service.

With drag racing still in the blood (does it ever leave?), McGrane hooked up with Don again during the period when he was running the Pro Mod–style 1962 Chevrolet. In fact, Don buttoned up the Chevy in McGrane's family garage before its first outing at Brown County, Indiana. When Don campaigned the Pro Stock Truck in 1998, McGrane was there once again, traveling the Midwest with Don just like it was the old days. McGrane had collected a Bronze Star, a Silver Star, and two Purple hearts in Vietnam, but he also brought home the remnants of the chemical Agent Orange. In 2010, cancer related to the defoliant took McGrane's life at the age of 63.

Dyno Don's final Pinto was sold to Bill Bagshaw then to Gary Dodd. Bagshaw never ran the car, instead he returned to a Ron Butler–built Dart Sport. Gary bought the car in 1976 and relied on Earl Wade's tuning skills to keep the Gapp & Roush Cleveland competitive. (Photo Courtesy Gary Dodd)

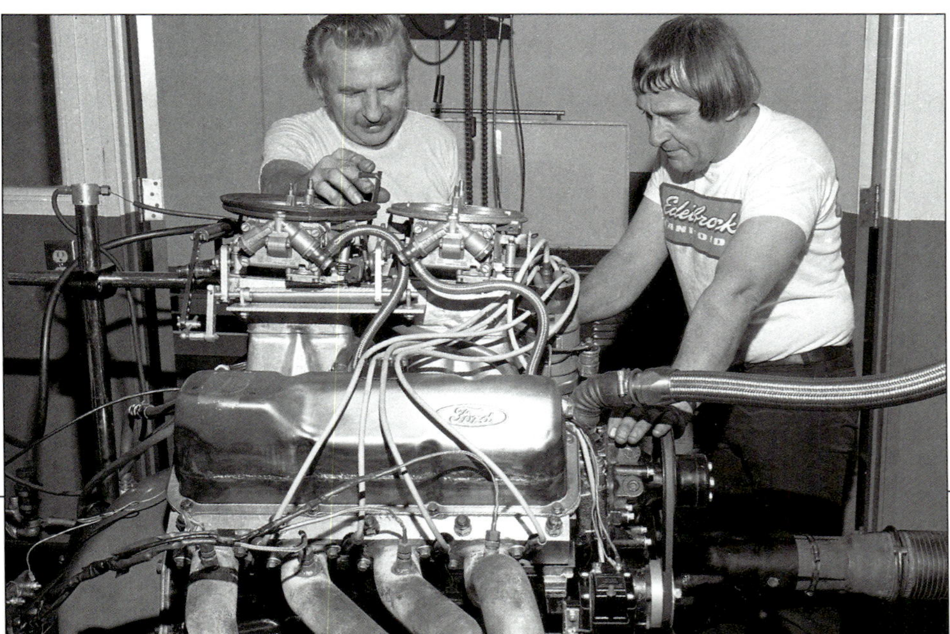

Earl Wade and Bob Mandel were real workhorses, adding to Don's success well into the 1970s. The pair is seen here in Edelbrock's El Segundo dyno room late in 1973, fine-tuning one of Don's Clevelands as it goes through a development exercise. (Photo Courtesy Edelbrock, LLC. Archive)

MUSTANG COUNTRY (1974–1977)

The Mustang II started out as an acid-dipped body in white and could be lightened all the way down to 1,900 pounds for match racing. Rack and pinion steering helped to get the lowered stance. Don set the IHRA class record at Southland Raceway in 1974 with an 8.845 at 151 mph. (Photo Courtesy Brian Beattie)

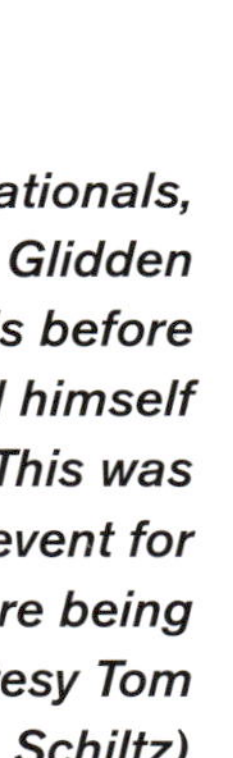

At the 1975 U.S. Nationals, Don defeated Bob Glidden in the quarterfinals before being eliminated himself in the semifinals. This was the last national event for the Mustang before being sold. (Photo Courtesy Tom Schiltz)

Increasing expenses combined with a gas crunch saw Dyno Don trim back his operation in 1974. Early in the year, the Pintos went bye-bye when Don debuted the first in a string of Mustangs. As well as giving up the Pintos in 1974, Don cut loose the no-longer required Ken Dondero. Dondero had no problem landing a job, taking up Grumpy Jenkins's open offer to come drive for him. The fresh start and the line of Mustangs proved to be a successful recipe for Don, as he earned two of his three World Championships during this period.

1974 Mustang II (1974–1975)

The first of three Mustang IIs started out as an acid-dipped body in white. Along with the new

The new Mustang II made a good showing during its debut at the NHRA Gatornationals but fell in eliminations to eventual category winner Wally Booth. The "$ Patty $" on the C-pillar was a nod to Don's wife, who handled the finances and traveled with him regularly. (Photo Courtesy Michael Pottie)

The decals tell the story: General Kinetics cam, Accel ignition, Brooks rods, and Hooker headers moved the Mustang along in a hurry. Lightweight Cragar Super Tricks mounting Firestone tires harnessed the power. A magnesium rear by way of the Ramchargers housed 5.57 gears. (Photo Courtesy Tom Schiltz)

The underpinnings of Don's first Mustang II consisted of a Pinto rack, Monroe coil-overs, and Hurst-Airheart brakes. Note the fabricated spindles and mounting of the rack. The tires are Firestone, wheels are Cragar. (Photo ©TEN: The Enthusiast Network. All Rights Reserved.)

Back from Don Hardy's, the first Mustang II was completed at Dyno Don's shop on Katella Avenue in Orange County. While on the West Coast, Don operated out of this shop between 1971 and 1991. Prior to 1971, he worked out of a building on Batavia Street, just a couple miles away. In 1991, he built a 1,200-square foot shop, with a full loft behind his home in Orange. Note the expandable foam used on the Mustang II to give support to the body panels. That Pinto up front was no doubt giving up parts for the new car. (Photo ©TEN: The Enthusiast Network. All Rights Reserved.)

By 1974, Don was extracting approximately 700 hp from his Cleveland and pulling the Lenco levers through the gears at 8,600 to 8,800 rpm. Dave McGrane hanging on to the left rear, retired after the 1974 season. (Photo Courtesy Tom West Collection)

The 1974 Earl Wade Cleveland measured 355 ci and featured Holley 4500 carbs, Edelbrock intake, and a General Kinetics camshaft. Tinwork was by Hardy, completed by Don. (Photo ©TEN: The Enthusiast Network. All Rights Reserved.)

Don ran the Mustang II at all AHRA and IHRA races he attended through 1975. The car is seen here at Great Lakes for the IHRA Summernationals, a race that Don won. Even though Riverside painted it, Don was more than competent in a spray booth and through the years he painted many of his cars. Note the pulled-in bumpers, helping to cheat the wind. (Photo Courtesy Dan Williams)

Through 1975, the two Dons, Carlton and Nicholson, butted heads, battling back and forth for the IHRA championship. Here, at Dragway 42 in August, Dyno Don dropped Carlton to meet and defeat Roy Hill in the final. Throughout his illustrious career, Don won 7 IHRA national events in 13 final-round appearances. Dyno operated without a major sponsor or help from Ford through most of his career. A good amount of what he earned from racing went right back into the cars. (Photo Courtesy Dan Williams)

car, Don called on a new chassis builder, Don Hardy of Floydada, Texas, to bend up the 96.2-inch wheelbase chrome-moly chassis. Featuring all the latest Pro Stock goods (rack and pinion, twin engine plates, etc.), Hardy had the Mustang out the door in a marathon 10 days. When it came to the engines that Don used, it was reported that builder Earl Wade sonic tested the walls of blocks in search of the thickest starting point. Blocks were opened up to 355 ci and were usually good for about 10 runs before the thin cylinder walls lost shape. Internals included Brooks Racing Component rods, Venolia pistons, Delta crank with turned-down rod journals, and wrapped with Chevy bearings. Compression was reported to be 12.4:1. A General Kinetics cam with .697 lift and 321/329 duration actuated the 2.19 and 1.72 valves. Bob Mullen of Mullen & Company was called on to prep the heads. Intake ports were left "rough," while the exhaust ports were opened up and fitted with raised plates. Induction came by way of a modified Edelbrock intake and a pair of 4500 Holleys that were said to have been tweaked by Grumpy Jenkins. A Hays clutch was in between the Cleveland and Lenco transmission. Out back were 5.57 gears in a Ramcharger magnesium housing. The horsepower was pegged at 692, which produced initial times of 8.72 at 154 mph. At the car's Gatornationals debut, Don qualified at number 12, recording a 9.124. He improved to a 9.03 in the first round, but it wasn't good enough to defeat Wally Booth, who turned an 8.97 on his way to winning the event.

Although NHRA national event wins eluded Don through 1975, he continued his winning ways in match racing, and he did more than all right for himself in IHRA competition, where he won the World Championship in 1975. In July, Don defeated Scott Shafiroff at the Summernationals held at Union Grove. Dyno Don used a slight holeshot to beat Shafiroff's Mustang II, turning in a 9.01 at 149.00 mph to Shafiroff's 8.98 at 150.50. At Dragway 42 in August, Don continued on his march to the championship by defeating Roy Hill in the ex–Butch Leal Duster. Don defeated the Duster of low qualifier Don Carlton in the second round when Carlton backed off after getting out of shape. In the semifinals, Hill defeated Larry Huff while Dyno put away "General" Lee Edwards. In the final go, Hill's 9.04 at 153.84 mph wasn't quite enough to beat Don's 9-flat at 154.84.

Newfound power for the little Cleveland that could came by way of C. J. Batten, who, as a favor to Don, took a look at his Bob Mullen–prepped cylinder heads. Batten, who was considered to be one of the best in cylinder head prep, picked up the heads from Doug Nash's shop in Romulus, Michigan. Don, who had enjoyed a friendship with Nash dating back to 1965, used Doug's well-equipped shop when he was in town. Mullen, situated on the West Coast, had built quite the reputation, building his own cylinder head business after having spent time as an engineer at Chrysler.

Batten recalls, "Don brought me the heads and challenged me to do better. The exhaust port on those Mullen heads was all brazed up, and I must say that the workmanship was excellent. The floor was raised and opposed to the square Cleveland port, they had a "W" shape with a center peak that improved the exhaust flow." On the intake side it was a different story. Batten found that the ports he was prepping for Super Modified cars actually flowed better than the Mullen Pro Stock head. Mullen's work on the intake was similar to that seen on a Hemi head; it didn't work on the Cleveland.

"Low and mid-lift wasn't too bad but when it came

Don enjoyed his most successful years in Pro Stock running a string of Mustangs, cars that earned him two world championships and bragging rights for having the first ever 7-second Pro Stocker. Even though he came up short here at the NHRA Springnationals, he did defeat the Camaro of Warren Johnson at the AHRA Spring Nationals in St. Louis on June 1. Riverside Autobody in Daytona, Florida, completed the multicolor paint. (Photo Courtesy Thomas Nagy)

to the high lift, they just didn't have it." Batten improved the situation by filling in the floor; he decreased the port size by approximately a third. This increased velocity and the results showed on the track. In addition, Batten did a little work cleaning up the bowl area.

The Mustang II, which ran mostly AHRA and IHRA competition after the 1970 Mustang came along, was sold to Marty Furlipa in 1976 and shipped to Lars Flodman in Sweden. According to Swedish drag race historian Jan Suhr, at the time the car was the fastest door car to ever run on a Swedish dragstrip. At its debut at Mantorp Park in 1976, the Mustang ran an 8.90 time, a tenth off of the existing NHRA record. Unfortunately, the chute failed to deploy on the run and the car crashed. The chassis wasn't damaged but, having rolled, the body was pretty banged up. New panels were flown in from the United States and the car was back in action two weeks later. Flodman took the car back to the United States a year later and raced it for a few years, where eventually, another crash finished it.

1970 Mustang

This car was all about taking advantage of the favorable NHRA weight breaks. As they stood early in 1974, cars with a wheelbase longer than 105 inches had to carry 6.45 pounds per cubic inch while cars with a wheelbase of less than 105 inches had to carry 6.85 pounds per cubic inch. For Don, it meant that if he used the same 355 that he ran in the Mustang II, the 1970 car, he realized a 120-pound weight savings. Don wasn't the only one looking to save a few pounds. Glidden was another who debuted a 1970 Mustang, while the team of Gapp & Roush left plenty of people shaking their heads when they parked their own Mustang II and debuted a 109-inch wheelbase four-door Maverick. Dyno Don had gotten wind of Gapp & Roush's plans early in the spring

Don ran the Mustang II at just two NHRA events in 1975, the Gatornationals and here at the Springnationals at Ohio's National Trail, before switching to the 1970 Mustang for the remainder of the season. Note the "Engine by Jack Roush" on the door. If not using the engine here, Don was using parts from Roush. (Photo Courtesy Tom Schiltz)

Don debuted his 1970 Mustang at the Grandnationals in Québec, where, on the first run, he recorded a 9.07. New-car bugs saw him bow in the second round. The yellow, blue, and red paint lent its self nicely to the longer-wheelbase Mustang. (Photo Courtesy Bob Boudreau)

and actually tossed the idea around. Clearer thoughts prevailed and out of that came the 1970 Mustang. In a period interview, Don stated that he wasn't crazy about the idea of a four-door race car and really didn't care for the looks of the Gapp & Roush Maverick. Even though no wind tunnel data was available, Dyno Don figured the Mustang had to cut a much cleaner path than the Maverick.

Dyno Don once again called on Don Hardy to build the car, hoping to debut it at the Summernationals in Englishtown. Rather than being built around a body in white, this car was assembled using separate body panels. To get the needed trim parts, a donor 1970 Mustang was purchased from a salvage yard. The debut of the Mustang was delayed when the car was damaged in a windstorm en route home from Hardy's. Remember, this was back when drag cars were still transported on open-ramp trucks. The needed repairs to the body delayed the debut until the Grandnationals at Sanair in August. There, the Mustang recorded a 9.07 on it first full pass but bowed out in the second round after falling to those dreaded new-car bugs.

As early as 1975, and through to the end of the decade, most of Don's engines were built on sleeved blocks. Why sleeved? Because the factory thin wall cylinders lost their shape after four or five runs. Don discovered just how bad they were when machinist Bill Coon ran a hone through one of the Cleveland's and it revealed numerous high spots ("the hone jumped all over the place"). Don presented the idea of sleeving the block to Coon, who then sourced chrome-moly sleeves in California. Replacing the factory cylinders with .275-inch thick barrels was a pretty straightforward process for Coon, a well-qualified machinist. After the factory cylinders were cut out, the block was cleaned and copper plated. This ensured a good bond when the works was furnace-brazed together. After the brazing, the block was then line honed, decked, and bored. The thick sleeves allowed Don to play with a variety of bore sizes, from 4.00 up to 4.145 inches. And play he did. A 4.145 x 3.50 stroke yielded him a killer 378 that "just screamed." Using the 4.145 bore, with a Boss 302 crank and a 2-inch Chevy rod bearing could see 324 ci. The possibilities were endless and Don was always experimenting, constantly thinking horsepower and how to make more.

Don's Mustang was said to run a NASCAR 366-ci Cleveland at one point, which was a rare piece produced in limited numbers between 1969 and 1972. The siamesed cylinder walls of the NASCAR block allowed higher compression while the big Cleveland valves loved the larger 4.08-inch bore. When power started to go south, Don borrowed a Jack Roush Cleveland. Running the engine at the U.S. Nationals in 1974, Don qualified the car third with a 9.01 behind Gapp & Roush (8.95) and Glidden's Pinto (8.99). Don handled Jenkins easily in the semifinals, but ran a redlight against Glidden in the final with a 9.016 at 151.77 to Glidden's 9.010 at 151.77 mph.

The best showing for the Mustang came in 1975 as Don won the seventh annual *Popular Hot Rodding* meet. Held at Michigan's Martin US-131 in August, Don had twice played bridesmaid at the meet, once in 1971 and again in 1972. In the tight field, Don qualified the Mustang with an 8.97, which was good for the 8th spot in the 16-car field, just 0.13 behind leader Bob Glidden. First-round action saw Don run a 9.15 against 16th-qualifier Dave Van Luke, whose Pinto ran into handling issues and ran a 9.53. Larry Ford, after dropping the Gapp & Roush Maverick on a tremendous holeshot in the first, fell to Don's 9.05 at 150.25 mph in the second. In the semifinals, Don faced Grumpy Jenkins, who was

Helping the sleek-looking Mustang grasp the Sanair track were Firestone slicks and a Don Hardy ladder-bar suspension. By the mid-1970s, Hardy was the nation's number-one Pro Stock chassis builder, and had five Car Craft Awards to prove it. (Photo Courtesy Bob Boudreau)

debuting his Chevy Monza. It took a holeshot by Don to spoil the Monza's coming-out party; Don took the win with an 8.99 at 149.00 to Jenkins's 8.92 at 152.80.

In the final round, Don faced the AMC Hornet of Maskin & Kanners. Richard Maskin was having a fairly easy day of it. He received a bye in the first round, got by a broken Glidden in the second, and defeated Fred Shafer's Vega in the third with a 9.17. In the final, Maskin & Kanners found a little extra oomph in their Nash and gave Don a run for the money. Through the traps, Don clocked a 9.091 at 149.75 mph to Maskin's 9.098 at 150.25.

The NHRA added .35 pounds per cubic inch to the long-wheelbase Clevelands in 1975, seemingly killing the advantage that guys such as Don, Glidden, and Gapp & Roush had enjoyed. Not surprisingly, Don was disappointed, feeling that it was a shame when a combination started winning; the NHRA felt the need to factor it.

Rumors have persisted for years regarding the demise of this car. Some facts are known. The Mustang was sold to Atlanta's Charlie Pepper. Pepper cut up the chassis and mounted

Indy 1974, and the still-fresh Mustang ran 9.0 times and played runner-up to Bob Glidden. Contrary to what was reported by some, there was never animosity between Don and Glidden. Each was a fierce competitor and independent. Neither racer received Ford support through the 1970s. (Photo Courtesy Thomas Nagy)

Yes, back when Pro Stocks were identifiable. At the Nationals in 1975, Don laid a holeshot on Dandy Dick Landy that Landy just couldn't make up. Don, among others, took advantage of NHRA's five-year rule that allowed the longer-wheelbase Mustang to run at a lower weight. (Photo Courtesy Pete Quinn)

Don figured that 1973 Pro Stock world champs Gapp & Roush were getting more power from their Cleveland than he was, so he briefly leased engines from Jack Roush. Trials were first made at Sanair in 1974 and ran through Indy. It's questionable as to whether the trial really made a difference. (Photo Courtesy Thomas Nagy)

a Mustang II body to it. According to Pepper, nothing remains of the car today. In his words, "It's gone, all gone." I'm sure Pepper made more passes in the car than Don ever did. Don only had 35 runs on the Mustang, seven national events in total before selling it.

1976 Mustang II (1976–1977)

Along with a new year came a new Mustang II for Don. Dyno Don called on Don Hardy once again to build his next panel car. Being a panel car, for that reason alone this Mustang II was much more precise, lighter, and cleaner than the first Mustang II. Moreover, it showed in match racing, where, with big-cubic-inch Cleveland's measuring anywhere from 390 to 406 ci, the Mustang was capable of running bottom 8-second times.

As the 1976 season opened, no NHRA Pro Stock car had to carry more weight than the Cleveland-powered Fords, and it showed in the results. The only national event win for Ford in 1976 came at the Winternationals, where Bob Glidden defeated Wayne Gapp in the final. This is where Don put in his best showing of the season, running a 9.30 and qualifying at number 8. He made it through the first two rounds. Mechanical ills saw him fall in the semifinals to Gapp.

Don came close to missing the show altogether after a near disastrous test and tune session at Irwindale prior to Wednesday's tech inspection. The Mustang went off the end of the track after losing brakes on the right rear and having the chute fail. The romp in the desert sand at 100 mph didn't do the engine or body any good. Don had the presence of mind to kill the engine, but the damage was done; the dominators, the manifold, heads, and

cylinders were full of sand. The Winternationals tech inspection started the next day, and ran through Friday morning. Don, with the help of Jon Kaase, rolled in on Friday with about an hour to spare. The two were worn out and the brand-new Mustang II looked like it had been hit by a sand blaster and was patched with duct tape.

At the Gatornationals, Don qualified in the middle of the pack with an 8.84 and fell to the Chevy of Jenkins in the first round.

A report from the NHRA Springnationals, where Don failed to qualify, stated, "Nicholson, who had been terrorizing the match-race circuit with a number of 8.0 and 8.1 clockings, was not able to make a smooth transition

Don's sponsorship agreement with Minolta was good for two years. Although Don's family can't remember what the deal was worth financially, his daughter does recall receiving a really nice Minolta camera for her birthday. Don had planned initially to run the Mustang for just a single season. He sure got a lot of miles out of that open hauler, first making use of it in 1969. (Photo Courtesy Thomas Nagy)

Don had a close relationship with the folks at Edelbrock, and he was friends with Vic going back to the early days of drag racing. Here, Edelbrock's Gene Thompson flow-tests a Cleveland cylinder head while Don stands by. (Photo Courtesy Steve Call/ Edelbrock Archives)

back to national event competition and his best clocking of 9.267 was .015 too slow to make the field." At the following Summernationals and U.S. Nationals, Don chose to run his Mustang in C/Altered and B/Altered. These were the last NHRA National events Don ran for the season. At the Summernationals, he lost a close one in the Comp Eliminator final to the B/A Rod Shop Dart of Don Carlton, turning an 8.58 to an 8.55. At the U.S. Nationals, Don took class but fell during eliminations.

1977

In 1976, a new face joined Don's crew. Jon Kaase came on board just as Earl Wade left to run a Funny Car with Sherman Gunn. Personal issues kept Wade close to home, but he was never too far off to lend Don a helping hand when necessary. With the bugs worked out of the Cleveland, Don and Kaase put a concerted effort forward to win the NHRA Pro Stock crown in 1977. To get the job done, Don ran a legal 340-ci mill (4.08 bore x 3.25 stroke) while the match-race engine, a rare aluminum Cleveland measuring 392 ci, destroyed bigger-inch competition. At

Although 1976 was a bit of an off year, by Don's standards, by the end of the season he had hired Jon Kaase full time and things began to turn around. Ford's strongest hope is seen here early in the season at the NHRA Gatornationals. Don fell to the Monza of Grumpy Jenkins, who was the 1976 points champ. (Photo Courtesy Tom Schiltz)

At Gainesville in 1976, Don qualified number 9 but made a quick exit after falling to Larry Lombardo in Grumpy's Toy in the first round. At the following Springnationals in Columbus, Don failed to qualify. Realizing that the unfair weight breaks had him fighting an uphill battle, at his next NHRA event, Indy, he ran Comp. (Photo Courtesy Dave Doctrow)

In 1976, Don was just one of a number of NHRA Pro Stock racers who chose to show their displeasure with the less-than-favorable weight breaks by running Comp Eliminator. Don is seen here at Indy, competing in B/A against the early Ford of Lou Sattel-maier. With the growing number of Pro Stocks in the Altered ranks, the NHRA resurrected Factory Experimental in 1977 and forced them all to run there. (Photo Courtesy Dan Williams)

the season-opening NHRA Winternationals, Don fell in the final round to Larry Lombardo in Jenkins's Monza. However, Dyno Don made it clear that he was back, having held the number-1 qualifying position with an 8.72. With a little help from Lady Luck, Don made it out of the

It may not look like it during this more serious moment in 1976, but Don thoroughly enjoyed the profession he chose. It's well known that Don lived with a nervous stomach and popped Rolaids like a kid popping candy. He never left home without them, carrying packs in his pocket and jars in his truck. His brother Harold had the same ailment but drank buttermilk for comfort. (Author's Collection)

first round, defeating old teammate Ken Dondero, who was now driving a Pinto for Gapp & Roush. Dondero took Don off the line with a half-car holeshot but saw it disappear when the Cleveland broke a rocker arm. Don drove around him with an 8.90 at 157.97 mph. In the final against 1976 World Champ Lombardo, Don redlighted away any chance of winning.

The tables turned at the following Gatornationals, where Don defeated Lombardo in the semifinals. As told in the *National Dragster*, the semifinal round was for all "practical purposes," the final round. While Wally Booth won the other semifinal match, he blew the engine in his Hornet and was unable to make repairs for the final round call. The Nicholson-Jenkins semi match saw Lombardo foul on the line, handing the win to Don, who took it with an 8.74 at 157.34 mph to an 8.84 at 155.70. As at the Winternationals, Don held the number-1 qualifying position, recording an 8.65. He also took low ET and top speed of the meet with an 8.64 at 157.61 mph, which gave him an early season lead in the Pro Stock points standings.

The Dyno Don train kept on rolling. At National Trail for the Springnationals, Don laid a gate job on Frank Iaconio in the final and hung on for the win, eliminating the SRD Monza with an ever-so-close 8.78 at 153.06 to Iaconio's 8.80 at 153.30. He'd face Iaconio again at the Summernationals, this time falling to the Chevy in the semifinals. After a prolonged staging battle that had the fans on their feet, Dyno Don moved first into the beams. Don had set the Pro Stock record in the second round with an 8.57 but hurt his good engine in the following round. Facing Iaconio with his back-up engine, Dyno lost with a quicker 8.67 to Iaconio's slower 8.75. Iaconio recalled, "I

The NHRA Fallnationals in Seattle wasn't one to remember for Don after he bowed out early. It was one of the few losses on the year for Don, who held the best record of all three pro category leaders. In match-race competition, Don held his own match racing with an ultra-rare aluminum Cleveland measuring 392 ci. The aluminum blocks were produced in 1968; it's believed that 50 blocks and 100 heads were cast. (Photo Courtesy Larry Pfister)

hated to stage first and after the burn down at Englishtown, we beat him on a holeshot. We shouldn't have because he had the quicker car. He had qualified number-1 and we were fifth or ninth or something. He said he never wanted to do that again. After that he wanted to flip a coin all the time to see who staged first."

It's hard to believe that with the amount of success that Don had throughout his career, it took until 1977 before he won his first NHRA Nationals. The victory came in convincing fashion, starting with Don setting the low ET of the meet with an 8.61 and finishing with him beating two-time world champ, Bob Glidden. In between, Don and the Mustang II eliminated a redlighting Warren Johnson in the second round and took care of Larry Lombardo in the semifinals. Lombardo was driving the borrowed Monza of Ronnie Manchester after *Grumpy's Toy* burned up after hitting the wall during qualifying. In the final, Don took a half-car holeshot lead and sailed on for the easy win with 8.74 at 154.10 mph after Glidden's Pinto suffered mechanical ills and slowed to a 13.99.

The U.S. Nationals win all but guaranteed Don the World Championship. At the close of Indy, Don held 13,374 points, 1,262 more than second-place Lombardo. The only way Lombardo could catch him was to win the World finals and set both ends of the national record. We know that didn't happen. The same Indy weekend, Don was awarded the coveted *Car Craft* magazine Ollie Award, recognizing his contribution and impact on the sport throughout his career. Chief wrench puller Jon Kaase, meanwhile, joined an elite crowd when S-K Tools welcomed him to its Hall of Fame.

At the World finals, Don and his fine line of 8.60s saw him defeat both Joe Satmary and Ronnie Manches-ter before an 8.67 allowed him to drive around Frank Iaconio in the semifinals. Bob Glidden took the final over Don with an 8.55. For what it's worth, Glidden's win moved him past Lombardo in the points standings. Regardless, Don had them all covered with a total of 14,589 points, more than 1,400 up on Glidden to win the World Championship.

In the nine NHRA national events that Don ran in 1977, he qualified number-1 three times, number-2 four times, number-3 once, and number-4 once. In regional points meets, he qualified number-1 at all of them. Dyno recalled in a *SS&DI* interview, "Our closest competitor was Larry Lombardo in Jenkins's car. They had won the championship the year before." Don took strategic measures to hold Lombardo at bay. "I had already won my allotted number of divisional points races, but went to the last one that Lombardo ran and beat him early in eliminations to keep him from winning any points." The move contributed to pushing Jenkins down to third in the final season standings.

The world-champ Mustang II racked up the miles, doubling down as a match racer and big-cubic-inch IHRA car through the year. According a competitionplus.com interview with Kaase, "We went to the big engines at the beginning of 1978. A 516 was built on an aluminum 429–460 block, with aluminum heads that Ford produced in a limited numbers back in 1970." The bore measured 4.53 while a 4.00 stroke was created by turning down the stock rod journals from 2.50 to 2.20. Horsepower for this torque monster was in the neighborhood of 900 ft-lbs, which helped produce consistent 7.9–8.0 times. It was on a Wednesday night in August that Don used the 516 to record Pro Stocks first 7-second pass. The

In first round action at Gainesville, Don eliminated the Vega of Gordie Rivera, recording an 8.66 at 157.61 mph. Rivera, who held the ninth qualifying position, recorded a 9.02 at 151 even. Don met Rivera just once more in eliminations during his career, at the Winternationals in 1979, where he beat him again. (Photo ©TEN: The Enthusiast Network. All Rights Reserved.)

historic moment came at a match race at Englishtown's *Crazy Eddie's Night of Thrills* (later renamed Summer Motorsports Spectacular) when, on a run against Grumpy Jenkins, Don recorded a 7.97 at 175 mph. The Mustang II was at a minimum weight of 1,900 pounds, featuring lightweight windowless doors and a humongous Formula 5000–style hood scoop to catch the good air.

When IHRA Competition vice president Ted Jones was looking at ways to revamp Pro Stock in 1976, he turned to the exploding big-cubic-inch match races of the South for inspiration. According to competitionplus.com, after viewing the racing down South, Jones told IHRA chief Larry Carrier, "We needed to come out with a new version of Pro Stock [that got away from weight breaks]." Jones presented Carrier with the minimal weight, maximum cube class idea, which Carrier jumped on and told Jones to "make it happen." New rules were implemented in 1977 and led to the first Mountain Motor Nationals in 1978.

Held at Maryland International Raceway in August,

this was no light-duty field. Competitors included Dyno Don in his 516-ci Mustang II, Ronnie Sox in the Sox & Martin Hemi Challenger, Lee Edwards's 490-ci Vega, Roy Hill in Pat Musi's Monza, Bob Glidden, Larry Lombardo in Jenkins's Monza, and the Camaro of Bill Clayton. The rules of the game were simple, any cubic-inch, any weight, and no nitrous.

As action got under way, both Edwards and Glidden fell with engine problems while Dyno Don, up next, broke his Lenco transmission. Roy Hill lost his doors in the lights, while Sox headed back to the pits after his first burnout. Bill Clayton was the first to make a full pass, opening up with an 8.56 at 159.23 mph. With repairs made to all the broken cars, action finally got under way. Edwards came to the line first and unleashed an 8.16 at 166.35 mph, followed by Hill who turned an 8.20. Dyno Don was next with an 8.26, followed by Glidden's 8.27, Sox's 8.32, Lombardo's 8.32, Frank Iaconio's 8.41, and Clayton's 8.56. With high evening temperatures and humidity at 97 percent, there'd be no 7-second runs this night.

Don's second national event win of 1977 came at the NHRA Springnationals, where he defeated the Monza of Frank Iaconio in the final. Sharing in the celebrations are Dave Dewitt (far left) and Jon Kaase (far right). (Photo Courtesy Nicholson Family Collection)

A different view of the Indy start line, courtesy of Dan Williams. Here, Dyno Don is about to face Warren Johnson in the second round of eliminations. Don advanced. Johnson, well, he'd have to wait until 1984 before he saw his first Indy win. (Photo Courtesy Dan Williams)

Just past 9 p.m., round action opened up with Edwards facing Sox. With burnouts complete, it was Edwards out first and taking the win with an 8.10. Next up was Glidden, who faced and disposed of Clayton with an 8.27 at 162.42 mph. Iaconio was up next in the Iaconio-Allen Monza to face Dyno Don. It was Don all the way, disposing Iaconio with an 8.21 at 162.16 mph to an 8.47 at 156. Lombardo used a holeshot to defeat Hill, 8.42 to an 8.41. The semifinal round opened up with Edwards facing Dyno Don. Lee took the redlight loss while Dyno Don took the easy win. In the other semifinal pairing, Lombardo lost out to Glidden after creeping through the beams. This gave the fans an all-Ford final. With Glidden having previously run an 8.27 and an 8.29 versus Dyno Don's 8.21 and 8.27, you knew it was going to be a close one. Well, it should have been. The pair left side by side but shortly out, Glidden's mill let lose, leaving Don to solo with an ever-so-quick 8.23 at 163.04.

Like many worn race cars, the two-year old Mustang was sold to finance a new car. For Don, the new car

There was no stopping Don at the 1977 U.S. Nationals. Here he is on the verge of quashing the hopes of AMC by defeating the Hornet of Maskin & Kanners in first-round action. (Photo Courtesy Tom Schiltz)

Don's championship season in 1977 was no walk in the park. Breathing down his neck were Bob Glidden, Bill Jenkins, and Frank Iaconio, who is seen here in the far lane. Don defeated Iaconio at the Springnationals. (Photo Courtesy Steve Call/ Edelbrock Archives)

Jon Kaase and Don "clicked" in late 1976, and it was a concerted effort by the pair to pursue the NHRA championship in 1977. Kaase could be seen guiding the mid-1970s cars of Don through the burnout box more times than not. Legal weight times in the 8.60s were the norm. (Photo Courtesy Michael Pottie)

By 1978, match-race times had hit the 7s, thanks to a big-inch Wedge. Kaase, seen here holding steady, was compared favorably by Don to Earl Wade. The pair's working relationship ran through 1981. PRO 1 on the window says it all. (Photo ©TEN: The Enthusiast Network. All Rights Reserved.)

came in the form of a 1978 Mustang II. Johnny Dowey purchased the world champ Mustang, and as luck (or no luck) would have it, Don faced and fell to Dowey at the Gatornationals. Things got worse for Don as the new Mustang was crashed after just a few outings. He was forced to buy the old Mustang back from Dowey, doing so in time for the Cajun Nationals. In debuting the old car, Don fell in the first round after creeping through the beams. Don match raced the Mustang into 1980. Today, the World Champ Mustang survives and is in storage waiting on Don's daughter to have it restored.

For Dyno, match racing was his bread and butter. Week in and week out, he faced Grumpy Jenkins, Ronnie Sox, and Dick Landy, and more often than not came out on top. The championship Mustang ran a 516-ci Wedge while facing Grumpy here at Union Grove in May 1978. For match races, fiberglass doors replaced the class-legal steel parts. (Photo Courtesy Mike Sopko Sr.)

After crashing his 1979 Mustang, the world champ Mustang was dusted off and run briefly in legal trim. This 1980 shot may best show the drooping front end. Although no competitive Pro Stocker admitted to performing the aerodynamic trick, many were. (Author's Collection)

Jon Kaase

According to his own website, Kaase was born and raised in Cleveland and started his drag-racing career at the age of 16. In high school, he went to work with a local mechanic, more or less so that he could learn to work on his own stuff. That "stuff" started with a 1966 Comet. He drag raced into his early 20s, all the while earning a degree in mechanical engineering.

Kaase first met Don in 1969 and kept in touch through the early 1970s, looking for tuning tips and sharing ideas. By then, Kaase was running a Pro Pinto with partner Larry Ford and occasionally match raced Don. The partnership ended when the Pinto was wrecked in a crash during 1976. Kaase, who had been filling his time repairing lawnmowers, pestered Don to take him on as crew. Picking up on Don's indecision, Kaase loaded his van and headed to Atlanta.

Frank Oglesby, longtime Nicholson friend, recalled, "One day, Kaase pulled up in an old van. He had brought his tools, which included a Gerstner toolbox and a small lathe. At the time, Don had little equipment and he asked me what I thought. I told him 'the guy's got a Gerstner toolbox and a lathe, for that reason alone you should hire him.'" Don liked what he saw in Kaase and compared his work ethic to that of Earl Wade.

Later, Don had nothing but praise for Kaase, stating the 1977 World Championship wouldn't have happened without him. "He put in more time than I could afford to pay him." Around the end of the summer of 1979, Kaase was tired of life on the road and the hectic schedule that Don maintained, so he struck out on his own. Taking what he had learned from Don, he eventually opened his own engine-building business in Atlanta, which continues to thrive today. Jon Kaase Racing Engines (JKRE) is located in Winder, Georgia, and, among other rewards, has built the Boss engine for 12-straight IHRA Pro Stock World Champions.

Don turned in some of his best performances at the winter meets. Running his three-year-old Mustang here at the AHRA Winter Nationals in 1980, Don became runner-up to Lee Shepherd in the Reher-Morrison Camaro. (Photo Courtesy Nicholson Family Collection)

FOXY BODIES (1978–1981)

The 105.5-inch wheelbase of the new Fairmont was a better fit to NHRA's less-than-favorable weight breaks. The first full pass netted a promising 8.68 at Suffolk, Virginia. Engine ills saw the Fairmont fail to qualify at Indy. (Photo Courtesy Tom Schiltz)

Ford introduced its popular Fox-Body platform in 1978. First came the Fairmont, followed by the Mustang, Thunderbird, and more, all produced in mass quantities through 1993. It didn't mean a lot to Don, but it did give him more options to choose from when it came to dealing with the always-fluctuating NHRA weight breaks. The Cleveland Fords were being hammered continuously with additional weight, and Don tried nearly everything, short of turning his back on the brand, to remain competitive. Frustrated, he focused more of his attention on AHRA, IHRA, and Mountain Motor events. At least there he stood a fighting chance of success.

After winning the World Championship in 1977, Dyno just couldn't seem to win for losing in 1978. As noted in a late-season talk with *SS&DI*, Don stated, "My season is completely reversed. In 1977, my match-race record was poor, but I was killing them at national events. This year I won 95 percent of my match races yet I couldn't win a big race for love or money." He started the new season driving his "narrow" 1978 Mustang II, often referred to as such because of its tucked lower body. After a pair of failed qualifying attempts at the Winternationals, Don headed to OCIR for some testing and tuning to try to figure out what was wrong. Back at

Pomona the following day, Don, figuring he had the bugs worked out, proceeded to scatter the engine. He and Kaase then made a quick engine swap and headed for the staging lanes, where Don sat and sat and waited and, after six hours, qualifying ended, two cars ahead of Don.

At the upcoming Gatornationals, Dyno qualified number 5 but lost in the second round to Bob Glidden after hurting the engine. The Mustang never survived its third race, crashing during a match race at Atlanta against Grumpy Jenkins. The car went back to Don Hardy for repairs and was sold to Alfred Williams immediately after. It passed through a couple more hands and reportedly gathered a couple more wrecks along the way. The car was patched up, restored to Dyno likeness, and sold at auction. It is often referred to as the narrow car, but there was nothing overly "trick" about the Mustang. It retained the stock width and was not narrowed, and the windshield was not laid back, as some suspected. The Mustang did run narrowed bumpers and was as about as low as it could go; these were typical modifications seen in most competitive mid-1970s Pro Stocks. By June, Don was finished with the Mustangs, or so he thought, and once again, called on Hardy to build him something a little different.

1978 Fairmont

Taking a 180-degree turn from the swoopy Mustangs, Don commissioned Hardy to build the boxy, longer-wheelbase Fairmont. Because of the wacky NHRA weight breaks, the Fairmont carried approximately 150 pounds less than the Mustang. The plan was to debut the car at the NHRA Summernationals in mid-July, but a week after hitting up Hardy, Bob Glidden came knocking, seeking a Fairmont of his own. Glidden hoped to debut his car at Edgewater July 8–9, which gave Hardy just a couple weeks to build the two cars. Needless to say, there was a lot of late nights put in by Hardy and crew.

Both Dyno Don and Glidden had their cars back in their own garages by July 1. Dyno Don, with the help of Jon Kaase, went to work completing the car before sending it to Rusty Greer for paint. Don got the car back July 7 and, by 6 p.m. that evening, he was on the road to Suffolk for a points meet. Even though the 340 was in place and had been fired, the car had yet to move under its own power. He drove the car for the first time through the Suffolk pits to the scales. The first full pass in the car netted Don an 8.68 at 154 mph. At Englishtown for the Summernationals, the Suffolk engine was found to have spun a few bearings and cracked the block at the main webs. After changing the engine and toying with a new 5-speed transmission, Dyno bowed in the first round. The Fairmont played runner-up to Shelby Jester at the AHRA Grand Nationals at Dragway 42 in August. At Indy the following month, Don failed to qualify.

After winning the NHRA championship in 1977, Don had hopes of repeating in 1978 but Lady Luck had other plans. After wrecking the new Mustang II, the Fairmont was built. It did great match racing and fared well in AHRA competition but came up empty at NHRA events. Rusty Greer, brother of famed Funny Car pilot Shirl Greer, painted the car. (Photo Courtesy Dan Williams)

The Ford Cleveland was more efficient than the much-praised small-block Chevy, and Don proved it over and over through the 1970s. The Fairmont wore competition number 205 in 1979 and closed the year number 3 in the points standings. (Author's Collection)

Don's biggest win behind the wheel of the Fairmont came at the 1979 AHRA Winter Nationals in Tucson. Those folks who were expecting the usual January temperatures of 70 to 80 degrees were met instead with near-freezing temps. The combination of a cold track and headwinds contributed to an off-pace field. Don qualified the Fairmont number-1 with an 8.87 at 154.37 mph in a field that saw the Camaro of Don Campanello hold the final spot with a 9.04 at 149.75 mph. Don faced Arizona's own Kevin Rotty in the

The Fairmont's 340 housed the best parts of the day: an Accel ignition, Holley 4500 carbs atop a modified Edelbrock intake, Ace pistons, and Childs and Albert rods. Jomar girdles and Crower equipment hid under the Moroso covers. Don avoided "trick of the week" parts; research and development were ongoing and change was constant. (Photo ©TEN: The Enthusiast Network. All Rights Reserved.)

A Moroso tach stands front and center in the Fairmont while the controls for the Lenco are at an easy reach. The Hurst line-loc runs from the tallest Lenco lever. The safety net became mandatory equipment in NHRA Pro Stock for 1978. (Photo ©TEN: The Enthusiast Network. All Rights Reserved.)

By the latter half of the 1970s, the 340-ci Cleveland was Don's NHRA legal "go-to" mill. Although he tried different combinations, down to 330 ci, he found no advantage. (Photo Courtesy Nicholson Family Collection)

For a match against Jenkins in May 1979, Dyno dropped in a big-cubic-inch Kaase engine and it sucked the side windows out at speed. To quote Don, "I thought that big engine was just going to be a weak suck. It ran a lot stronger than I thought." The side windows wouldn't stay in the fiberglass doors, so he left them out. Jenkins was running a 494 here and Don a 516, which propelled the Fairmont to a best of 8.01. (Photo Courtesy Mike Sopko Sr.)

final, but not before downing Sonny Bryant in the semis with a 9.07 at 150.75 mph to a 9.12 at 151.26. Rotty, meanwhile, took a semifinal win over a redlighting Roy Hill. In an attempt to warm up the cold start line, both Dyno Don and Rotty laid down the VHT and performed numerous burnouts. As ready as they were going to be, the pair played a little psychological warfare, taking their time staging before Rotty crept forward. On the green, the pair was out, bumper to bumper. About 300 feet off the line, the big-block in Rotty's Camaro let loose, making it an easy win for Dyno, who recorded an 8.87 at 150.25 mph.

The Fairmont last ran as a match racer with the aluminum 516-ci Wedge. It was during a match at Darlington that Don flipped the car, sliding it a distance on the roof before coming to a stop. Thankfully, Don suffered no injuries. Considering the length of his career and the few crashes he had, Don never received serious injury or

Earl Wade

One constant throughout Don's career was master tuner/ engine builder Earl Wade. The pair first met at El Mirage in the early 1950s after Wade snuck a ride up with friends who ran the Price Brothers Fuel Coupe, a flathead-powered, nitro-induced 1936 Ford five-window. Lucky Wade; at age 15 it was the first "real" car he ever drove. Wade's father, a mechanic, no doubt fueled his interest in cars. His dad couldn't have been too happy in the trade, though, as he forbid Wade to become a mechanic. He wanted his son to go to school and become a mechanical engineer, something that paid good money. No doubt Wade did okay by himself without formal schooling.

Wade became a fine driver in his own right but decided to focus his attention on turning wrenches after an incident while campaigning Gas Ronda's Thunderbolt in 1965. While working on the front suspension, a coil spring let loose and nailed him square in the face. It was while laid up in the hospital recovering from his near-death injuries that Wade made the decision to give up driving. Having worked alongside Dyno Don back in the early 1960s, Wade hooked up with him once again late in 1965. He razzed Don, saying he (Wade) was still the better

driver. On at least one occasion, the pair hopped into the two Mavericks and had at it. No doubt Wade had a sense of humor. One time back in 1966, a camera crew was holding a trackside interview with Ed Schartman, just after one of the rare times he actually defeated Don. Wade picked the ideal time to butt in and add, "Yeah, but you're still number two."

A shrewd operator, back in the mid-1960s he took time to help Hubert Platt tune his Ford. When he returned to his own pits, he told Don that he "got the car running real well, but not good enough to beat us." Wade said he only had one employer in life and that was Don, later adding, "I've known a lot of guys in this business but never a better driver, sharper mechanic, or more considerate man than Don. He was always thinking about doing something new to get times down just a little." And as Don recalled, he doubted if he ever had one serious disagreement with Wade, on or off the track.

Wade was just as diverse as Don. In 1968, he took a year off to team with his old business partner, Dick Bourgeois, in running the Chevy-powered Doug Thorley Corvair. The car morphed into a Javelin Funny Car, which the pair ran into 1970. Nevertheless, Wade was never far off and continued to assist Don. At the same time, his reputation saw him building blocks for cars such as Sherman Gunn's Chevy-powered Altered, the SOHC for Ken Hedman's Husler Maverick, and the Cleveland for Ed Terry's 1971 Pro Stock effort. No doubt his work with Terry helped out when Don made the switch to Cleveland power in 1972. Wade was thick in the development and helped Don win the AHRA World Championship that season. He left Don at the end of 1974 and briefly teamed with Sherman Gunn, of M & S Race Cars, in campaigning a Funny Car.

Wade and Don teamed once again in the mid-1980s and remained side by side until Don's retirement in 2001. Wade continued to plug away and for many years was regarded as the go-to guy when it came to FE Fords. He spent the last 10 years or so of his life working out of Frank Sicinski's shop in Texas, building engines for numerous drag cars as well as for local oval track racers. Drag racing lost one of its greats when Wade passed suddenly in 2012 at the age of 77.

Earl Wade and Don stand proudly during a break in late-1967 action. The dynamic duo was one of the most successful pairings in drag racing history. Don's niece Linda (right) sits pretty in the new Mercury Cyclone. (Photo Courtesy Nicholson Family Collection)

The last Cammer that Earl Wade built resided between the rails of Larry Knapp's *Stampede Mustang*. When this photo was shot in 2009, the Mustang was capable of bottom-9-second times. Here, Wade stands ready to guide Knapp to the line. (Photo Courtesy Bob Wenzelburger)

Don closed out the 1979 season 3rd in the NHRA Pro Stock points standing behind Bob Glidden and Frank Iaconio. Longtime friend Gil Younger of TransGo sponsored Don into 1981. At this point in his career, Don was still match racing up to five times a week. Shown here is the revitalized world champ Mustang II. (Photo Courtesy David Ball)

This Kil-Kare Dragway photo was snapped during a 1980 match race. The tall studs out of the Holleys are used to retain the formula-style scoop. Don relied on big cubic inches to get the job done and only used nitrous once; that was back around 1977 during a match race against the Chevy of Pat Musi. After burning a piston, he said no more, until his Pro Mod Bel Air. (Photo Courtesy Jeff Wright)

The Fox-Body Mustang, its unorthodox scoop hiding a big-cubic-inch Jon Kaase Boss, was one of the nation's most feared match racers. According to Kaase, the biggest big-block Don ran was a 589. Wilwood disc brakes and a Deist chute helped bring the 7-second ride to a halt. Underpinnings included Lamb Components' MacPherson strut suspension. Summers axles, Monroe shocks, and fabricated ladder bars supported a narrowed Jack Chrisman 9-inch rear end. (Photo Courtesy Jim Kampmann)

Having to carry 7.20 pounds per cubic inch in NHRA competition, it's no wonder that Don and other Cleveland-powered Fords suffered in 1979. Here at Cayuga, Ontario, Don is caught making adjustments to the Mustang's suspension. Components included a ladder bar–suspended Jack Chrisman 9-inch, Summers Brothers axles, and adjustable Monroe coil-over shocks. (Photo Courtesy Rob Potter)

Warming the hides at Buds Creek, Maryland, in 1979. The Mustang was powered by a 342-ci Cleveland, which pushed the car to legal 8.40 times. NHRA weight breaks saw the Mustang weigh in at a legal 2,462 pounds, which could be brought down to 2,200 pounds for match racing. (Photo Courtesy Dave Bishop)

One of six NHRA national events that Don ran in 1980 was the U.S. Nationals, where his 8.724 left the Mustang on the outs. Greater success with the Mustang came from running big-cubic-inch engines in IHRA competition and match racing. Don won the IHRA Northern Nationals at Milan, Michigan, in July by defeating the Chevy Monza of William Parris in the final. (Photo Courtesy Tom Schiltz)

Old friend Gil Younger at TransGo got a great deal when Don signed with him in 1979. The sponsorship ran into 1981 and was said to be worth $5,000 a season. Don did a bunch of experimental work for TransGo, including attempting to run a convertor in front of his Lenco. Testing took place at Orange County but the experiment went nowhere. (Photo Courtesy Steve Reyes)

Dyno Don's first Fox-Body Mustang was received just 10 days before the 1979 Springnationals, and it was destroyed less than three months later. Gene Branham of Alpharetta, Georgia, painted this one. (Photo Courtesy Tom Schiltz)

At the NHRA Springnationals in 1979, Dyno Don in the new Mustang lost a close one in the semis to Larry Lombardo in Grumpy Jenkins's Camaro, 8.80 to 8.89. There was a lot of mutual respect between Don and Grumpy. Often on early swings East, Don maintained his Pro Stocks at Jenkins Competition. (Photo Courtesy Tom Kasch)

broken bones. The Fairmont was shipped to Don Hardy's for a new roof skin and other repairs, and it was sold shortly after as a roller to Billy Takaki in Honolulu. Takaki painted the car black and labeled it *Super Fairmont* before debuting it at Hilo Dragstrip as Hawaii's first Pro Stock. Southern California's Lee Hunter drove the car during its debut. It's known that Takaki raced the Fairmont through 1980, but the car seems to have fallen off the map after that.

1979–1980

When Don made the decision to build a new car, he didn't waste any time "gettin' 'er done." The Maverick, the Fairmont, and his Fox-Body Mustangs all attest to that. Looking for a new Mustang, Dyno went knocking on Don Hardy's door in June; within 10 days, the Fox-Body car was sitting in Dyno's Atlanta shop. For Dyno Don, this was the sixth of seven cars that Hardy built for him.

With the weight that the Cleveland-powered cars had to carry, I question how any of them were competitive as the 1970s wound down. The Cleveland in Don's new Mustang was similar to the engine that he ran back in 1975. When it came to the heads, Don did make use of rare factory aluminum parts. He replaced the head bolts with a more supportive stud kit. Studs were also used in the bottom end along with Milodon caps. The block was supposedly honed and re-ringed every 35 to 40 runs. The engine started out at 340 ci; it's said that the blocks were used up by the time they reached a 4.10 bore

breakage. To hold the Mustang steady, Don used both a Hurst line lock and a Lamb trans brake. The line lock held the car while heating the tires; the trans brake held the car on the line. The trans brake prevented any drag on the wheels that a line lock might cause when the light turned green.

Don used two different transmissions through the late 1970s: the Lenco 4-speed and a trick Doug Nash 5-speed. Quirky NHRA rules of the day limited the Lenco and Liberty transmissions to four forward gears while the less popular Nash was allowed to run five forward gears. This was ideal for the Cleveland, which loved the higher RPM; Don shifted at 9,500. Unlike the planetary Lenco that was shifted without using a clutch, the Nash required engaging the clutch with each gear change. The downside of this, of course, was the time lost during gear changes.

According to a *SS&DI* magazine interview, Don and Jon Kaase spent approximately 500 hours ingeniously rigging up the Nash so that it could shift without the need to engage the clutch. The pair determined that if they could cut the power to the engine for a "millisecond," the full-throttle shift could be made without engaging the clutch, thus preventing the engine RPM from going off the chart. A pressure-sensitive switch mounted on the vertical gate shifter activated an electronic "cutout" timer. When the switch sensed enough pressure at the lever to make a shift, it made contact with the timer, which was wired into the ignition. When the timer was triggered, it cut the ignition for that millisecond. Cutting the power took the strain off of the synchro and

Don was an innovator, he used to beat everyone with that trick 5-speed.

(343 ci). When it came to compression, Don maximized at 12.5:1. Induction was by way of a pair of 1050 Holleys on a much-modified Edelbrock intake. Lighting the fire was an ignition created from Mallory and MSD parts.

Behind the engine was a McLeod 30-pound flywheel and a "soft" pressure plate. Don felt that the soft pressure plate was easier on the driveline and helped prevent

then the full-throttle power shift was made without fear of damage.

Of course, a number of critical issues had to be hammered out to ensure that the system worked. For instance, if the pressure switch on the shifter lever was set too low, the lever could be pulled out of gear without enough force to engage the next gear. If the switch was

The old Mustang was still seeing active duty as late as 1980. Here at a Mountain Motor race held at Connecticut International, Dyno Don faces the Monza of Grumpy Jenkins. Note the ill-fitting glass doors and tall tail spoiler. (Photo Courtesy Jon Graves/Mick Smallridge Collection)

The final Mustang is seen here in the Pomona staging lanes for the 1981 NHRA Winternationals. Don's frustration with the less-than-favorable NHRA weight saw him focus most of his attention elsewhere between 1979 and 1981. He attended just three NHRA national events in 1981. (Photo Courtesy Bob Bayles)

Seven-second runs became the norm when Don started running the big-cubic-inch aluminum Can-Am–based block in 1980. Topping the Boss were Holley Dominators on a much-modified Weiand intake. Toward the end, Don toyed with various-size Wedge and Boss engines, measuring anywhere from 366 to 396 ci and 512 to 589 ci. (Photo Courtesy Jim Kampmann)

Dyno Don heats the hides during Brainerd International Raceway's Quaker State Spectacular in 1980. For two years prior to Brainerd getting an NHRA National Event in 1982, it booked several Top Fuel and Funny Cars as well as the Mountain Motor Pro Stocks, which had never been there previously or since. Attendees included Dyno Don, Ronnie Sox, and Harold Denton, as well as Warren Johnson, who was running IHRA at the time with Jerome Bradford. (Photo Courtesy Jim Kampmann)

When it came to IHRA Mountain Motor Pro Stock, an older Don schooled many young guns. His exploits have him ranked number 15 on the list of all-time greats. Quite impressive, considering his short time running Mountain Motor. (Photo Courtesy Jim Kampmann)

set too high, the ignition could come back on before Don had the chance to move the shifter out of one gear and into the next, causing a missed shift. Just as critical to the setup was the ignition cutout. Too short a cutout would not allow the gear to free itself from the engine strain; too long and it would cost engine speed and quarter-mile times would suffer.

Fellow racers complained about the setup, while at the same time trying to mimic it. Pro Stock competitor Frank Iaconio was one. "Don was an innovator, he used to beat everyone with that trick 5-speed. A clutchless transmission when they were illegal. Somehow he made it work and got away with it. We tried to figure it out, buying electronics and all, but found we were

chasing our tails." The car was more than a tenth faster and more than a mile per hour quicker with the Nash. They spent more than a year experimenting with the transmission. Nevertheless, the NHRA had banned its use by the end of the 1979 season. Dyno Don never did run the Nash behind the big-inch match-race engine; he believed that the transmission would never have survived the increased torque.

The Mustang weighed in at 2,462 pounds legal. However, by bolting on fiberglass doors and dropping ballast, the Mustang could drop to as little as 2,200 pounds for match races. The match-race engine remained the tried and true 516 through 1979. Although some of his competition was already running more than 600 ci, Don had no

This image was captured in late 1980 at Billy Herndon's Orlando Speed World Dragway in Florida. Don drove the 512-ci Boss Mustang against Jenkins's 494-ci Monza and buried Grumpy's Toy *in three rounds. (Photo Courtesy Carl Weisinger)*

problem holding his own. The engine featured Venolia pistons swinging from Childs & Albert rods. The heads were similar to his NHRA legal engine; it featured the same size titanium valves and, the now-standard-equipment exhaust plates. Topping the 516 were twin Holley 1050s feeding through a gargantuan IMSA-style scoop drawing clean air from way up. The carbs mounted on a much-modified Weiand tunnel ram.

This Mustang had a short life, meeting its demise on August 25 during a match race against Ronnie Sox. The car lasted just 11 weeks, a mere half dozen races before (it's said) meeting a guardrail at Dragway 42. The incident unfolded when the 516 blew a head gasket at approximately 130 mph and spewed fluid under the tires. The Mustang then veered from the right lane to the left. In doing so, it clipped the Omni of Sox & Martin, sending it across the lanes. The Mustang hit the guardrail hard, taking out eight support posts and 200 feet of railing. In the opposing lane, Sox and the Omni barrel-rolled numerous times before coming to rest. When the dust finally settled, there was little left of either car. Both drivers limped away, Don with a sprained ankle.

Work began almost immediately at Hardy's on a replacement Mustang. In the meantime, Don dusted off the World Championship Mustang II and made do. All of the salvageable pieces from the wrecked Mustang found their way either onto the new Hardy car or were added to Don's growing parts bin. Don received the new Mustang a week before the August 1980 Mountain Motor Nationals at Buds Creek, Maryland. The car was painted the night before the race and was still being pieced together the next day in the pits.

Into 1981 . . .

Don ran just three NHRA national events in 1981. His class-legal engine was a destroked Boss 429 measuring 372 ci, which Don worked out late the previous season with Kaase. After spending a decade thrashing on the small-block, revised weight breaks (how quickly they changed) leaned favorably to the Boss engine. Running the short 100.5-inch wheelbase Fox-Body Mustang, the car only had to carry 6.45 pounds per cubic inch, which was down from the previous year's 6.60. Compare that to the Cleveland, which was forced to carry 7.05 pounds per cubic inch in 1981, and you can see why Don, among others, was taking a second look at the Boss engine.

Don professed that it was Kaase who pushed the Boss and that Kaase put a lot of time, money, and development into the engine. "I never tried to run one before. I always ran the Ford SOHC engine. Gapp & Roush were running one quite a bit. Eddie Schartman worked with Holman-Moody on it but none of them at that time [1970–1971] showed me anything." Even though Don had all the parts to build a Boss, he felt he was better off with his Cammer, so he never deviated. Obviously, camshaft and valvetrain technology had come a long way since the early days and the gear really woke the engine

match at Connecticut. While Jenkins relied upon a 572-ci Rodeck, Don was now running a 589, based upon an aluminum Can-Am block. Venolia pistons on Miller rods helped squeeze out 13:1 compression. The valve gear consisted of a Crower cam with a lift in the neighborhood of .800 inch and 285/290 duration. Rockers were 1.75 inches and the deep-breathing valves measured 2.40 and 1.98 inches. Fuel from the 1150 Holleys passed through a much-modified Weiand intake. The big mill was limited to 9,000 rpm; any higher and the valves would kiss the pistons. In the match against Allen, Don took him two-straight with a best of 7.87 at 176.17 mph, which stood as a new track record.

In class action, Don ran seven IHRA national events in 1981 and really shook them up at Darlington on March 22 at the Octane Plus Winternationals when he qualified number 1 with a 7.88 at 176 mph. At the time, this was the quickest speed ever turned in Pro Stock at an IHRA national event. In defeating Keith Albritten in the first, Dyno improved on his 7.88 when he ran low ET of the meet with a 7.81 at 176 mph to take the win against Albritten, who turned an 8.26 at 167. Unfortunately for Don, he took a nap in the second against Rickie Smith and his 7.86 at 175 was not enough to catch Smith's 8.07 at 171 mph.

Don's last national event win came in 1981 at the IHRA Pro-Am Nationals at Rockingham.

up. The "tweaked" valvetrain allowed the engine to zip to 10,000 rpm.

Don retired from NHRA competition shortly after the Gatornationals in March. At the time, Dyno had just the one engine so was a little reluctant to "lean" on it. He qualified seventh at the Gators with an 8.48, won the first round, and lost the second to eventual event winner Frank Iaconio. Losing power to a worn cam, Don ran an 8.62 at 157 mph against Iaconio's 8.41 at 161.

Don was surviving off of what he was taking in match racing and by 1981 was running three times a week. In April, it was just like the old days when Don faced Ray Allen in the *Grumpy's Toy* Camaro for a best-of-three

Don's last national event win came in 1981 at the IHRA Pro-Am Nationals at Rockingham. The IHRA Pro Stock category varied from the same-named NHRA category by having an unlimited cubic-inch displacement rule and a minimum weight of 2,400 pounds. It was a true reflection of the "run whatcha brung" mentality of the southeast. Rockingham had no problem filling its 16-car field and the top contenders proved to be the Shotgun-powered Mustangs of Dean Thompson/Ronnie Sox, Rickie Smith, and Dyno Don. Sox counted on a Jack Roush engine, while both Dyno and Smith were running their big-inch Kaase engines. Rounding out the top four was the lone GM standout Monte Carlo of Warren John-

With match-race dates disappearing due to dwindling tracks, Don took Harold Denton's generous offer to buy the Mustang and sold it while he was still on top. Due, in part, to his own success with the car, Harold was voted number 17 on the list of top IHRA Mountain Motor Pro Stock racers. (Photo Courtesy Jim Kampmann)

son. Don held the low qualifying position with a 7.82 at 176 mph and change followed closely by Smith. It was no surprise that when the semifinals rolled around, these four were the last men standing. In the first pairing, Sox made it an easy win for Dyno after he dropped the driveshaft. Next up, it was Smith in the Oak Ridge Boys–sponsored Mustang II taking care of Johnson with a 7.96.

The all-Kaase final saw Smith jump to a car-length lead, a lead that would have seen a lesser opponent counting his loss. Not Don. He kept his foot in it and when Smith's Shotgun expired before the first lights, Nicholson sailed on by for the win with a 7.90. "It was a quick light," Don exclaimed after the race. No doubt, the man still had it.

The Mustang's 7.80 times made the car an easy sell in the spring of 1981 when Harold Denton offered up a reported $50,000. Denton's first outing with the car netted him a runner-up finish at IHRA's high-dollar Bristol race. Don hung around for the next few races, pulling wrenches and guiding Denton until he was familiar enough with the car to carry on. A year later, Denton crashed the Mustang and then sold it to Dick Estevez, who made the necessary repairs before selling it to Vernon Summer in South Carolina.

IT'S IN THE BLOOD (1983–2001)

Don painted the Olds at his Orange, California, shop, retaining the same colors and a similar scheme as his earlier Mustangs. Ford fans can take solace in knowing Don didn't own this car. (Photo Courtesy Ray Cunningham)

Like Mark Twain and his, "The reports of my death have been greatly exaggerated," so too was the talk of Dyno Don's retirement back in 1981. The cost of owning and maintaining a Pro Stocker had reached the stratosphere by the early 1980s, which forced Dyno to take a brief hiatus. For years, Don had relied upon match-race bookings to keep him going, but, looking at his calendar, he had a lot of open dates because half of the tracks where he once raced were gone. In addition, it's been said Don was feeling a little slighted by Ford, which (apparently) had made promises that just never materialized. Don returned to performing body and paint at his Orange shop after selling the Mustang, where, for the next 18 months, he busied himself rebuilding Mercedes-Benzes and other "preferred cars."

In match-race trim, and with a few extra cubes, the Oldsmobile clocked 7.54 at 182 mph in 1984. As owner Ralph Woodall recalls, in legal trim the car ran a quick 7.74 at 178.21 at Atlanta. The team finished 15th in the 1984 Pro Stock standings. (Photo Courtesy Jim Kampmann)

1983–1984

By spring 1983, Dyno Don's hiatus was over. He hooked up with Washington's Ralph Woodall, who had landed himself an Oldsmobile Pro Stock deal. It was a deal that Dyno had been rumored to be interested in landing himself. Woodall, a well-known Super Stock racer in the Northwest, landed the deal when he called Oldsmobile's Tom Erb directly. It seems that Woodall was on GM's radar thanks, in large part, to his work with the big-block Chevy. Erb stated that he'd be interested in having Woodall join Oldsmobile and flew into Washington the next night to get him under contract. Woodall, who operated a number of transmission shops at the time, readily admits that he was worried that he had gotten in over his head. Dyno Don, an acquaintance of Woodall's, called shortly after the deal had been signed and inquired how he got the Oldsmobile deal. At the time, Woodall was still asking himself that same question. Knowing Dyno had sold his Ford mount, Woodall took the opportunity to ask

Ray Cunningham was called on to build the chassis and complete the tinwork for the Olds. All body panels were sent directly from General Motors, eventually. The car is nearing completion at this point, and the Dyno colors are not too far off. (Photo Courtesy Ray Cunningham)

The nearly completed interior gives a good feel for how the inside of a Pro Stocker used to look. The clutch on the Olds was set up similar to a line-loc and could be controlled electronically. Push a button and release the pedal; when the tree turned green, you released the button. (Photo Courtesy Ray Cunningham)

him if he wanted to run an Oldsmobile. Dyno's response was, "sure." And so was formed the brief, and unlikely, partnership between the Chevy racer, the Ford racer, and Oldsmobile.

Woodall immediately requested Ciera body panels from Oldsmobile: a roof, quarter panels, doors, etc., so that he could get to building. After a comedy of errors that saw Oldsmobile send him a total of three complete Cieras, a body in white, and a semitruck, he finally received the panels he had originally requested. Ray Cunningham, out of the Fremont area, was called on to build the chassis.

General Motors supplied the NHRA-legal 500-ci cast block, aluminum heads, and nitrite crank. Woodall assembled it and Sonny Bryant in Anaheim performed a good part of the machine work. Brooks pistons squeezed out 14:1 compression and the Holley 1150 carbs, reworked to 1230, fed the fuel. Horsepower was said to be right around the 1,100 mark. For IHRA and match racing, the team relied on a 560-ci mill. Records show that on the car's first full pass, Dyno recorded a 7.88 at 174 mph.

The first national showing for the car was the NHRA World Finals. Dyno qualified but fell in the first round. At the 1984 Winternationals, he ran a 7.83 to qualify but on a subsequent run, the clutch went south. He broke a rod on another run and was not able to make eliminations. Dyno and the Olds ran eight national events through 1984 and qualified at five of them. His best showing was a number-8 qualifying position at the Cajun Nationals in Baton Rouge. Reflecting on this, Woodall felt that they could have gone higher in the season standings if the parts had held up. Dyno Don had no financial stake in the car, and, when money dried up at the end of the season, he moved on.

It was a good partnership; even after Don and buddy Dick Estevez made the decision, without Woodall's knowledge, to shorten the car late in 1984. During a trip back East, the pair decided to take advantage of the NHRA rules and chop 4 inches out of the car, forward of the firewall. NHRA rules allowed it, as long as the number-1

Don stated that he never worked as hard on a car as he did on the Olds. Keeping the car in the thick of competition were Carburetor Shop dominators, Venolia pistons, and a Crane valvetrain. Sonny Bryant should be given credit for performing a lot of machine work for the team. (Photo Courtesy Ray Cunningham)

At Don's shop on Katella Street in Orange, he and Ray Cunningham are caught in the process of piecing together a fresh mill for the Olds. According to car owner, Ralph Woodall, "The initial 500-ci engines were built on high-nickel 427s that weren't available to the general public." The Drag Racing Competition Engine (DRCE) blocks came later. Larry Olsen at Edvanced Engines & Performance (EPD) did the initial work on the heads, and then approximately another 100 hours were spent on the flow bench. (Photo Courtesy Ray Cunningham)

At the 1984 NHRA Summernationals at Englishtown, Don faced reigning Ford champion and eventual event winner Bob Glidden during eliminations. Seeing Don in an Oldsmobile was a tough pill to swallow for the Ford faithful. (Photo Courtesy Keith Hudak)

cylinder remained aligned with the front spindle. The reason behind the modification was to move the weight of the engine and transmission closer to the rear wheels.

Outside of drag racing, Woodall and Don got along exceptionally well. Woodall recalls one humorous incident when Don's wife, Patty, wanted to get the kitchen in their California home painted. She had everything off the walls for three or four days and was waiting impatiently while Don and Woodall worked on the Olds. Woodall made a trip to Sonny Bryant's for parts and, while he was gone, Don volunteered him to go paint shopping with Patty. When Woodall returned, there was no discussion, no ifs, ands, or buts, just off to the paint store they trooped.

Says Woodall, "To Don, this was the funniest thing ever. Well, Patty and I get to the store and after an hour, she's still deciding on what color she wants. So I say to myself, 'It's time to get even with Don.' We buy this fancy tape for making straight lines. 'This is very important,' I say. So we get back to their house and Patty is not letting me go until the painting is done. So I am putting this tape up and, on purpose, it's anything but straight. So I tell Patty, 'You know, Don is a body man and really good at taping.' Long story short, with a few threats she gets Don home to do the taping. I suggest to Patty that if Don and I did the painting now it would be all done in no time. Don was stuck so he says, 'Okay, let's do this!' So

I took the paint out of the bag and it was Glidden paint. He just stared at it and said, 'Payback can be a b&#%h.' Patty and I both were killing ourselves laughing. When we finished, Don took the leftover paint and threw it into the garbage."

A big-cubic-inch nitrous engine finally wore the Ciera out and, in 1985, Woodall replaced it with a Don Ness car he rebodied as a Ciera and painted exactly like the Cunningham car. The first Ciera was sold to Paul Wiechmann, minus the iron block Chevy and transmission. Those parts went to Dyno Don and were plugged into his Nostalgia Pro Mod Bel Air. Today, Wiechmann runs the Ciera in Pro Gas, hitting 8.60 times, which is about a second behind Dyno Don's best times.

1985

In 1985, the Nicholsons vacated Atlanta, moving permanently back to their Orange, California, home. Since 1962, the family had been splitting its time between Atlanta and California, usually making the "western swing" prior to the Christmas holidays then heading back east in time for the Gatornationals in March. It was around 1985 that Don reconnected with old acquaintance, Frank Sicinski of New Caney, Texas.

Sicinski first met Don in 1977, introducing himself

Qualifying Frank Sicinski's Thunderbird in the number-14 position at the 1985 NHRA Winternationals, Don faced old friend Butch Leal in the first round. Butch was at the top of game in the mid-1980s and trailed the Thunderbird in a close one. (Photo Courtesy Steve Reyes)

Frank Sicinski's Boss 500-ci, Earl Wade mill cools between rounds at the sweltering 1986 NHRA Summernationals. Dyno Don drove the Thunderbird at a handful of national events between 1985 and 1987. (Photo Courtesy Nicholson Family Collection)

Don was more than happy to be back behind the wheel in 1985, and he teamed once again with Earl Wade. The Wade-built 500-ci Boss propelled Don to a best of 7.60. Frank Sicinski later tried out a Greg Good Boss in the 'Bird. (Photo Courtesy Jim Kampmann)

Frank Sicinski's Thunderbird wasn't the only Pro Stock that Don hitched a ride in during 1985. At an eight-car IHRA Mountain Motor race the same year, Dyno drove Ernie Fore's Thunderbird to a number of 7.90 times. Don drove the ex-Rickie Smith Thunderbird on and off in 1985 and into 1986. Fore, who hailed from Fairfax Station, Virginia, campaigned the Kaase 615-ci powered–car through 1988. (Photo Courtesy JL Ervin)

At some point in 1986, Don dropped one of his dated 500-ci Chevy engines into the Firebird of Ken Thurm. The Firebird was a chassis research car that had previously been run by Fred Taylor at the 1985 World Finals. Don drove the car at the NHRA Winternationals in 1987 but failed to qualify with a 7.72. (Author's Collection)

Not familiar with the Litening Bolt name? Well, you can be forgiven. The brainchild of Scott Alder, the modern-day version of the 1964 Thunderbolt was built with help from Don and Bill Stroppe and with parts from Crites Industries. Powered by a Jon Kaase 519 FE, Don drove the car to 10 teen times during a Hot Rod magazine shoot-out in 1995. With Don on board, Alder had the idea of going into business building tribute drag cars, starting with the DDN 1 (Dyno Don Nicholson 1). The over-inflated asking price of $75,000 dollars scared off any interested parties and, in the end, the DDN 1 was the only car built by Litening Bolt Performance Cars. (Photo ©TEN: The Enthusiast Network. All Rights Reserved.)

> ## It was Wade who suggested that we put Don behind the wheel of the Thunderbird

and his seven-year-old son Stacy to the legendary racer. Half a dozen years later, Sicinski was racing a SOHC Mustang II of his own, counting on friend Earl Wade as his engine builder and top wrench. In 1984, Sicinski stepped up with a Willie Rells Pro Stock Thunderbird. Powering the car was a 500-ci Boss engine built by Wade.

"It was Wade who suggested that we put Don behind the wheel of the Thunderbird," said Sicinski. "We had been having some misfire issues that had popped up and I wanted to get out of the seat so I could see for myself what was happening on the track." Well, the Thunderbird continued to misfire until Sicinski finally hunted the issue down to a hot wire on the fuse panel. Don ended up driving the car at the Winternationals, Phoenix, and Gainesville in 1985. He failed to qualify at the latter two races and his number-7 qualifying position at the Winternationals was the last time Don qualified at a NHRA national event. The best time Don managed with the Thunderbird was a 7.60 at 183 mph.

Just like the old days, Don's Bel Air ran a 409; this one measured out to 434 ci. This "truck" engine, which initially pushed the Chevy well into the 9s, was replaced with a 500-ci Pro Stock engine. (Photo Courtesy Nicholson Family Collection)

Roger Gustin and his AutoStar Productions put on the Super Chevy magazine shows that booked Don and his retro Bel Air to run a quick-8 program. Longtime rival Arnie Beswick was the lone "non-Chevy" in the program and ran his Pontiac for three or four years. Don is being interviewed here at the 1997 Hot Rod Reunion. (Photo Courtesy Bob Bayles)

A few different engines propelled the nostalgia Bel Air. Don and Dick Estevez built this 632-ci nitrous engine. It was fellow racer Arnie Beswick who felt the need to add nitro to the equation, leaving Don little choice but to do the same if he wished to continue his domination. (Photo Courtesy Bob Bayles)

An interior shot of the Bel Air shows the vastness of these old Chevys. With its easily identifiable Lenco levers, and AutoMeter gauges, Don's bubble top was all business. The red interior mimics that of his original Bel Air. (Photo Courtesy Nicholson Family Collection)

Caught with the wheels up off the line, Don faces longtime friend Dick Estevez in the Daddy Warbucks *Falcon. Don ran up to 25 matches a year with the Bel Air. (Photo Courtesy Steve Reyes)*

1988–2001

In 1988, Don still had the desire to run Pro Stock, but without the help of a big-dollar sponsor, he couldn't afford to play, at least not at the level he was used to. It was the desire to go big and go fast, in conjunction with a little peer pressure that saw Don build his Nostalgia Pro Mod 1962 Bel Air. Don started out with a steel body, gutting it of excess metal before adding fiberglass doors, front clip, decklid, and bumpers. To reduce the weight further, he added Lexan windows.

Don called on Victory Race Cars of Victorville, California, to complete the stock wheelbase (119 inches) chassis, tinwork, and wiring. Finished weight of the Chevy, with Don onboard was 2,600 pounds. An early W engine measuring 434 ci initially powered the Bel Air before Don dropped in a 500-ci engine left over from the Oldsmobile Pro Stocker. After throwing the rods out of that engine, Don borrowed one of Butch Leal's Pro Stock engines.

Leal recalls the first time Don ran the engine: "My engine ran one-to-one linkage on the carbs, meaning all eight barrels on the Holleys opened up at once. Dyno wasn't used to that, as he had his set up to come in more gradual. It ran so fast out of the chute it scared him." The Leal engine filled the void for a couple weeks while Don and Estevez built a 632-ci engine for the Bel Air. With a shot of nitrous, the Chevy ran a best of 7.42. Not bad times at all, considering the amount of air that the car was pushing. Rounding out the drivetrain was a Lenco transmission and Ford rear end. Don loved the car and was having a lot of fun with it but hated the

Don made his last pass in the Bel Air in 2001, the same year his wife Patty passed away. The Victory chassis measured 116 inches and carried a four-link rear suspension and 9-inch housing as well as Strange brakes, springs, and struts. Don admitted that by this point his sight was so bad he was guessing at the lights. (Photo Courtesy Jim Kampmann)

continuous maintenance. Engine breakage and repairs increased after the nitrous was added. Don put a lot of miles on the car, running the Super Chevy shows and quick-8 programs, as well as competing against Arnie

> ## It ran so fast out of the chute it scared him.

Beswick and his *Tameless Tiger* GTO, Dick Estevez and his *Daddy Warbucks* Falcon, and others.

Don made his final pass in the Bel Air in 2001, after which the car went into storage at crewmember Greg Davis's place in Norco, California. Davis owed Don a large sum of money against a promissory note that wasn't being paid. It seems that kindhearted Don had bought Davis equipment to help get his fabrication business off the ground.

Sadly, the story of the Bel Air goes south from here. Prior to Don passing, his daughter Cindy received word from some of Don's friends who said that they were worried about the car. Davis had sold his house and never mentioned a word to Cindy that he moved from Alta Loma to Las Vegas. The Bel Air was left in storage at a neighbor's house. Cindy paid a visit to Davis, who assured her that there was no problem and she'd get the car back. He had no intentions of keeping it.

The next thing Cindy knew, the car turned up on eBay. Friends contacted the seller and went to look at the car. Once the new location of the car was known,

Cindy was notified. She arrived only to be threatened with harm if she didn't leave. Instead, she remained in the area until the next day with her daughter and son-in-law, trying to figure out what to do next. It was then that they were approached by friends of the guy in possession of the Bel Air with drawn guns, forcing them to leave. The following day, Cindy got a court order to retrieve the car but when she returned to the house, the car was gone. A private investigator on retainer to find the car promised to get it back.

Cindy spent a ton of money, upward of $45,000 dollars, and then went to court, where the judge couldn't believe what Cindy had gone through. The judge told her that the car needed to be impounded and all of this settled. Cindy got a writ to get the car back, and, once again, it had disappeared, this time out of state. The writ was only good for California. The PI traced the car to Missouri. The people who had it knew they had it illegally but basically told the PI to get lost because they weren't giving the car up. The PI sent all the information they had on the car to the local sheriff, who chose to call it a civil matter. No one wanted to do anything about it, and to this day, this seems to be the general consensus. Pass the buck, it's someone else's problem.

Cindy has a living trust that states the car is to go to her. The last word has the car passing hands and now residing in New York. The person possessing the

> **We had plans on placing it in the NHRA museum.**

car has it up on blocks in his garage; he's afraid that someone is going to take it. He has apparently endured some harassment from those who know where the car belongs. Cindy hopes the car is returned to her someday. "We had plans on placing it in the NHRA museum. It belongs in a museum."

Don was the first to drive the completed Pro Stock Truck of Frank Sicinski and commented at the time that it was the easiest race car he had ever driven. This was the last class-legal car/truck Don ran in competition. Eventually, the truck ran a 7.41 at 181 mph. (Photo Courtesy Allen Tracy)

Earl Wade put his 50 years of experience into building the potent 357 engine for the Sicinski truck. Ford trucks saw limited success in part due to the manufacturer's lack of participation in the category and its lack of small-block development. (Photo Courtesy Frank Sicinski)

1998–1999

Don joined Frank Sicinski and Earl Wade for one more kick at the can. Sicinski called upon Willie Rells once again, this time to assemble a Ford Ranger for NHRA Pro Stock Truck. For those who missed it, Pro Stock Truck ran from 1998 through 2001. The NHRA, following the lead of NASCAR, created the category to cash in on the growing popularity of the mid-size pickups. The rules followed closely to NHRA Pro Stock cars. The biggest difference is the allowable cubic inch, which was maxed out at 358. Apart from nitrous oxide, pretty much any modification to the mill was acceptable. Transmission choice was limited to a clutch-activated 5-speed because the Lenco planetary transmission was not allowed. Wheelbase was pegged at a minimum 125 inches and truck weight could be no less than 2,300 pounds. One category rule that didn't last beyond the first season was that the top four quickest trucks of each of the three manufacturers were guaranteed a spot. The final four spots consisted of the quickest of the remaining trucks.

While NASCAR's Truck Series enjoyed the support of Detroit's Big Three, the NHRA never did; Ford refused to "buy in" to the series. Some thought that the category was doomed without the support of all three manufacturers. This view was justified and it seemed that from the get-go Ford racers were at a disadvantage. Don wasn't overly involved in this build and actually advised Sicinski and Wade that the Ranger would not be competitive enough, but it seems Sicinski's heart was set on it.

Propelling the Ranger was a 910-hp, Earl Wade–built 357 Windsor. Backing it up was a G-Force 5-speed, a 9-inch rear, and four-link suspension. Gears were usually 5:38s although 5:68s were tried. Oh, and remember that seven-year-old son of Sicinski's, Stacy, who was introduced to Don back around 1977? Well, he now crewed for his boyhood hero. Records show that Don competed in three races with the truck: one in 1998 and two in 1999. He failed to qualify the truck at all three races and recorded a best of 7.886 at 172.36 mph before giving up the reins to Stacy.

Through no fault of the crew, without factory R&D and newly developed parts, the truck lagged behind the front-runners. Sicinski and Wade built their own version of a splayed-valve engine to compete against the dominating 358-ci splayed valve Chevys. Before having the chance to run the new engine, the NHRA killed the category. Today, this engine sits on the same engine stand that it was built on while the truck sits in storage in "as raced" condition at Sicinski's New Caney shop.

Frank Sicinski's truck ran a G-Force 5-speed transmission that mounted behind an East West Engineering 6-inch dual disc clutch. Parts by Trick Titanium and AutoMeter were standard Pro Stock gear in the late 1990s. (Photo Courtesy Frank Sicinski)

Frank still owns the Ranger as well as the previously mentioned Thunderbird, maintaining them in as-raced condition. Decals and wrap are vinyl. Check out the drum of VP racing fuel on the right. Yup, they went through plenty of it. (Photo Courtesy Frank Sicinski)

THE LEGEND LIVES

Don spent half of his time on the phone at any given time during his career; booking matches, chasing parts, returning calls, and taking calls. He's shown here at his rented shop in Orange, wrenches in one hand and phone in the other. (Photo Courtesy Ray Cunningham)

A man of Don's caliber isn't soon forgotten, attesting to that are the countless numbers of fans who Dyno chatted up and always had time for. Unlike many so-called stars of our sport, Don freely gave autographs, T-shirts, and tuning tips, as well as his time.

His granddaughter recalls handing out T-shirts at the drags: "He'd have us chasing down dejected kids who felt they missed an opportunity to get a shirt. He always went out of his way for his fans."

Being raised in a Christian home helped instill strong family values and ethics in Don. These same standards live on

Jim Sottie takes model building to a whole new level with his pair of Dyno Don 409 Chevys. Lindberg produced the 1961 kit and AMT the 1962 kit. Auction sites are your best bet to find these two nowadays. Be prepared to spend some long green, though. (Photo Courtesy Jim Sottile)

Not only did Don have the most model kits of any drag racer but also his Super Cat Cougar may have set a record for drag cars when an unopened kit sold for $400 in 2017.

in his daughter and his grandchildren. Says Cindy, "He taught us to give to others and to make the most of life, without drugs or alcohol. A little known fact is that in the 1970s Don turned down a lucrative offer to join a race team sponsored by Coors, a deal said to be worth $250,000, all because he thought it set a bad example for the youth."

When it came to life on the road, Don was no stick-in-the-mud but preferred hanging out with his wife and daughter rather than fellow racers. More often than not, when he wasn't at the track he was back at the hotel playing Yahtzee, Boggle, and Rummy. That was life on the road for the Nicholsons.

"When Dad did finally retire, he enjoyed watching racing on TV. And the Lakers; he was a pretty big Lakers fan as well. He loved playing all the handheld games back when they started. No doubt he would have been crazy about these phones." Cindy spent a lot of time on

the road with her mom and dad and people would ask her if she missed not being home, playing with friends, and doing the things other kids were doing. Her response was that she loved traveling with her parents.

"Few people got to enjoy the company of their parents and be as much a part as their lives as I did. I had friends all over the country and saw them at each race. I never wanted it any other way." Away from the track, Cindy did enjoy the company of neighbor friends and family in both Atlanta and California. The Nicholsons were a close lot and, away from the cars, Don and Patty enjoyed the company of his brother and sister-in-law, who were their best friends.

Dyno's Ongoing Popularity

When speaking of drag racing in the 1960s and 1970s, Pat Minick of *Chi-Town Hustler* Funny Car fame

Talk about fan appreciation! This replica of Don's Nostalgia 1962 Bel Air is carved from wood. A family friend gifted it to Don's nephew. Bet he could sell a ton of them! (Photo Courtesy Nicholson Family Collection)

When it came to cars replicated in plastic kit form, no drag racer ever enjoyed the same popularity as Don. You have to love the original AMT artwork on the box of this Eliminator II *kit. (Photo Courtesy Rob Potter)*

said, "It was drag racing's heyday. We lived through it and didn't even know it." With a twinge of sadness, I believe that's the way many "more experienced ones" look back on the sport's golden age. It seems the more drag racing evolves, the more we long for the way it used to be. The preference for all things nostalgic, specifically drag racing, isn't going away anytime soon and proof of this can be seen all around us. On the Internet, we have websites, Facebook pages, and online forums and groups where people are chatting it up. Whether it's Funny Car or Pro Stock, at the center of many of these discussions is Dyno Don. Skimming through Internet search engines looking up Dyno Don reveals nearly 2 million results.

Talk about ongoing popularity. And every day new fans are coming on board.

Having to start somewhere, many fans young and young at heart begin with model kits. When it comes to these plastic kits, no other person in any form of racing has ever enjoyed the same level of popularity as Don. From his 1961 Impala to his first Mustang II, nine of Don's cars were replicated by manufacturers: AMT, Jo-Han, MPC, and Revell. Oddly, when Revell chose to replicate his Cobra Jet Mustang, it used a 1969 body. A number of Dyno's kits are available at hobby stores and through online sources. Obsolete kits such as his 1969 Super Cat Cougar fetch big dollars; one sold at auction in 2017 for just short of $400.

You say that your favorite Dyno car wasn't made in a 1:24 or 1:25 kit form. Here's an easy fix: pick up any Mustang, Maverick, or Comet kit that you see on the shelf and build your own by ordering a Dyno Don decal kit from Slixx.com. If you can't find the kit, companies such as Competition Resins and Bandit Resins form bodies that fit existing kit chassis. The world of plastic model kits has come a long way since its introduction back in 1936.

Joining the kits in scale are a number of

Don's rides have been replicated in all sizes. Here are just two of the cars produced in 1:18 scale, his 1970 Mustang and the 1963 Impala. Produced in limited numbers, these die-casts became instant collector pieces.

Those aluminum FE engines sure are popular, and rightly so. This beautiful tribute runs out of Colorado and has a G-Force 5-speed transmission behind its aluminum mill. Times for the wagon are an unreal 8.70 at 151 mph. (Photo Courtesy Bob Wenzelburger)

Dave Powers runs this beautiful Dyno Don tribute 1964 Comet. Times in the 9.70s come by way of an aluminum FE Ford and Jerico transmission. Powers runs with the Pennsylvania-based 422 Motorsports group, an all-Ford team of veteran racers. (Photo Courtesy Bob Wenzelburger)

Pennsylvania's Steve McBlane's tribute to Don, seen at the York US-30 reunion in 2010, has run 8.80s at 149 mph. Power comes from an aluminum FE with twin fours backed by a C4. Steve is another member of the 422 team of racers. (Photo Courtesy Bob Wenzelburger)

quality Dyno Don die-cast cars. Welley Supercar Collectables has released his 1963 Impala in 1:18 scale and Supercar Collectables has released the 1968 Super Stock Cobra Jet car and his 1970 Pro Stocker. Another manufacturer, Action, has produced the 1963 Impala in 1:64 scale. Produced in limited numbers, these cars all became instant collectables.

Between 1961 and 1981, Don campaigned more than 30 cars. Of those, more than a dozen survive. Rumors persist that a number of the other cars remain, but until someone steps forward with documented proof, they remain rumors. Apart from his nostalgia Pro Mod Bel Air, all his Chevys are lost to history, as are his four flip-up Funny Cars. A number of tribute cars honor Don.

Those at 422 Motorsports on the East Coast are carrying on tradition and run a few tribute cars under its banner. Don has influenced generations of drag racers and these tribute cars honor him by helping keep his memory alive.

Dyno's Final Shows

When Don's wife, Patty, had a severe stroke in 1986, doctors felt the chance of her living another five years was pretty slim. With Don's care, she lived another 14 years before passing in February 2001. Drag racing was Don's living and she was his life. Even after her stroke, Patty traveled everywhere with him. The year she passed

John Jodauga was responsible for the colorful 1971 and 1978 Dyno Don press kits. In addition to doing the artwork, Jodauga also wrote the included history, added photos, and had the works printed. With a track record as long and strong as Don's, little touting was ever necessary.

was the same year Don made his final exhibition run in the Chevy, doing so at Pomona.

After retirement, Don attended a lot of car shows, but eventually his Alzheimer's became too much. At the recommendation of his doctor, Cindy pulled Don off the road. "I wanted all his fans to remember him as he always was," she said.

It wasn't a happy time for anyone. Cindy endured a lot of backlash from fans and promoters who wanted more of Don. She was the brunt of uncalled-for abuse because they thought she was forcibly keeping him away.

"People thought I had him locked up in a closet or something. It was nothing like that." The last show Don attended was the 100 Years of Ford Racing in 2003. Fans loved it, and they appreciated him being there, but they had no idea how rough it was getting through it. They never realized that his daughter was standing beside him telling him what to sign because he couldn't remember his own signature. He'd start then draw a blank. Those promoting the show wanted Don to join in a question and answer session, and the only way he got through it was with the help of Carroll Shelby, who answered many

Don and Patty were married for more than 50 years, and a person would be hard pressed to find a couple who were more in love. When they met, Don was introduced to Patty as "Nick." That was his nickname before "Dyno" and it was tattooed on his upper left arm. This was Don's only tattoo. (Photo Courtesy Nicholson Family Collection)

At the celebration of Ford's 100 years of racing in October 2001, Don received one of 11 produced cast-iron replicas of Ford's first racer. The Sweepstakes award was given to Don for his exceptional contribution to the advancement of Ford motorsport. With it came a personal letter of thanks from Edsel Ford II. (Author's Collection)

of the questions for him. It was a wise decision to retire at that point, as Don had literally given his all.

Dyno Don, A Man to Remember

Don's on-track accomplishments have been recognized in many ways. He has been inducted into the *Super Stock* magazine Hall of Fame, the International Drag Racing Hall of Fame, the Motorsports Hall of Fame of America, and the *East Coast Drag News* Hall of Fame. In 1997, he received a lifetime achievement award from the NHRA in the form of another Wally. The same year, he was chosen to be Grand Marshall at the California Hot Rod Reunion.

As part of NHRA's 50th anniversary celebration in 2001, the NHRA, along with a panel of expert journalists and drag race historians, sat down to hammer out who

Why quit something you enjoy so much?

they felt were the top 50 drivers of all time. Don came in at number 18 on the list. Think about all the greats who have come and gone, and let that sink in. On the other side of the fence, the IHRA has ranked Don number 15 when it comes to all-time Mountain Motor Pro Stock competitors.

When it was all said and done, Don figured that he had racked up around a million and a half miles traveling from track to track. He was a lucky man to have been able to make most of those miles with his wife, daughter, and Fang by his side. (Fang, by the way, was his silver teacup poodle. The dog's registered name was Dyno Don's Silver Dollar, but it picked up the name Fang after taking a bite at Earl Wade's nose. It seems Wade failed to realize that dogs don't like people blowing in their faces.)

In a 1995 interview with *National Dragster*'s John Jodauga, Don stated, "I remember people asking me when I turned 40 if I thought about retirement. It seemed like a silly question then, and I feel the same way now. Why quit something you enjoy so much?" Three years later, at the age of 71, it was time for Don to renew his NHRA license. He astounded the examining doctor, who told him he had a body of an 18-year-old. And it's no wonder, he worked seven days a week, ate sensibly, and exercised when he felt the weight coming on. He looked forward to living to be 100, and there's no doubt if it weren't for the Alzheimer's, he would have.

Sadly, complications related to the disease took Don from us on January 24, 2006, at the age of 78. He is resting peacefully at the Good Shepherd Cemetery in Huntington Beach, California. Dyno Don Nicholson left his mark on the world, ensuring that he won't soon be forgotten.

Don and his poodle, Silver Dollar, pose during the Christmas of 1969. "Fang" was Don's constant companion and went everywhere with him. At races, the poodle would crawl out of the Lincoln's side window, walk along the door ledge to the hood, and lie there watching Don work away. (Photo Courtesy Nicholson Family Collection)

In Memoriam

Butch Leal

"He was my hero, the nicest person in the whole world. When it came to those early Chevys, he was magic. He knew the whole deal better than anyone else. He beat my 348 El Camino by half a length and complimented me on how well it ran. He taught me how to drive my (1962) Biscayne out."

Jerry Jardine

"Dyno was a good, honest guy. He'd do anything for anybody. You just couldn't match him."

Hayden Proffitt

"Out of all of them guys, Sox & Martin, Gas Ronda, Arne Beswick, Dyno was the best and the toughest."

Al Turner

"Don was an innovator and did a lot of things people didn't know about. He was very intuitive, a genius in his mechanical skills."

Ronnie Sox

"The Mercury Comets were absolutely flying. Dyno Don was hard to do anything with. We could outrun Schartman every now and then, but Dyno was tough. Don was the hardest to beat."

Ed Schartman

"Don was a hard worker and put in a lot of late nights to win. As far as a tuner, he was better than most people."

Arnie Beswick

"He was a hard, hard racer that never stopped trying, always coming up with something new to make his cars faster."

Tommy Grove

"He was very strong, just a tough competitor who I had a lot of respect for. Like me, Don grew up without people telling him what to do and how to do it. He learned what to do and how to do it on his own. In his era, he was doing things that hadn't been done yet."

Frank Oglesby

"Don could drive. He was technically orientated and he could come back after a run and tell you when the car was laying down or did this or that, he knew. He was one of finest people I've ever met and we remained friends to the end."

Austin Coil

"My dealings were mainly with (mechanic) Earl Wade, who was just meticulous, and he never blamed anyone but himself if things screwed up. The first time I met Don was during a meet at York US-30 during the early days of Funny Car. We set low ET with the *Chi-Town Hustler* and Don came over and asked, 'Who the %$#@ are you guys?!' He was tough competition, tough to outrun."

Dick Brannan

"Don was for sure a great friend even while driving his 409 Chevys. Since my department (at Ford Motor Company) controlled all the engines, from time to time I was told what to release to the Lincoln–Mercury team guys, but I always did work close with Don. He used to stay at my home some while at the factory."

Barrie Poole

"Don was a very smart man and taught me a lot. He and Earl were really competitive and made the Cammer come alive."

Jack Roush

"Don was always the guy who figured out things faster than his contemporaries did, so I went to the Don Nicholson school on a lot of things for several years. He had the answers, knew the secrets, and amazed people who were just getting started like I was in 1970–1971."

Bill Jenkins

"You knew with Nicholson there would be no starting-line antics, he was a real pro. He had a very likable personality; he was a man you couldn't dislike."

Bob Glidden

"Don was a real fierce competitor, one of the front liners in innovation in Pro Stock. He was the first to use the 5-speed, first to use titanium rods. People really didn't give him enough credit for what he did."

Frank Iaconio

"Don was always one up on us. He had that trick transmission that we tried to duplicate but could never figure out. I don't know how he got away with it."

Mark Yuill

"Dyno was always a gentleman whether he was winning or losing. We were night racing at Buds Creek and the lights lit up the quarter-mile but not the shut off area. I said to Don, 'I can't see anything in the shutdown area.' Don said, 'Think you can't see, I surely can't see anything.' He said that he just pulls the chute, turns the engine off, and listens. 'If I hear rocks in the left wheelwell I just turn right and the same thing if I hear them in the right wheelwell, I turn to the left.'"

David Reher

"Don was just a really nice guy we enjoyed hanging out with and talking with. We didn't hang out with many guys but Don was so approachable and funny. He was one of my heroes and when I got into Pro Stock I found out what kind of genuine guy he was. And there are a few of them out there that I wouldn't be able to say that about."

In Memoriam

Dick Estevez

"Don was attuned to what went on, on the track. He could tell you what the car was doing at any spot on the racetrack. He was good with setting the power up so the car would leave the starting line good. He never lost a step."

John Jodauga

"It's no accident that Don Nicholson was one of the leading pioneers in the Super Stock, Funny Car, and Pro Stock ranks. Not only did his engines produce record-breaking horsepower, but he also excelled with his chassis setup and tuning for the track. He had an unmatched tenacity in looking for the edge, and that enabled him to become one of the quarter-mile's most successful door slammer racers."

Bob Frey

"I have been very fortunate in my years of following the sport to be able to meet a lot of the 'superstars' in drag racing. Many have made favorable impressions but few more so than Dyno Don Nicholson. I first met Don at Atco Dragway in 1966, my first year of announcing, and to say I was starstruck would be an understatement.

"I followed Don throughout his career and was always glad when our paths crossed, whether it was at Atco, a match race somewhere, or at one of the big NHRA or IHRA events that I worked. There have been a lot of people who have drag raced but few had the impact that Don did, and by that I mean not only on the sport but on my life as well. He was the best!"

Appendix

Dyno Don's Racing Record

Very few racers can match Don's phenomenal run of final-round appearances. And no other racer can match him in the number of categories in which he did the winning.

National Event Wins and Runner-Ups

1961	Winner	Stock Eliminator	NHRA Winternationals, California	1961 Impala
1962	Winner	Stock Eliminator	NHRA Winternationals, California	1962 Bel Air
1962	Runner-up	Stock Eliminator	AHRA Winter Nationals, California	1962 Bel Air
1963	Winner	Stock Eliminator	NASCAR Winter Nationals, Florida	1963 Impala
1964	Runner-up	Factory Stock	NHRA Winternationals, California	1964 Comet
1966	Winner	Funny Car	AHRA Grand Nationals, Wisconsin	1966 Comet
1966	Runner-up	Funny Car	NHRA World Finals, Oklahoma	1966 Comet
1967	Winner	Unlimited F/C	AHRA Winter Nationals, Arizona	1966 Comet
1968	Runner-up	Super Eliminator	NHRA Nationals, Indiana	1968 Cougar
1969	Winner	Street Eliminator	NHRA Springnationals, Texas	1965 Mustang
1970	Winner	Super Stock	AHRA Grand-American, Nebraska	1970 Maverick
1970	Winner	Super Stock	AHRA Nationals, Tennessee	1970 Maverick
1970	Runner-up	Pro Stock	IHRA Rockingham, North Carolina	1970 Maverick
1970	Runner-up	Super Stock	AHRA Grand-American, California	1970 Maverick
1971	Winner	Super Stock	AHRA Grand-American, California	1971 Maverick
1971	Runner-up	Pro Stock	NHRA Springnationals, Texas	1971 Maverick
1971	Winner	Pro Stock	NHRA Summernationals, New Jersey	1971 Maverick
1971	Winner	Super Stock	AHRA Grand-American, Ohio	1971 Maverick
1972	Winner	Pro Stock	AHRA Grand-American, Florida	1972 Pinto
1972	Runner-up	Pro Stock	AHRA Gateway Nationals, Missouri	1972 Pinto
1972	Runner-up	Pro Stock	AHRA Grand-American, Kansas	1972 Pinto
1972	Winner	Pro Stock	AHRA World Championships, California	1972 Pinto
1972	Runner-up	Pro Stock	IHRA Summernationals, Ohio	1972 Pinto
1973	Winner	Pro Stock	AHRA Winter Nationals, Arizona	1972 Pinto
1973	Winner	Pro Stock	NHRA Winternationals, California	1972 Pinto
1973	Winner	Pro Stock	NHRA Gatornationals, Florida	1972 Pinto
1973	Runner-up	Pro Stock	IHRA Springnationals, Tennessee	1972 Pinto
1973	Winner	Pro Stock	IHRA All-American Nationals, Tennessee	1972 Pinto
1973	Winner	Pro Stock	IHRA Nationals, Florida	1972 Pinto
1974	Runner-up	Pro Stock	IHRA All-American Nationals, Tennessee	1974 Mustang

Year	Result	Class	Event	Car
1974	Winner	Pro Stock	IHRA Pro-Am Nationals, North Carolina	1974 Mustang
1974	Runner-up	Pro Stock	NHRA U.S. Nationals, Indiana	1974 Mustang
1975	Winner	Pro Stock	AHRA Spring Nationals, Missouri	1974 Mustang
1975	Winner	Pro Stock	IHRA Summernationals, Wisconsin	1974 Mustang
1975	Winner	Pro Stock	IHRA Nationals, Ohio	1974 Mustang
1975	Runner-up	Pro Stock	IHRA World Nationals, Texas	1974 Mustang
1976	Runner-up	Comp Eliminator	NHRA Summernationals, New Jersey	1976 Mustang
1977	Runner-up	Pro Stock	AHRA Winter Nationals, Arizona	1976 Mustang
1977	Runner-up	Pro Stock	NHRA Winternationals, California	1976 Mustang
1977	Winner	Pro Stock	NHRA Gatornationals, Florida	1976 Mustang
1977	Winner	Pro Stock	NHRA Springnationals, Ohio	1976 Mustang
1977	Winner	Pro Stock	NHRA U.S. Nationals, Indiana	1976 Mustang
1977	Runner-up	Pro Stock	NHRA World Finals, California	1976 Mustang
1978	Runner-up	Pro Stock	AHRA Grand Nationals, Ohio	1978 Fairmont
1979	Winner	Pro Stock	AHRA Winter Nationals, Arizona	1978 Fairmont
1980	Runner-up	Pro Stock	IHRA Summernationals, Tennessee	1980 Mustang
1980	Runner-up	Pro Stock	AHRA Winter Nationals, Arizona	1980 Mustang
1980	Winner	Pro Stock	IHRA Northern Nationals, Michigan	1980 Mustang
1981	Runner-up	Pro Stock	AHRA Winter Nationals, Arizona	1980 Mustang
1981	Winner	Pro Stock	IHRA Pro-Am Nationals, North Carolina	1980 Mustang

At the North Carolina Motor Speedway in Rockingham on May 3, 1981, Don earned his final national event win. It was home of the IHRA Pro-Am Nationals and in the final round, Don defeated Rickie Smith. Don held the class record at the time with a 7.81 ET. (Courtesy Nicholson Family Collection)

Appendix

Other Significant Wins

1964	Super Stock	*Cars* Magazine S/S Invitational, Maryland	1964 Comet
1966	Funny Car	UDRA Nationals, Wisconsin	1966 Comet
1967	Funny Car	Smokers Meet/Bakersfield, California	1967 Comet
1967	Funny Car	*Drag News* Invitational, New Jersey	1967 Comet
1969	Super Stock	Mr. USA Super Stock Eliminator, Maryland	1965 Mustang
1970	Pro Stock	Capitol Raceway King of Kings, Maryland	1970 Maverick
1970	Pro Stock	Detroit Dragway Pro Stock Championship, Michigan	1970 Maverick
1971	Pro Stock	Super Stock Nationals, Pennsylvania	1971 Maverick
1971	Pro Stock	PDA Pro Stock Nationals, Pennsylvania	1971 Maverick
1975	Pro Stock	*Popular Hot Rodding* Meet, Michigan	1970 Mustang
1977	Pro Stock	PRO National Challenge, Wisconsin	1976 Mustang
1978	Pro Stock	Mountain Motor Nationals, Maryland	1976 Mustang

Index

Index

Index

"DYNO DON"

Additional books that may interest you...

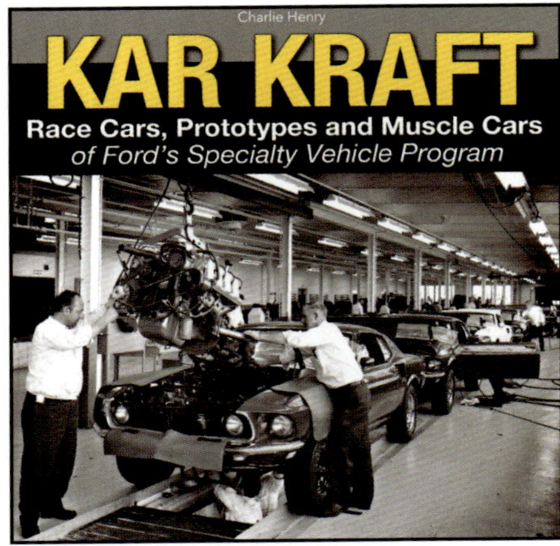

Kar-Kraft: Race Cars, Prototypes and Muscle Cars of Ford's Specialty Vehicle Activity Program by Charlie Henry
The story of Kar-Kraft began, as did many others in the automotive industry, with an axe to grind. In 1963, Ford was seriously interested in purchasing Ferrari. Ferrari was a legendary brand with considerable success in racing, and Ford saw the acquisition as a great way to be instantly successful in the racing arena. When Ferrari backed out of the deal late in the process it set in motion a vengeful response against Ferrari. The Kar-Kraft relationship was established and Ford organized an all-out assault on racing in general. Author Charlie Henry (a former Kar-Kraft employee) has enlisted the help of many of his former co-workers to bring you the very first book ever published on Ford's all-encompassing special projects facility, Kar-Kraft. 10 x 10", 192 pgs, 332 photos. *Part # CT569*

MATCH RACE MAYHEM Drag Racing's Grudges, Rivalries and Big-Money Showdowns *by Doug Boyce* During the golden age of drag racing, fans didn't care as much about class racing as much as they wanted to see scores settled and interesting match-ups. Match races were also a great way to feature wildly popular cars that no longer had a class in which to compete, yet the fans still wanted to see them. So popular were these races that many track promoters didn't bother to promote class racing at all. Instead, they used the match races as headliners, similar to the marquee at your local arena or a billboard in Las Vegas, all resulting in putting more fans in the stands. And the drivers loved it too. Many of the most popular pro drivers quit class racing altogether just to go match racing. Softbound, 8.5 x 11 inches, 176 pages, 201 color and 96 b/w photos. *Part # CT582*

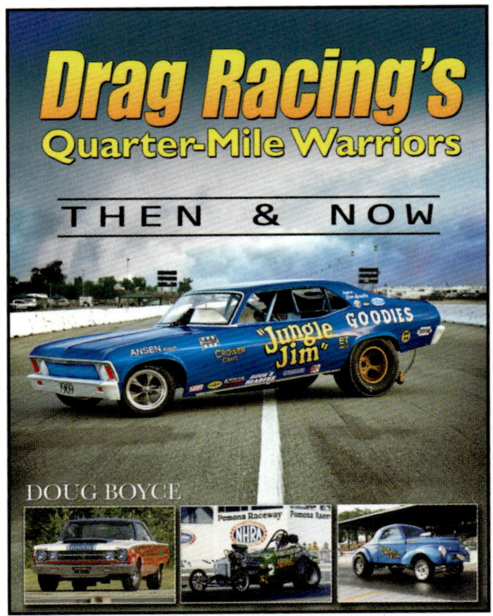

DRAG RACING'S QUARTER-MILE WARRIORS: Then & Now *by Doug Boyce* This book takes a unique look at the most memorable, interesting, and successful cars from the golden age of drag racing, the late 50s through the early 70s. Chronicled are Diggers and Rail dragsters, Funny Cars, wild Altereds, door slammers like Super and Junior Stock cars, early 70s Pro Stock cars, and more. Vintage and modern photography in a unique "then and now" format cover the cars as they first competed, through their evolution (or inactivity) over the years, and how they look today. See cars driven by legends such as Mickey Thompson, Tommy Ivo, Dick Landy, Grumpy Jenkins, Sox & Martin, Don Nicholson, Bob Glidden, and more. Hardbound, 8.5 x 11 inches, 192 pages, 500 color and b/w photos. *Part # CT528*

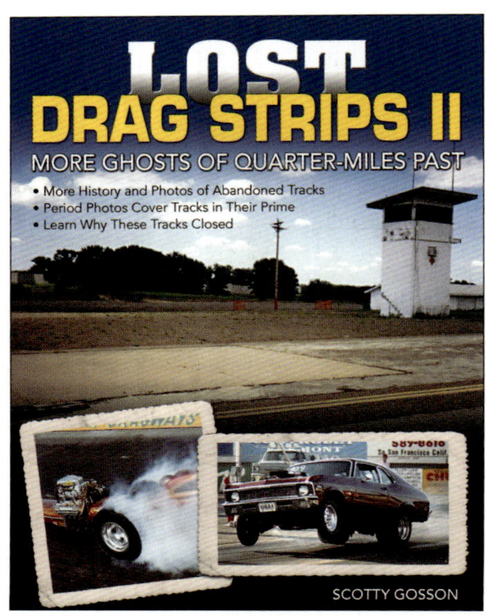

LOST DRAG STRIPS II: More Ghosts of Quarter-Miles Past *by Scotty Gosson* This book picks up where the best-selling first volume left off, covering even more tracks with archival photos of racing in the tracks' heyday and coverage of the notable cars that ran there. This volume also includes some of the tracks that survived, those that fought off the economic demons and the urban sprawl and that against all odds, continue to operate today. Softbound, 8.5 x 11 inches, 176 pages, 265 photos. *Part # CT550*

www.cartechbooks.com or 1-800-551-4754